For years, Hagar was hidden from my
Kuhn turned the spotlight on her in 1.
see her in three dimensions. Since then, I have read that book several times.
Now Mike turns the spotlight on Peter in his book, *In Quest of the Rock*. Peter
is painted by the Master Artist on the canvas of the Old Testament and the
historical setting of Peter's time. Seeing Peter in three dimensions is life transforming. Both books are a must read.

Nabeel T. Jabbour, ThD
Lecturer in Islam and Geopolitics
Colorado, USA

One thing I have learned in pastoring a congregation over the past twenty-
three years is that the spiritual journey often does not look the way we expect
it will. Mike Kuhn does an excellent job exploring how Peter must have often
felt the same way about his own journey as a follower of Jesus. As he traces
the story of Peter with a specific focus on the process of transformation in his
life, we begin to identify with that journey, noting the signposts that become
evident as the spirit guides us toward Christ. This book reminds us that often
the times we feel God is the most distant or times when we have reached a
point of deep failure are often the times that God is working to strip away our
false self as he renews us into the image of his son. Kuhn's honest look at the
life of Peter with practical application to our own spiritual journey is a gift to
the church, one that provides deep insight as well as great encouragement.

Jeff Kuhn
Teaching Pastor,
Grace Baptist Church, Hope, Canada

I see myself too much like the "act first, think later" apostle Peter, so it will cause
activistic readers like me to pause and reflect and be granted hope that, like
Peter, we can become the man or woman our savior so desires us to become.

Greg Livingstone
Founder, Frontiers, UK

Mike Kuhn's *In Quest of the Rock* is a rich guidebook for the journey of spiritual
formation. Walking the road with Peter in following Jesus involves pain and

the Middle East and his love of Scripture, Mike will challenge, encourage and embolden you on the path. Read and learn. Read and grow.

Perry Shaw, PhD
Researcher in Residence at Morling College, Sydney, Australia
Former Professor of Education,
Arab Baptist Theological Seminary, Beirut, Lebanon

I believe that Jesus's death on the cross accomplished justification for me. But for some time now, I have wrestled with God's promise of his sanctifying work in my life. You can't see justification; you accept it through faith. But it seems to me a person ought to be able to clearly see the work of sanctification in his or her life. This book, by showing how Jesus shaped Peter, has given me an understanding and hope of how Jesus is shaping me; that the sanctification of the soul is the work of, and requires the power of, the spirit of Jesus. Mike challenges us to push back against cultural and religious influences that have distorted our view of ourselves and of what God is doing in his world; to take a fresh look at who we are, honestly acknowledging the "shadow-self," and to humbly submit to the redemptive work, the shaping, that God wants to do in our lives in order to bring us to the "real-self" that God uniquely created each of us to be.

Jon Woodroof, PhD
Founder and CEO,
Sedona Systems, Tennessee, USA

There is no doubt that Mike Kuhn's most recent publication is not only creative, but captivating. The author takes readers on a profound journey, compelling them to reflect on their spiritual life using Peter's own narrative as a paradigm. The reader cannot but engage with the depth of Peter's experiences, the failures and the triumphs. As this project was partially birthed in the Middle East, it is a timely and relevant resource for theological educators like myself who are embedded in the soil of the Middle East and entrusted with the spiritual formation of Arab Christian leaders. This resource is a call and a challenge to examine our spiritual standards transparently, thoroughly and reflectively in light of Kuhn's methodology of discipleship.

Grace Al-Zoughbi
Lecturer in Theological Education,
Arab Baptist Theological Seminary, Beirut, Lebanon

In Quest of the Rock

Langham
GLOBAL LIBRARY

In Quest of the Rock

Peter's Transformative Journey with Jesus

Michael F. Kuhn

Illustrated by Bethany Giles

Langham

GLOBAL LIBRARY

Published 2022 by Langham Global Library
An imprint of Langham Publishing
www.langhampublishing.org

Langham Publishing and its imprints are a ministry of Langham Partnership

Langham Partnership
PO Box 296, Carlisle, Cumbria, CA3 9WZ, UK
www.langham.org

ISBNs:
978-1-83973-604-9 Print
978-1-83973-718-3 ePub
978-1-83973-719-0 Mobi
978-1-83973-720-6 PDF

British Library Cataloguing-in-Publication Data
A catalogue record for this book is available from the British Library

ISBN: 978-1-83973-604-9

Illustrations and Cover picture: © Bethany Giles

Cover & Book Design: projectluz.com

Dedication

To my parents M.F. and Barbara Daniels Kuhn and my grandmother Margaret Daniels, with gratitude for placing me on a good path in the early years of spiritual formation.

Contents

Introduction

A Spiritually Formative Journey

Before we dive into Peter's journey of spiritual formation, I would like to share a little of mine. This book is the fruit of reflection that originated from a discipleship class I taught at the Arab Baptist Theological Seminary in Beirut, Lebanon. However, my quest to help believers grow in Christ started years earlier. Many of the believers I related to in the Middle East were from Islamic background. They faced immense pressures with some being incarcerated and tortured because of their embrace of Jesus as Lord. Having read stories of those who suffer for their faith, I had a naïve expectation that these new believers would emerge from these trials mature and strong in their faith. In fact, they came out of those experiences traumatized as anyone would. My friends from Islamic background were courageous, but suffering in and of itself, did not grow them in Christ.

Walking alongside these brothers and sisters pushed me to think about what constitutes growth. How do we make progress in following Jesus, becoming more like him in our lived experience? Looking back, I can identify four streams that fed into my thinking over the years. The first was my evangelical upbringing with its emphasis on study of the scriptures as a means of growth. I did a lot of that with my friends in the Middle East. They seemed to benefit and grow from it as I had so that was a good beginning. In fact, I would say it was foundational.

A second stream was the distinction made in my own tradition between justification and sanctification. The former is a free gift of God in which he declares that we are made right with God on the sole basis of Jesus's righteousness. Joining ourselves to Christ in his death and resurrection, by faith, we are given the status of children of God (adoption). It is, as Luther said, an "alien" righteousness, given from outside ourselves. A clear understanding of justification frees us from trying to elevate our status by works of devotion and obedience. We are "in the family" by faith in Jesus. We could never improve on what Jesus accomplished, so elevating our status or commending ourselves to God is out of the question. The gospel is a gift . . . an unspeakably great gift.

Sanctification grows out of justification. An experiential knowledge of God's love through the Spirit outpoured in the believer's heart incentivizes the disciple to press in and follow Jesus closely. I see myself more objectively and realize innately how much progress there is to be made – a life's worth! "For the grace of God has appeared, . . . training us to renounce ungodliness and worldly passions, and to live self-controlled, upright and godly lives . . ." (Titus 2:11–12). Like justification, sanctification is God's gift to me, not solely the fruit of my effort. However, unlike justification, it is a life-long process of dying to the old sinful nature and living the reality of my status and calling as an adopted son or daughter. Both justification and sanctification express the gospel. God so loved the world that he gave his only Son. Through faith in Jesus I am reconciled to God. Sanctification is not about moving beyond the cross, but penetrating ever deeper into its truth and implications. By the way, I tend to use the terms – discipleship, spiritual formation and sanctification – synonymously.

The third stream was the spiritually formative writings of the ancient church. I found Catholic and Orthodox writings penetrating and insightful. I especially appreciated contemporary writers who express those ideas in a more accessible style (many are cited in this book). However, I sometimes felt that the justification-sanctification distinction was lost or minimized. Some of those writings tended towards asceticism – a denial or suppression of the needs of the body – as the means of drawing near to God. While I recognize the need to discipline the body, I became convinced that the body and its appetites were God-given and disciples are free to enjoy them as good gifts within scriptural limits.

The fourth stream is similar to the third but represented by contemporary Protestant and evangelical writers on the spiritual disciplines. Being a devotee of discipline, I was naturally inclined to those writings. Practicing the disciplines (prayer, fasting, meditation, silence, etc.) was helpful but I inevitably slipped into thinking of the disciplines as the end of spiritual formation rather than the means. The thought that I could earn God's favor kept lifting its ugly head. I know that is not what these writers intended. Nevertheless, I felt the practice of the disciplines was only partially helpful to me in spiritual formation. Looking back I realize that I lacked a community to sustain these practices and keep them in their proper place as a means and not an end of spiritual formation.

Those four streams are really only part of what was driving me. A famous Arabic saying captures what I was feeling about my own spiritual journey: "He who has lost something can't give it away!" All my thinking about spiritual formation was worth nothing if my own heart was not being formed in the way of Jesus. My Bible study, good as it was, did not deal thoroughly with my heart issues. I struggled to lay hold of Jesus' promise that "he who believes in me, as the Scripture has said, out of his heart will flow rivers of living water" (John 7:38). I realized that spiritual formation requires a deeper awareness of myself than I had attained. The goal was not self-awareness but Christlikeness. Nevertheless, the layers of my soul had to be exposed gradually, like the geological layers of an archeological dig site. The artifacts of an alienated self were lodged deeply and required concentrated effort to bring them out.

When the seminary in Beirut asked me to teach on discipleship, I was honored and eager but I was also haunted by an awareness that leading my students further in sanctification required that I go there myself. Also, despite all those streams mentioned above, I had yet to land on a good "methodology" of discipleship. The reality that I was passing on my experience to future servants of Jesus in the Middle East raised the stakes. I felt an urgency to land on a solid understanding of how disciples are formed spiritually.

So I started looking into how Jesus formed the soul of his protégé, Peter. I noticed that Jesus zeroed in on Peter's shadow-self as a direct confrontation of Peter's expectations and responses. I could relate to that as I had often experienced my growth in Christ as a response to disillusionment. Realities of life forced me to release false expectations. It was a spiritually formative journey with Jesus. We might call it "pilgrim spirituality." In Peter's case, the encounters are with Jesus, constituting Peter's stations of spiritual formation. For us who follow Jesus post-Pentecost, it consists of encounters led by the Spirit of Jesus as we journey through life. It requires faith. My real-life encounters must be seen as divine appointments and opportunities to be mentored and shaped in the Jesus way. I can enter each new station of spiritual formation aware that the Spirit of Jesus is fully supplied to me such that I can be transformed. It requires careful listening to my life journey in the context of my community of faith, especially those who care enough to tell me the truth about myself. It also requires a solid mooring in the story of Scripture.

I should be careful not to claim more for this book than it is, but I suggest that if you have hit a dead end in your desire for conformity to Christ, this book might open some doors for you. It is neither the approach of disciplines as such nor the mystical spirituality of the church Fathers and Mothers. This book draws on those riches but seeks to locate the impetus for spiritual formation in the lived experience of each disciple. It is spiritual formation for the common person in his or her normal, everyday life. It is not a recipe or a series of steps that one takes to grow in Christ. No overnight transformations here. No shortcuts. Spiritual formation is a committed, relational following over a lifelong journey. The good news is that every disciple has the resources – the Word and Spirit in the community of other Jesus followers – to take this journey.

Finally, I want to express my indebtedness to a few friends and family members who have read the book and offered their feedback. While I alone am responsible for the content, they have enriched and encouraged me greatly. Those seminary students in Beirut were the first to interact with these ideas. I am in their debt. Jon and Stacy Woodroof have been friends through the journey. Jon has engaged with each chapter. He has a keen editorial eye and his own discovery of the biblical story added depth to these pages. My friend Ivan Fawzi has helped me realize what it means to see Christ in the Old Testament. His comments on the Epilogue ("Centering Christ in the Old Testament") were invaluable. Recently, I led two groups of disciples through this material. The first was a class at Cordata Presbyterian Church (Bellingham, WA) and the second was a group of refugees from Syria who live as displaced, but joy-filled disciples in a Middle Eastern country. I am indebted to these friends for their eager participation and application of the book's ideas.

I had some help from family members too. My brother, Jeff Kuhn, is a pastor. He has delved deeper into spiritual formation than I and brought a wealth of insight from his own reflection as he engaged with me in this book. Jeff suggested concepts and quotes from his wide reading which I deeply appreciated. Jake Giles is married to my daughter, Beth. Jake read this work and offered helpful feedback and encouragement. Beth did the illustrations. As in a former book (*Finding Hagar: God's Pursuit of a Runaway*), Beth's images add texture and depth, inviting the reader into Peter's journey. My other adult kids – Hannah and her husband, Nick, and Emily are also lurking among these pages. Their insightful curiosity and their pursuit of justice, not to mention their authentic walk with Christ, inspire and push me to keep changing and growing. Finally, Stephanie is my life partner. I find that everything I write needs to be run by her. She always helps me bring it down to earth, to make it a little more accessible. She often offers a different perspective that inevitably makes my writing better. More importantly, she makes my life better.

I am again indebted to Langham Partnership. I have always admired the spiritual and intellectual legacy of John Stott. For that reason alone, publishing with Langham is a privilege and honor. Vivian Doub and her husband Brian are long-time friends. Though she politely refuses any credit, she helped bring me into the Langham family while serving as their liaison with writers. I was delighted that she served as Langham's editor for this book.

Lastly, I now enjoy a deep and lasting friendship with the apostle Peter. I hope to thank him personally some day, but till then, I acknowledge gratefully his companionship. In these pages I refer to him interchangeably as Simon (his given name), Peter (the Greek translation of the title Jesus gave him, "the rock") and Cephas (Aramaic for "the Rock").

It seems fitting to introduce this book with one of my favorite sayings of Peter:

> *To whom would we go? You have the words of real life.*
> (John 6:68 *The Message*)

I offer this book in that hope – the source of life is available to us normal folks just as it was to Peter.

Mike Kuhn

Prologue

Spiritual Formation

The Art of Shaping a Life

The Spirit broods over us as we read this book, to straighten out our bent thinking; the worldviews that have got twisted so that they are like the world's worldviews.

N. T. Wright, "How Can the Bible Be Authoritative?"

Luke 24:44

Then he said to them, "These are my words that I spoke to you while I was still with you, that everything written about me in the Law of Moses and the Prophets and the Psalms must be fulfilled."

I need a moment.

When the women told us, I couldn't believe it. I couldn't allow myself to hope for it . . . after all that's happened these past ten days.

I had to see for myself. I got there as fast as I could, but not as fast as John. Then I went all the way in. I had to see for myself.

This is the place. That must be the cloth they wrapped him in. But where's his body?

Oh man . . . Jesus, will following you ever be straightforward? Will it always be this road of blind curves? My expectations never pan out! Where are you now?

I'd like to put the blame somewhere else. It's like I set the perfect trap for myself. Jesus saw it and told me, but I still walked right in . . . in front of everybody. I said I wouldn't deny, even if they all did . . . and they all heard him say I would. And then John was there when I swore that I never knew him. And cursed.

I can't get away. Everybody knows. Even if they don't, I do. It's killing me.

That rooster crow has been reverberating in my brain for the past three days! I can't let it go. I'm so ashamed . . . What happens to me now?

It's like I'm sinking.

The women said he was alive but how? It's too much to hope for. Even if he is alive, it will never be the same.

8

An Artist's Medium

As a master artist, Jesus shaped Peter's life.

Every work of art requires a master artist. King Lear only exists because Shakespeare brought him to life. The *Brothers Karamazov* would be unknown if not for Dostoevsky. Beethoven's genius gave birth to the *Moonlight Sonata*.

Artists use media. Whether it's Emily Dickinson's poetry or Shakespeare's drama, each master artist depicts a facet of our human existence that we recognize is true, beautiful and enduring. The artist pursues her craft, interpreting reality in ways that help us to see it as beautiful and worth preserving.

We can think of spiritual formation in similar terms.

The master artist of spiritual formation is God – Father, Son and Holy Spirit. The medium in which he works is the human person – the soul. The end goal is the shaping of the human soul to regain its original beauty, to be re-created in the image of Jesus Christ himself.

Peter

Nowhere in Scripture or in history that I know, do we find a more true, beautiful and enduring shaping of the human soul than in Jesus's relationship with Peter. Observing Peter, we step into the artist's workshop to closely observe the master artist at work. The unthinkable privilege is that we amateurs and spectators are allowed to violate the sacred space of the artist's work. There is no "keep out" sign posted. We are invited, even compelled, to check it out.

The reason for that lies in the intentionality of this artist. His design for Peter is not for Peter only. It is for anyone who dares to expose himself or herself to the artist's creative genius. It is for all who are drawn to the master's touch. The artist is prolific. Peter provides the case study for multitudes of master works of art.

To be shaped by God – Father, Son and Holy Spirit – does not require isolation in a desert cave or even scrupulous disciplines. Disciplines enable us to rehabilitate the body so that we reflexively do what we most deeply desire but they are not *the source* of spiritual formation. Nor are programs, sermons and catechesis the real "stuff" of this spiritual shaping. All of those may serve as implements in the artist's toolbox. Think of them as the artist's brush or the poet's pen. But, none of them is the medium – the human soul – and none of them can replicate the master's creative genius.

Peter talks a lot. We may be inclined to ridicule him for putting his foot in his mouth. In reality, his impetuous nature supplies the open door to the artist's workshop. Peter's chatter allows us to observe his motives, core pivotal

*To be shaped by God – Father, Son and Holy Spirit – does not require isolation in a desert cave or even scrupulous disciplines. Disciplines enable us to rehabilitate the body so that we reflexively do what we most deeply desire but they are not **the source** of spiritual formation. Nor are programs, sermons and catechesis the real "stuff" of this spiritual shaping. All of those may serve as implements in the artist's toolbox. Think of them as the artist's brush or the poet's pen. But, none of them is the medium – the human soul – and none of them can replicate the master's creative genius.*

beliefs and assumptions and how these are reshaped by the master artist. Peter's talking more than any other disciple is not a fluke. It's intentional. Through his word, God pulls back the veil, allowing us to see how Jesus shapes the man.

Perhaps no scene of Peter's life portrays that reality more powerfully than his denial of Jesus. We will come back to that pivotal scene, but Peter's self-deception regarding his faithfulness to Jesus reveals that his core assumptions must undergo major rescripting. Peter's internal self-talk (imagined above) attempts to capture the pain of Peter's awakening to the reality that he is not who he thinks he is.

To enter life-shaping spiritual formation, the heart must be open to the master's direct touch. Peter's certainly was. The process was not without pain and confusion. It was a long-term production with many stations of growth in Peter's self-awareness and trust. But it produced a masterpiece – a human being of rare humility and spiritual fruitfulness who continues to serve as a model for our own spiritual formation.

Spiritual formation: the word "spiritual" is often misunderstood. By using it, I don't mean something other-worldly or merely internal that leads one away from real-life commitments. It may begin internally as core pivotal beliefs are reshaped, but it doesn't end there. It works its way outward through the actions of the body, the thoughts of the mind and the attitudes of the heart to impact the totality of life. If we are spiritually formed, it will be obvious in our relationships. Peter became a fruitful servant-leader because he was spiritually formed. His spiritual formation made him useful, trustworthy, inspiring, insightful, practical and powerful. However, none of these things was the objective of his spiritual formation. They were benefits. The objective was conformity to Jesus.

The purpose of this book is to guide the reader into an intentional contemplation of Peter's spiritual formation, inspiring the reader's own spiritual journey. The purpose is not to become more "spiritual," but to be spiritually formed. It is not to draw us away from the realities of life but to make us more present in those realities as the implements of the master artist's toolkit.

Before we begin down this road, we should consider two elements in Peter's spiritual formation that are easily overlooked – his story and his community.

Peter's Story

Many readers were shaped in a culture that is individualistic rather than collective. I am from the United States – the most individualistic country in the history of the world. The signs of that individualism are widespread in the US and other Western cultures. It is the air we breathe which means we tend not to be very conscious of it. Slogans like "be kind to yourself" or "you deserve the best" or "follow your dreams" betray our inclination to individualistic thinking.

What's more, individualists tend to be oriented towards the present and future rather than the past. Our technological age and the seeming inevitable "progress" of science causes us to view the cultures of the past as antiquated and ignorant.

Peter's spiritual formation subverts those assumptions. Peter's ability to grasp truth and translate it into deep personal transformation grew out of the rich soil of a collective history. Peter's story was woven into the fabric of a people and their history. His identity was rooted in the collective story of his people.

Using our artist theme, the history of Peter's people served as the canvas on which Jesus, the master artist, would do his deep work.

It's important to get a grip on this now. When we read the stories of Peter's transformation, it may seem that it is an individual effort. Jesus is dealing with Peter. Peter's core assumptions are being rescripted. Peter's values are being shaken and reformed. So it would be easy for us to simply overlook the canvas – the backdrop – of this intense personal formation. That's why we need to understand it before we start the journey. When we become aware of it, we can see how central the story of Peter's people is to his discipleship. But it is rarely stated explicitly. In fact, that doesn't happen until the end of Peter's journey with Jesus.

The scene from Luke 24 takes place after Jesus has risen from the dead. Jesus meets the disciples who are shell-shocked. They now understand the tomb is empty. They hear the report from the two disciples on the Emmaus Road, insisting that Jesus is alive. Mary Magdalene and the other women bring the news . . . but who could believe that a man just walked out of the tomb? Don't think for a moment that it was easier for the disciples in AD33 than it is for us in the third millennium. People in that day saw death and its realities more closely than we do. So when he stood among them and said, "Peace to you," they naturally thought they were seeing a ghost. Tenderly, Jesus encourages them to touch him, his hands, his feet, so they can understand he's not a ghost, but a real person. Then, driving home the reality that he is physically alive, he asks them for something to eat.

But after these preliminaries, Jesus gets to the point. He says, in effect, "I told you so." I told you that all that was written about me in the Law, the Prophets and the Psalms had to be fulfilled. The Law, the Prophets and the Psalms were the three divisions of the Hebrew Scriptures – the Old Testament – the collective story of the Hebrew people.

Please pause here and ask yourself how important the Old Testament is for your spiritual formation. On a scale of 1 to 10, with 1 being "unimportant" and 10 being "extremely important," what number would you assign the Old Testament in your spiritual formation?

Peter's Exposure to the Old Testament

In our day of proliferation of media, it is difficult for us to understand the centrality of the Old Testament story for the social and faith formation of the Jewish people at the time of Jesus. It was the meditation of every synagogue gathering, the subject of every holiday, the point of seasonal pilgrimages to Jerusalem, the curriculum of childhood education. Unlike our day of cultural and ethnic diversity, the Jews of Jesus's day built their collective life around their shared history, recorded in the sacred writings.

Peter's home in Capernaum was adjacent to the local synagogue. We can be reasonably sure that the fisherman-apostle spent ample time listening to the recitation of the Law, the Prophets and the Psalms. Jewish boys would normally begin Torah study at the age of five.[1] As copies of the text were difficult to obtain, a pious Jew would have committed long sections of the Torah to memory. He may have engaged actively, or at least listened passively, to Rabbis

---

1. Card, *Fragile Stone*, 16.

searching out the meaning of these texts and their implications for the Jewish people of his time, especially their anticipation of the Messiah.

For Peter, there was no news outlet menu of CNN, BBC, etc. He didn't click on the *Times* or Reuters to get up to speed on current events. There was no Amazon Kindle, or a bookshop offering an array of literary genres. Doubtless, there were political rumblings in Galilee but the interpretive grid for it all was the Hebrew Scriptures. Those Scriptures and their interpretation in the temple and synagogues formed the worldview of Peter and the other disciples.

My, what a narrow view of the world! How poor they were compared to our wealth of accessible information! (Pause.)

Are you tempted to think that way? If so, admit it. If left unchecked, my internal monologue tends to go like this: "Those poor people! They had such a restricted view of the world. How sad. No wonder they lacked imagination!" (Pause again.)

When the Father chose a canvas on which to produce the masterpiece of Peter's spiritual formation, he chose this time, these people, this story, this canvas. The collective story of the Hebrew people was the story Jesus came to fulfill and to conclude. He chose to paint on this canvas because it was the right one. It was the true story which was told in the sacred writings.

The Old Testament was a story "in search of a conclusion."[2] It was the story of humanity alienated from God, and God's pursuit to re-establish a relationship with humanity through the progeny of Abraham. The high points of the story in the Exodus led by Moses, and then David's kingdom, are amazing, but also disappointing. No one lives "happily ever after!" The plot quickly devolves into idolatry, debauched leaders and ultimately the loss of the promised holy land as God's chosen people go into exile.

Though some of Abraham's seed are sent back to the land, the return is far from glorious. The entire Jewish narrative depicted in the Exodus, the temple, the priesthood, the law, the kingdom and the prophets awaited a consummation. When Jesus met with his disciples in that room, he said to them in no uncertain terms, "I am the subject and the conclusion of that story. It's not just your story. It's my story. Now let me help you see me in it." So Jesus "opened their minds" to understand the story.

When Jesus wanted to create a masterpiece of spiritual formation, he chose to paint on that canvas. That's important.

---

2. Wright, *New Testament and the People of God*, 217.

Peter's Story and Ours

So, we should reconsider. Perhaps we are the underprivileged ones whose media-rich age has deprived us, at least to some degree, of the real story, the true one, the one that Jesus came to fulfill. Maybe it is we whose imagination is limited, who cannot see the forest for the trees. Maybe a carnival of narratives and the pseudo-freedom to choose the narrative we want is not so great after all. Maybe we've been duped. Access is not knowledge.

But let's be honest; the Old Testament is hard going – endless genealogies, religious wars, vindictive leaders, misogyny, polygamy, sibling rivalries, genocide, and the list could go on.

In reality, we need to think long and hard about *how* we read the Old Testament. It simply will not work to read it as prescriptive; "Jacob or Noah or David did this, so we should too." Sometimes that works but more often, it's a disaster. The Old Testament characters are rarely role models that we should imitate. That's not the purpose.

Nor does the Old Testament provide a pristine account of religious history so that we now have all the facts we need for drawing informed conclusions about origins and the history of the world's varied peoples. The Old Testament is often read that way, but the results fail to satisfy. Some read the Old Testament as a spiritual puzzle, a cryptic foretelling of the future that only informed insiders can understand. The fact that their predictions do not come to pass does not seem to deter them. They end up undermining faith and showing themselves to be as clueless as the rest of us! So what do we mean when we say that the Hebrew Scriptures are the canvas on which Peter's spiritual formation was painted?

We mean that the story of the Old Testament is the story of God's interaction with and pursuit of a people whom he intended to use to bring blessing to all the nations of the world.[3] Jesus fulfilled that purpose and also relaunched it. He expanded the people of God, sweeping in peoples of all tongues and tribes and nations, and he continues to use that diverse and inclusive people as his people to bless all the nations of the world. Like ancient Israel, the people of God today are often obstinate, slow to understand and uncooperative. Nevertheless, God is pursuing that people, indwelling them, imperfect as they are, to bring about his purposes in the world.

---

3. N. T. Wright's article is helpful to understand how the story of the Bible can exercise authority in contemporary life. "How Can the Bible Be Authoritative?" The article is accessible online: https://biblicalstudies.org.uk/pdf/vox/vol21/bible_wright.pdf.

This story expresses God's original purposes for humanity. In fact, it is the story of humanity's betrayal of God and how God undertook to subvert humanity's arrogance by bringing his own Son – the perfect image of God – to indwell humanity, redeem them and ultimately effect a full reconciliation of human beings to himself.

This story expresses God's original purposes for humanity. In fact, it is the story of humanity's betrayal of God and how God undertook to subvert humanity's arrogance by bringing his own Son – the perfect image of God – to indwell humanity, redeem them and ultimately effect a full reconciliation of human beings to himself.

So we do not read the Old Testament as prescriptive (though some parts certainly are). We don't read it as an idealized history. We don't read it as cryptic symbolism that must be discerned by elite insiders. It is a story of brokenness and long-term restoration that awaits fulfillment. Though Peter and the other disciples had internalized that story, they had to learn how to read it and understand it in a new way. Jesus used the canvas of the Old Testament story and supplied its interpretation. This story, including its surprise interpretation, is the one we must internalize if we are to be formed spiritually. Epilogue 1 of this book titled "Going Deeper: Centering Jesus in the Old Testament" suggests ways to read the Old Testament with Jesus as its focal point and fulfillment. If the concept seems strange to you or you struggle to reconcile the God of the Old Testament with the Jesus of the New Testament, consider reading that chapter now, before going further in Peter's journey.

Peter's Community

After Peter's story, the other important element is Peter's community. We've already described the historic community of the Jewish people, but what we're after here is the immediate community in which Peter interacted with Jesus.

From the time Jesus called Peter to follow him and promised him he would become a fisher of men, he was embraced in a brotherhood, which also included a sisterhood. But for now, let's focus on the twelve.

One of them was Peter's brother, Andrew. The two knew each other intimately, having grown up together and collaborated in their father's (John/Jonah) fishing business in Capernaum. The other set of brothers, James and John (sons of Zebedee), were also associates in the fishing venture. They could have been cousins or part of Peter's extended family by marriage. Although we don't know for sure, it is possible that these two families lived together in the home in Capernaum which became Jesus's home during his Galilean ministry.[4] Some suggest that Mary, the mother of Jesus, may have been a sister of Siloam, wife of Zebedee, mother of James and John. If it is true, James and John were Jesus's first cousins. Others suggest that Peter may have married a sister of the same family, making him related by marriage to James and John. Although this is unconfirmed, it fits well with the cultural practices of the time. What is certain is that the two sets of brothers knew each other well and worked together in a fishing partnership.

Additionally, Philip (one of the twelve) was from Bethsaida (same hometown as Peter) as was Nathaniel. They, along with Thomas, assisted in a fishing expedition. So Peter was a close associate and possibly a family relation of three disciples. He may have also been a work associate of three others. What emerges is a deeply interwoven community linked by threads of work and family.

We should consider that *Peter was known.*

With all his foibles, his past, his impetuous temperament, he was known and accepted. He had a long history with four of the twelve disciples and possibly more. The women who followed Jesus knew him as well and one of them was likely Peter's mother. Presumably, Peter's wife and mother-in-law who lived in the same house played some role in the collective life of the twelve. The point is that Peter's spiritual formation took place in a rich social context involving many family relations and close colleagues in Jesus's traveling band.

Peter's spiritual formation did not take place in isolation but in community.

It is noteworthy that, even when Peter was at his lowest point as a disciple, his community stuck with him or perhaps he stuck with them. After his denial of Jesus, he gathers with the disciples and decides to go fishing. They accompany him. Through the ups and downs of Peter's spiritual journey, his community held firm, bonded by deep family relationships in a culture that valued family and a shared vocation.

---

4. Archeologists have determined which home likely served as the base of the Capernaum fishing business that Zebedee and John/Jonah ran. It was a large house with a central courtyard and surrounding rooms. Helyer, *Life and Witness of Peter*, 28–29.

Peter's Community and Ours

The richness and depth of Peter's social relationships should reassure us. As we trace his spiritual formation, we do so in a context rich with relational acceptance. His journey does not lead us to a monastic cell, a hermit's cave, or even a one-on-one Bible study, but to a group of friends and family. How freeing!

On the flipside, we aren't like Peter. Peter's relationships were the natural by-product of life in a collective culture that placed a high value on family relationships and work associates. I suspect many readers live in a highly mobile culture. Some hope to see family members once a year. Extended family members might connect through social media or occasionally at holidays or reunions. Jobs relocate us far from the place(s) of our upbringing. Even in church, small groups form for six months and then reform around a different purpose. Many people today are not good at long-term committed relationships. In fact, we may view Peter's relationally rich community with skepticism that it is too enmeshed, overly interdependent!

There's a reason the master artist works in and through our community. It has to do with his nature and our being in his image. But that gets a little ahead of our story. For now, let's recall that Jesus worked out of a story – the collective story of his Old Testament people. He also worked in and through a community – Peter's close associates, family and friends. Spiritual formation is not done in isolation. We are being woven into a tapestry, joining our lives to the threads of many other lives. It's what we were made for!

So before we take off on this journey, we must ask ourselves if we have a community of committed friends, a relational network that provides a natural source of accountability, direction and encouragement? If that is not in place, then spiritual formation is *not* likely to happen. Even if we have great intentions, without being known to others, we may be doing little more than data collection as we read and think through these stations of Peter's transformation.

For spiritual formation to take place, we will need to nurture a community around us. Consider asking two to five friends to walk with you through a journey of spiritual formation. The more natural your relationship with these people (e.g. family, church members, colleagues), the more likely they can be a community to you.

They will likely want to know what being a community involves. For starters, it involves a willingness to be honest about struggles and assumptions. It involves the will to share those struggles in a non-judgmental context where the goal is growth in character towards the attitudes and actions which Jesus and his disciples taught. That's the starting point. If you find two to five people who say "yes" to that, then your prospects for spiritual formation in community are good.

1

Facing the Shadow-Self

A Disciple's Starting Point

*The gospel is this: We are more sinful and flawed
in ourselves than we ever dared believe, yet at the
very same time we are more loved and accepted
in Jesus Christ than we ever dared hope.*

Tim Keller, *The Meaning of Marriage*

*True spirituality is not a superhuman religiosity;
it is simply true humanity released from bondage
to sin and renewed by the Holy Spirit.*

Richard Lovelace, *Dynamics of Spiritual Life*

On one occasion, while the crowd was pressing in on him to hear the word of God, he was standing by the lake of Gennesaret, and he saw two boats by the lake, but the fishermen had gone out of them and were washing their nets. Getting into one of the boats, which was Simon's, he asked him to put out a little from the land. And he sat down and taught the people from the boat.

And when he had finished speaking, he said to Simon, "Put out into the deep and let down your nets for a catch." And Simon answered, "Master, we toiled all night and took nothing! But at your word I will let down the nets." And when they had done this, they enclosed a large number of fish, and their nets were breaking. They signaled to their partners in the other boat to come and help them. And they came and filled both the boats, so that they began to sink.

But when Simon Peter saw it, he fell down at Jesus' knees, saying, "Depart from me, for I am a sinful man, O Lord." For he and all who were with him were astonished at the catch of fish that they had taken, and so also were James and John, sons of Zebedee, who were partners with Simon. And Jesus said to Simon, "Do not be afraid; from now on you will be catching men." And when they had brought their boats to land, they left everything and followed him.

Drop the nets . . . again!?

If it were anyone but him, I'd just say "I'm not that stupid."

All night and into the early morning this water was still as death. I've fished this lake hundreds of times. I know when it's time to hang the nets and call it a night.

And he says, "Cast the net again."

What can I say to a man like Jesus? "I'm not that stupid?!"

. . . trying to put it all together . . . been following him a while . . . me and my brother . . . James and John too. But the week at Capernaum rocked my world. He rolled into my hometown. He stayed at my house, taught at my synagogue. This place will never be the same.

Around here, we know about evil spirits. We know what they do to people. But never have I heard an evil spirit say those things. I clearly heard him say, "We know who you are, Jesus, Qadosh Elohim."

What does that even mean?! How does a demon declare Jesus to be the holy one of God?!

And it didn't faze Jesus! He just commanded the demon to come out . . . like he knew it would . . . and it did! That demon slung Bin Zadok to the ground like a sack of grain. And then it left him, unharmed. What do I do with that?!

Later at the house, my wife's mom is in bed with a high fever . . . He rebukes the fever. Who does that? But she immediately gets up, the perfect picture of health!

After we eat together, we're all out in the courtyard. By now, news of Bin Zadok has spread through the village. So everyone is bringing sick family members. He touches them, puts his hands on them, and they get better. Every single one of them!

He casts out more demons. We never knew there were so many. We heard them shrieking, "You are the Son of God!"

So I can't say "no" to Jesus. At least I want him to know that I've already been there and done that. I am an experienced fisherman, after all. It's my specialty. I tell him we've already tried, all night, in fact, but, because it's Jesus, I give in to his request.

And now, just look out there! That water that was still as death is overcome with signs of life . . . movement, splashing, frenzy. It reaches a boiling point, like a pot over a fire as we raise that loaded net to the surface. Fish. Way more than I've ever seen in a net.

"James! John! Can you guys get the other side of the net? Throw me a rope. It's gonna take all of us to haul these in."

All those fish in my net . . . my wife won't believe this! I'm not sure I can believe this!

It's hard work getting them all in. The net is brimming, heavy. I'm aware that Jesus is watching, amazingly calm and unhurried. He's not surprised.

There's a moment when all the heavy lifting is done. The morning sun beats down hot on our bare skin. The water returns to a placid stillness. We fall back in the boat exhausted, with the fish filling the hull of the boat.

At that moment. It all converges. I realize who he is.

And it's like his presence is shining on me, exposing me. And I realize who I am. I can't be here. He can't be here. Not with me . . . not in my boat.

At that moment, the weight of it all throws me forward and down into that mountain of fish. I desperately want to hide my face from this man. But I find myself lunging toward him. I can't hide from him. Either he leaves or . . .

At that moment, I never wanted so badly to be accepted by another person and I never knew so surely that I could never be accepted by him.

His reply was the last thing I expected. In that scene of shame, while I lay prostrate, face-down in the fish, with Andrew and our friends looking on, he said, "Don't be afraid. You're going to catch men from now on."

He poured honor on my shame. I'd never felt such an embrace . . . and I know I'll never forget it. He poured honor on my shame!

Beginnings of Transformation

A Middle Eastern proverb preserves a wise principle of communication: "The best words are few and to the point."

The author of the gospel economizes verbiage allowing the reader to infer from Simon's body language and words. A modern novelist wouldn't let the moment pass without detailing the disciple's emotional response. But not Luke. It's there for us to contemplate, but the author leaves us to our own conclusions.

What provokes Simon's response? He falls face down, on a mound of squirming fish, in the hull of the boat and asks Jesus to get away from him! That response is meant to stun us. It is intended to provoke questions. "But why, Peter? Why ask Jesus to get away from you? What's up with that?"

It doesn't fit. He doesn't even say "thank-you for this amazing catch!"

Simon's response reveals his heart.

If Simon's heart's desire was the profitability of his business, inviting Jesus to join the fishermen for a share of the profits would have been the right move. Apparently, he's not interested in the bottom line.

From a ministry impact standpoint, Simon could easily have strategized a PR campaign, promoting Jesus as "the prosperity Rabbi." Thankfully, it never occurs to him.

So what is in Simon's heart?

Picture the scene, mid-morning as the sun begins to warm up the Sea of Galilee. Simon and a few of his fellow fishermen hauling in a catch of fish the likes of which they've never seen. Jesus, seated, I imagine, in the stern of the boat, perhaps amused by the frenzy as the catch is hauled in. Once the fish are securely in the boat, filling the hull with their freshly captured life, Simon falls at the knees of Jesus. There's nowhere to fall but in the fish!

"Depart from me for I am a sinful man, O Lord!"

But why that thought?

We will tease that out in this chapter, but for now, let it surprise you. You've probably read it a few hundred times. It was a powerful turning point in the disciple's relationship to Jesus. It was the entry point of his discipleship, the making of a servant-leader. At this moment, Simon realizes fully that what he presents is not actually who he is. Somehow, in Jesus's presence, the mask is off. The reality is laid bare. His misalignment, estrangement, is fully apparent when he is with Jesus.

His plea for Jesus to depart represents a visceral acknowledgment of this internal alienation. There is no way that he can carry on normally in the presence of Jesus. One of the two, Jesus or Simon, must go!

Jesus however sees a third way and calmly calls Simon to it – transformation.

In effect, Jesus invites Simon to join him. What Simon has seen Jesus doing the past few days in Capernaum – healing the sick, casting out demons and teaching with authority – has left Simon overwhelmed. The unthinkable reality is that this is his destiny. Fear not! From now on *you* will be catching men, just as you've seen me do.

Reviewing the Relationship

It might help to see that this stunning response of Simon was not the product of one event, or even a weekend in Capernaum. It was the outgrowth of a relationship that had already grown deep and strong.

Each gospel writer records an initial call of Jesus to his disciples.[1] Putting the four accounts together leads to the conclusion that there must have been at least two different events, perhaps three. Simon was introduced to Jesus by Andrew, his brother and a disciple of John the Baptist (John 1:35–42). This took place where John was baptizing. At some point, Jesus called Simon (along with Andrew, James and John) near the Sea of Galilee (Matt 4:18–22; Mark 1:16–20). The Luke 5 event that we are considering here may have taken place later, after Simon's initial call. The fact that Jesus, after preaching in the synagogues of Galilee, went to Simon's home, suggests there was already a relationship. So Simon's response to Jesus comes as a result of a history of interaction that may have been months long.

Simon already knows Jesus. His heart is already drawn to him. Still, the events of Capernaum catapult him to a new level of response. Observing Jesus's compassion and authority forces Simon to confront himself. He sees himself in a new light and what he sees is not pretty.

Capernaum was abuzz with the new Rabbi. He taught with authority, not like the other rabbis (Luke 4:32). A precipitating event occurred when one of the marginalized locals came into the synagogue shrieking, "Ha! What have you to do with us, Jesus of Nazareth? Have you come to destroy us? I know who you are – the Holy One of God" (Luke 4:34). If that had happened in your church, it would have made quite an impression, right? It was a demonic manifestation. When Jesus commanded the demon to be silent and come out, the demon violently threw the man to the ground, but it did come out, to the amazement of the locals. You can imagine the talk around the Galilean countryside. "What kind of authority is this?! He commands demons and they have to obey him!"

---

1. Mark 1:16–20; Matthew 4:18–22; Luke 5:1–11; and John 1:35–42. John 1:43–51 also relates the call of Philip and Nathaniel.

His plea for Jesus to depart represents a visceral acknowledgment of this internal alienation. There is no way that he can carry on normally in the presence of Jesus. One of the two, Jesus or Simon, must go! Jesus however sees a third way and calmly calls Simon to it – transformation.

Archeologists are relatively certain they have uncovered the remains of Simon's house, a large two-story home beside the synagogue. It was shared with other fishermen families such that it became a small community linked to the synagogue and connected through family and work relationships. It seems this house became Jesus's center of operations in Galilee.

That Capernaum community has never seen a visitor like this. First, he heals Simon's mother-in-law. Yes, Simon Peter is a married man. Jesus heals her so completely that she immediately gets up and begins to serve. No recuperation time needed!

Then the village people bring their sick. Imagine a two-story house built around a spacious open courtyard, normally used for communal meals and family interaction. A steady stream of Galileans flow into that courtyard where Jesus graciously receives and heals each one by laying his hands on them. Demons also leave their victims, crying out, "You are the Son of God." Part of Simon's response to Jesus must owe to the consistent confession of the dark spiritual forces of his village that Jesus is indeed the Son of God.

Those must have been dramatic days for Simon. By now, he realizes that he is not dealing with your typical rabbi. This Rabbi heals the sick. He commands spiritual evil forces who readily acknowledge his divine identity. And now he unveils his mastery over creation as fish from every nook and crevice of the Sea of Galilee make a beeline for Peter's net.

He has a right to be overwhelmed. We would be too. But the question remains: why did Peter react the way he did? What led him to such a dramatic and total acknowledgment of his own unworthiness as he threw himself at the knees of Jesus in that boat?

Simon's Preparation

In the last chapter we saw the importance of Simon Peter's story. Simon saw himself as part of a collective history recounted by the Hebrew prophets. That history, and its lack of a satisfying conclusion, had led to confusion for the people of Jesus's time. Various groups set out to revive the notion that the Jews were in fact an exceptional lot, God's chosen people. Any of those might have influenced Simon.

We know the Pharisees for their scrupulous observance of the written law to prepare for Messiah's arrival. Then there were the Zealots. One of them, the other Simon, made his way into the community of Jesus's disciples (Luke 6:15). These nationalist patriots wanted to break the bonds of subjugation and cast off the heavy tax burden that filled Rome's coffers. They looked for a new warrior-king in the style of David to re-establish Jewish sovereignty.

The Essenes were separatists who held themselves to be the true expression of Israel's return from exile. They were the righteous remnant, a human embodiment of the temple. They fled to isolated communities to purify themselves ritually and morally in preparation for the coming Messiah(s). It seems they anticipated a priest-Messiah for the temple and another one as King in the line of David.[2]

Though Simon was well-aware of these and other movements, there is no evidence that any of these was significant in Simon's preparation. The Gospel writers recognize only one person as the legitimate forerunner of Messiah. A new prophet, John, emerges, clad in animal skins and restricting his diet to wild locusts and honey, calling his people to come out to the wilderness of Judea and wash themselves as a sign of repentance in preparation for Messiah. He was a charismatic revivalist calling for personal and corporate purification before Israel's visitation by Yahweh. We know that John's prophetic call had found its way deep into Simon's family as Andrew, his brother, was one of the inner circle of John's disciples.

As a desert herald, John prepares the way of the Lord, echoing Isaiah:

> Behold, the LORD God comes with might,
>   and his arm rules for him;
> behold his reward is with him
>   and his recompense before him.
> He will tend his flock like a shepherd;
>   he will gather the lambs in his arms;
> he will carry them in his bosom,
>   and gently lead those that are with young." (Isa 40:10–11)

The promised visitation of Yahweh to his people reverberated through the hills of the Judean wilderness as the Jews made their way to John to be

---

2. Wright, *New Testament and the People of God*, 203–8.

washed in the Jordan River. By calling his people into the wilderness, John was recalling the Exodus. He was calling his people out, collectively, corporately. The repentance he called for was both personal and societal. The Jewish systems of purification were not working. John envisioned a radical transformation of the heart.

Simon's spiritual roots were sunk deeply in the soil of John's call to repentance. If you have come under the influence of a spiritual renewal movement, a revival, you will find no difficulty in understanding Simon's reaction. Strong conviction of personal and collective sin is nearly always a feature of revival. It often leads to confession of sin accompanied by emotional and physical manifestations. People may weep or fall to the ground, overwhelmed by their own guilt and shame as they are brought face to face with the purity and holiness of God's presence.

With the Capernaum events fresh in his mind, Simon now had no doubt that Yahweh was visiting his people as promised. No disguise, no mask, no cover-up operation would suffice in the presence of Jesus. Simon could not stay there for his heart was estranged, alienated from the purity and love of God.

Like the frenzied fish in his net, Simon has been taken unawares. He gasps for breath as a force greater than he lands him in the new and alien environment of God's presence. Like his catch, he flails in a hopeless attempt to get away with nowhere to go.[3]

Is it a particular sin that troubles you, Simon? We have that much in common with him. Thoughts and actions cling to our memories, accusing us before God. But the Gospels give us no hint of particular sins that plague Simon. The blazing light of the Hebrew Scriptures lays claim to the totality of life and provides a better guide than our curiosity.

> Hear, O Israel: The LORD our God, the LORD is one. You shall love the LORD your God with all your heart, with all your soul and with all your might. (Deut 6:4–5)

The Pharisees had done a disservice to the Mosaic law by requiring external, legalistic conformity. Jesus had no use for that. The law itself clearly demanded an internal purity – a heart conformed to the righteous requirements of a holy God. It was this internal purity that would break sin's power of alienation over individuals and societies. Of this law, Jesus declared that even the smallest stroke of the pen would not be annulled until all was fulfilled.

---

3. Card, *Fragile Stone*, 39.

Simon was caught. In the presence of the righteous law-giver, who demanded a heart attuned to God's righteous law, he had no claim. No leverage.

Simon was forced to face himself, a self that was alienated and estranged from God.

Our Alienation

Jesus becoming a human being (the incarnation) may be considered the distinctive feature of the Christian faith. God with us – Immanuel. It is a unique reality; it is the grounds of the good news, the gospel.

But there is a danger. In coming to be with us, God has *not* become altogether like us. This scene on the Sea of Galilee reinforces this fact. As Simon contemplates the human being before him, he sees eyes, ears, nose, arms and legs . . . all the parts of a human being. Yet Simon is supremely aware that Jesus is so unlike him that he cannot be in his presence. The holiness of Jesus is incompatible with the sinfulness of Simon. Oil and water. Light and darkness.

The dangerous aspect of the incarnation, of God's eternal Son becoming a human being, is that we may subtly think that he is altogether like us. We take him as a buddy, boyfriend or therapist. This scene on the Sea of Galilee reinforces the fact that God in Jesus is still the Holy One of Israel. He is not altogether like Simon and Simon is not altogether like him.

The dangerous aspect of the incarnation, of God's eternal Son becoming a human being, is that we may subtly think that he is altogether like us. We take him as a buddy, boyfriend or therapist. This scene on the Sea of Galilee reinforces the fact that God in Jesus is still the Holy One of Israel. He is not altogether like Simon and Simon is not altogether like him.

The two cannot coexist. One must depart, and Simon frantically asks Jesus to leave.

Jesus mercifully declines and unveils the reality that Simon will be transformed through relationship with him, following him. From that place of transformation, Simon will venture forth among his own people as an agent of collective change, forming a new society of those who will enter Jesus's kingdom. The healing of Simon's guilt will lead to the breaking of sin's power.

We weren't created in this state of alienation. Our spiritual parents tragically broke faith with God which resulted in an alien instinct to hide from his presence. Hearing the sound of the Lord God walking in the garden, Adam and Eve ran and hid! It was, in fact, the very same presence which Simon asked to depart from him. Having left the presence of God, the human soul became a *shadow* of its former self. Alienation invaded the heart – alienation from God, from our true selves and from each other. It invades us as individuals, but it also invades every human relationship, institution and society.

"Alienation" is a good word to describe what Simon is experiencing. Traditional Christian teaching uses the word "sin." That good word is over-used and often misunderstood. We usually think of "sin" as the things we do that make us feel ashamed such that we hide them from others. That is a mere effect of alienation, but it doesn't get to the crux of the idea. Alienation implies that though we once were in relationship, we no longer are. We've become aliens, strangers, unknown.

The fact of our alienation implies a certain revulsion. The beauty of God, once freely shared with humanity, is no longer found in us, or it is so badly skewed that it is unrecognizable. That's a hard word for us to hear. We're quite positive about human ability and creativity. We're all about self-actualization and reaching our full potential.

There will be a time, of course, when Peter's abilities are redeemed and elevated to be useful to Jesus ("Follow me and I will make you fishers of men"), but he's not there yet. This is the gateway, the entry point, the starting blocks for a life-marathon of spiritual formation. Peter's gaze into his alienated soul was the entry point to spiritual formation. We, too, must start here.

Our issue is the posture of our heart. Some will refer to it as the self or the soul. Here, we prefer "heart" which is the seat of how we think, act and feel. Simon's alienated heart makes him, like Adam and Eve, want to run and hide. The alienated heart is the state of humanity. Cut off from the source of life, we go about searching for something to fill the void, often dressing up our shadow-self with the externals of position, wealth and pleasure – proxy gods. The reality is that we can look pretty good dressed up in these externals. Simon had them as well – a leader in the community, a respected tradesman, a pillar of the local synagogue. His dressed-up shadow-self had served him well and had prevented the need to search for his true self. The true self is what we were created to be – image-bearers of God. Our positions and pleasures were meant to flow from that center – a life lived from the inside-out – but that direction was reversed by a great betrayal. We now live outside-in, seeking to fill the void of our alienated hearts.

Simon's anguished cry, "Lord, depart from me!" is a deeply felt acknowledgement that it is not working. In an instant, Simon grasps that his life does not correspond to the image of divine beauty who sits in the stern of that boat. He is repulsed and he fully expects that Jesus is too.

This is the entry point because every station of Simon's spiritual formation from here on out will be a progressive stripping away of Simon's false self, rescripting his core beliefs and assumptions – a ruthless extraction of his idols. The treasonous posture of his heart will undergo radical corrective surgery. Nothing will be left intact. Simon begins his journey with no conditions. He brings no chips to the table, no skills to the draft, no qualifications to the job. He starts from zero, emptying himself in order to be filled, releasing to receive, wiping the hard-drive so that the divine programmer can do his work.

The fact that Peter gets there so early in the relationship and comes to such a radical recognition likely owes to his preparation. It commends him to us as an example and anticipates how he will be instrumental in bringing a similar transformation to others.

Many of us will spend long years getting to the starting blocks, the place where we realize that what we hold on to so tightly is only an impediment to our spiritual development. The Spirit pursues us into "inside-out" life. Peter got there dramatically, in a way that we can see, contemplate and learn from.

Simon's "face-in-the-fish" plea punches his spiritual formation ticket. For Peter, as for us, the journey will be long but well-worth the pain. He is returning to the life he was intended to live – a life that flows from the center.

Perhaps, like me, you were taught that this transformation happens at the point of the new birth. For some, that may be true. But I venture that many come to Christ with hardly an inkling of how misaligned our hearts really are. That miscalculation masks a crying need for deep spiritual transformation which is why many believers make little progress as disciples. We only come to that realization as we progress in our spiritual journey. So don't read Simon's confession as synonymous with his new birth. It was a station of his spiritual journey, the starting point, but the journey to inside-out living has many more stations.

My journey of spiritual formation, of discipleship to Jesus, begins with a full-faced confrontation of my own spiritual bankruptcy, my own self-seeking, my own idolatry, no matter how cleverly concealed. The mask must come off. I am alienated from God, from those I love and even from my true self.

Now we can begin.

Peter's Alienation and Ours

This chapter has been a long reflection on Peter's spiritual self-appraisal that took place on the Sea of Galilee. No one enters into spiritual formation from zero. We have all undergone some preparation. Relationships, teaching, reading, upbringing, etc., may all play a role in our spiritual formation.

Try to describe your own preparation for spiritual formation up to this point in your life. If you feel you have already progressed in the journey of formation, you may want to describe the events which led to the early stages of your journey. Write those events, noting how they played into the formation of who you are today. A key question: Did your spiritual formative influences lead you along a similar path as Peter? Did you realize you were hopelessly alienated from God? Perhaps sharing the content of this chapter with a few friends in your community, allowing them to ask clarifying questions, can help you determine if you've passed through this station. Getting perspective from others is vital.

We will see that Peter's experience on the Sea of Galilee will continue to exert an influence on his subsequent formation. Similarly, the early stages of our journey will continue to influence our formation through the years of our life. Peter shows us the way. A deep, even visceral, realization of our alienation from God is the starting point. Reflect on that. As you do so, consider the following:

1. When was your "Sea of Galilee" moment? Can you identify one or two instances when you came to a profound spiritual awakening? (i.e. when you realized something about yourself and your relationship to God that you had not previously recognized?)

2. Articulate the lesson(s) that you derived from those significant moments.

3. Can you identify key persons who influenced your spiritual preparation? (much as John the Baptist influenced Peter; e.g. parents, relatives, friends, teachers, public figures)

2

Stepping into Chaos

The Disciple's Risk

Immediately he made the disciples get into the boat and go before him to the other side, while he dismissed the crowds. And after he had dismissed the crowds, he went up on the mountain by himself to pray. When evening came, he was there alone, but the boat by this time was a long way from the land, beaten by the waves, for the wind was against them. And in the fourth watch of the night he came to them, walking on the sea. But when the disciples saw him walking on the sea, they were terrified and said, "It is a ghost!" and they cried out in fear. But immediately Jesus spoke to them, saying, "Take heart; it is I. Do not be afraid."

And Peter answered him, "Lord, if it is you, command me to come to you on the water." He said, "Come." So Peter got out of the boat and walked on the water and came to Jesus. But when he saw the wind, he was afraid and beginning to sink he cried out, "Lord, save me." Jesus immediately reached out his hand and took hold of him, saying to him, "O you of little faith, why did you doubt?" And when they got into the boat, the wind ceased. And those in the boat worshipped him saying, "Truly you are the Son of God."

Another crazy night . . . one of those "Jesus nights." We never know what will happen next with him.

He tells us to feed all these people. James and I just look at each other and shake our heads. We have nothing! One of the guys has the presence of mind to suggest those few loaves and fish. That was all it took. We could live for weeks off the leftovers!

I am exhausted, but what happened there gave me new energy. I think we all feel it . . . as long as Jesus is with us, there is nothing to worry about.

Of course, the people want to make him king. Right? He feeds them. They're feeling it too . . . nothing to worry about as long as Jesus is with us. So what does he do? He puts us in the boat while he goes up the mountain. What was he up to? Sometimes, the things he does make no sense – until later.

We set out, with some dark clouds over Mt. Hermon, but nobody could have predicted what would happen. They sweep down over the sea, turning our little fishing boat into a death trap! The sea throws us around like a kernel of grain! We drop sail and put in oars, but we all know how this could end up. We fight the whole night, trying to make it across.

We're exhausted and at the point of despair when we see something coming toward us. We think it's a ghost! He must have known because he says, "Don't be afraid. I am." It's like you're surprised, shocked even, but then, in the next instant, you realize, no, this is his normal. Despairing one moment, thinking my life might come to an end. The next moment he's here and I want to go to him. I'm caught up in him, inspired.

So I call out that I want to go to him. And he says, "Come on." And I get out of the boat. For a minute, I'm walking on the water. It's amazing. Don't ask me how. All I know is that with him, I'm doing what he does. At least, I did for a minute.

I'm not sure what happened. The waves are mounting up and the wind is howling. I'm drenched from head to toe. I begin to go down so I yell to him to save me. He does . . . takes me by the arm and asks why I doubted. Why I doubted?

We get in the boat and it's like it always is when he's with us. That's Jesus. He does something like that and then he's just with us again, like we always were, like normal. We're beginning to get it. He's with us but he's not like us. He's more. In that moment, he said "I am." I can't get away from that.

This morning I'm thinking about my walk on water. I wish I hadn't sunk! His question is still turning around in my head. Why did I doubt? What I saw and heard and felt overwhelmed me. I knew the sea was stronger than I was. I knew it could take me down.

I wouldn't have ever tried that if he hadn't been there. Knowing he was there got me out of that boat. Even the "normal" days with him stretch and challenge me, but what happened yesterday!? I can't even put it into words. Yeah, I sank, but I'd do it again. Jesus gets to me right here (the heart). He gets inside me.

Experiential Learning: When Failing Is Good

I recall going to a retreat center with a ropes course. The idea was to learn valuable lessons – trust, teamwork, overcoming fear – through an experience on the ropes. I remember my first step on to the high rope as I held two guide ropes that were intended to help me cross to the other side. My leg began to shake, causing the rope to oscillate under my feet. The more my leg shook, the faster my heart beat. I began to perspire. My grip on the guide ropes tightened, as did my jaw. My whole body was responding to the stress brought about by walking across a rope elevated about 30 feet. The experience brought me face to face with my limitations and how a small change in environment can make a drastic difference in my response and ability to cope. The retreat leaders called it "experiential learning" and, believe me, there was a lot to learn!

This event in Peter's life is similar. Panic sets in. The fear of being overcome by waves and a rolling sea was real. Peter's mind and body responded as he calls out to Jesus. Once again, Jesus designs an ideal learning scenario for his mentee.

Every church-goer is familiar with this story. Drawing on a reserve of sermons and devotional reading, we intuitively understand the moral of the story: "Keep your eyes on Jesus and not on the waves." Let's begin by admitting that our instant application oversimplifies the story. For Simon Peter, the lesson is deeper and richer than keeping his mind focused on Jesus, important though that may be. Our familiarity with the story also reassures us because Jesus is calling someone else's faith "little." Peter becomes a negative example which, frankly, leads to missing the point. We should be careful not to see ourselves as the "courageous faith walkers" while those who disagree with us are small in faith, sinking under the waves. Jesus can call Peter's faith a "little-faith." We must not.

Simon Peter serves as a model disciple, reflecting human nature in the heart of every disciple. So let's try to look at the story with fresh eyes.

The Setup

John's version informs us that, after feeding the multitude, the people were intent on making Jesus king (John 6:15). Jesus sent the disciples away hurriedly; they were to have no part in the king-making tendencies of the masses. As the disciples set sail, Jesus ascends the mountain to commune with his Father.

The disciples were far out into the sea, possibly 3 or 4 miles. They had passed the night struggling against this storm as the time was now between 3 and 6 a.m. (the fourth watch). It appears, yet again, that the scene is set for deep learning. That's when Jesus starts toward them, walking on the water.

We have seen that one of the key movements of spiritual formation is expanding one's perception of Jesus. That is happening here. Jesus's statement, "Take heart. It is I. Do not be afraid," is the apex and turning point of the drama. The statement "it is I" is better translated "I am" as it uses the emphatic form of the pronoun. You will recognize this as the phrase used by Yahweh to reveal his name to Moses (Exod 3:14).[1] That's not coincidence. The realization of Jesus's identity is dawning on the disciples. The scene ends with the disciples worshipping Jesus, acknowledging him to be the Son of God, the confession Peter will assert later in north Galilee (Matt 16:16).

Peter's response, "If it is you," may not be an expression of doubt but something more like "since it is you, enable me to do as you are doing."[2] Peter is often labeled "impetuous." If that's what it is, it served him well. There were at least eleven others in that boat. Only one took steps towards Jesus on the surface of the water.

Jesus extends the invitation and Peter gets out of the boat. You've gotta love this guy. He does, in fact, walk on the water and almost gets to Jesus. How far did you make it, Peter? I wish we knew. That might prevent us from using Peter as a negative example of faith and put our own faith in perspective. Peter got out of a boat, on a raging sea and put his feet down on water at the command of Jesus. He left the relative safety of the boat for complete exposure to a storm-tossed sea simply because Jesus gave the invitation.

Following into Chaos

As a disciple with my fair share of failures, I'd like to stop here and applaud Peter. He had a victory, although it was short-lived. He saw the wind. He must have felt the spray of the water, heard the crashing of the waves, felt the deep darkness of the night. He doubted and began to sink and cried out to Jesus to save him.

Following Jesus's command to "come" put Peter in harm's way, or so it seemed. He found himself sinking, in imminent danger of death by drowning. As a master mentor, Jesus offered Peter a custom-designed lesson. Following Jesus will get him in over his head. He will face adversity. The resulting chaos will be beyond his control. Panic and pain will result.

Will he be able to keep his head in those circumstances? Jesus has already modeled dealing with resistance (Matt 10:25; 12:24; 13:57). Later Jesus warns

---

1. Blomberg, *Matthew*, 235.
2. Blomberg, 235.

*Following Jesus's command to "come" put Peter in harm's
way, or so it seemed. He found himself sinking, in imminent
danger of death by drowning. As a master mentor, Jesus
offered Peter a custom-designed lesson. Following Jesus will
get him in over his head. He will face adversity. The resulting
chaos will be beyond his control. Panic and pain will result.*

Peter (and the disciples) that this is the normal life of a follower (John 16:33; Matt 24:9). As Simon reflects on his scene, he has a clear case in point – an experience of following Jesus that resulted in exuberant victory but also left him exposed, vulnerable to grave danger. I can't imagine a more effective learning scenario.

Help, I'm Drowning!

In the Bible, the sea is usually symbolic of chaos. During creation, God speaks as his Spirit hovers over the waters, described as "without form and void" – chaotic. His word brings order out of the chaos of the waters. The psalmist expresses his disorientation and confusion by proclaiming "all your breakers and your waves have gone over me" (Ps 42:7). Jonah's disobedience lands him in a tempestuous sea (Jonah 1:11–12). The apocalypse of John includes a great beast rising out of the sea (Rev 13:1) and a renewed earth with no more sea (Rev 21:1).

When we read this story about Peter, we should read it with a view to the Bible's imagery of the sea as a place of chaos, void of the order and harmony (God's shalom) brought about by the word of God. As Jesus walks over a tempestuous sea, he demonstrates that the chaos of a world estranged from him is no match for him. He subdues the disorder and rules in the midst of it. Jesus's invitation to Peter to join him in his mastery over the chaotic sea recalls God's original purpose for humanity – that they should have dominion over the world. Adam and Eve received the garden as the outpost of God's creative order. They were to extend its boundaries and fill the earth with the beauty of the garden of Eden and with their offspring, image-bearers of God, filling the earth to tend and care for it. In a sense, Jesus is inviting Peter to regain the place of Adam, to join him in his mastery over the chaotic sea.

That's a lot to take in but stay with me for another step. This image will help us access a key building block of Jesus's way of spiritual formation. Jesus will very soon call the disciples to "take up their cross." For the disciples, the cross was a means of execution, a very cruel and inhumane one. The image could not be more terrifying, suggesting that following Jesus would result in serious opposition. So, why all the pain? Was Jesus a masochist? To follow him, do we need to be masochists too? Is following Jesus a means of self-harm? Is spiritual formation only for those who love pain?

Those questions are answered best by understanding the whole story of the Bible. Though God's intention for humanity was that they join him in restoring order to the world through dominion, human beings (represented by Adam and Eve) abandoned trust in God and embraced the word of their spiritual enemy (the serpent). Dominion is best understood as loving care, not "lording over." When human beings opted to usurp the place of God and cast off his dominion, chaos re-entered the world with humanity as its ally. That state of affairs continues to affect God's creation till today, alienating us as individuals from God and imposing chaos on our world. Our sin unleashed powers in this world which are antagonistic to God's creative order and shalom. Paul refers to these as rulers, authorities, cosmic powers and spiritual forces of evil (Eph 6:12). Jesus's incarnation, then, is not only a touching story of a baby's birth. It is also a story of a warrior invading enemy territory, confronting the powers, wresting the prey from the hand of the enemy and restoring his rightful reign.

Jesus is not merely saving us. He is restoring us to our rightful role in this world. We will join him in the Father's family as sons and daughters. We will also join him in dominion – loving care for creation – that will be fully realized when the earth is renewed. But as we follow Jesus in the present world, we are following him into chaotic territory. The earth's desperate need is to be set right, to be restored to shalom and harmony with God. Peter sinks into chaos as he follows Jesus. It is a warning that Jesus's invasion of the earth's powers has implications for us too. We are not mere individual recipients of restoration. He invites us to join him in a cosmic invasion, to regain our place of dominion (loving care of creation). That's why the inevitable result of following Jesus is opposition, resistance, chaos.

The Illusion of Order

Approaches to spiritual formation generally seek to order our world, to put the pieces together in a snug fit like a jigsaw puzzle. We reflexively want to avoid chaos so we internalize the message that following Jesus makes everything work well. If we follow well, we will be "a success" and our lives will be well-ordered. That is a seductive illusion. Peter's story subverts that neat and tidy approach.

We reflexively want to avoid chaos so we internalize the message that following Jesus makes everything work well. If we follow well, we will be "a success" and our lives will be well-ordered. That is a seductive illusion. Peter's story subverts that neat and tidy approach.

Jesus's way to spiritual formation inevitably causes the follower to pass through chaos; there will be moments when we do not know how to put life back together again.

Think about it carefully. Conventional wisdom would assign the safest place in the story to the people who were fed and remained on the shores of the Sea of Galilee. They were satisfied and wanted to make Jesus an earthly king to perpetuate their pleasure. The disciples in the boat were in a less safe place, or so it appeared. Their lives were threatened by a severe storm. Peter took the riskiest position, stepping off the boat and into absolute chaos.

The story upends conventional wisdom. If we reverse the order of the characters, the spiritual reality becomes apparent. Peter is in the most secure place. He sinks but within reach of Jesus and is saved. The person who willingly subjected himself to chaos out of trust in Jesus becomes the person whose life is ordered, who is safe, even though the storm is raging on all sides. The disciples, though at risk from the storm, are in the next most ordered position and role. They will receive the Lord into their boat and worship him as the Son of God. The satisfied followers on the coast remain in their illusion of an earthly king who will serve them by meeting their needs. Their lives will return to chaos again and again.

Lest we begin to think of ourselves as more advanced in taking risk, it is good to recall that we all fall into one of the three categories at various points along our life journey. Inevitably, there will be points when we are well-satisfied, casually asking Jesus to give us our daily bread, like the well-fed disciples who remained on the seashore. At other moments, we will get into the boat and join our community of friends and followers in a venture. As we progress, we encounter chaos, brokenness, hopelessness. We confront ourselves and look for our Lord to show up in the waves, calm our fear and restore order to our world. At some point in our journey, all of us will be like the disciples.

There are also points in our journey when we will be like Peter. Courage and faith take hold and we ask the Lord that we might do as he does, come to him, walking on the water. As we do so, we will experience both the thrill of following and our brokenness. We learn quickly that proximity to him is our only hope. We are not saved *out of the chaos*, but by his presence *in the chaos*. The whole experience deepens and broadens our perception of who Jesus is. The experience of walking in risk-taking faith brings a deeper communion with Jesus that we would never trade for the security of being well-fed and safe on the shore.

Spiritual formation is not merely ordering our internal world. It is something much deeper. It requires us to pass through uncertainty, disillusionment, danger, risk, to be in the world as Christ was in it. Until Jesus's return or our entrance into heaven, we will deal with chaos.

Peter's Progress through Chaos

As this lesson plays out in Peter's life, we see that he grows in his willingness to assume risk. He stands before the Jewish crowds to proclaim Jesus whom they crucified only weeks previously. He heals in Jerusalem and then stands before the high council of Jewish elders to say pointedly that they nailed Jesus to a cross. His trust in Jesus's saving presence *in the midst* of apparent or potential chaos becomes Peter's reflex. He walks headlong into adversity, knowing who he believes in. However, before he gets there, chaos and failure will again invade his life. There will come a moment when he will not know how to put his life together again. His brief walk on the water was an initial taste of authentic spiritual formation – the thrill of following and the threat of falling. There was much more to learn, but Jesus's protégé is on the path. In his brief walk on the water, we discern the elements that will lead to maturity further down the road.

Peter serves us by shedding light on the path of spiritual formation. Following Jesus into the tempestuous sea led to failure. Peter sank. Being formed spiritually in the way of Jesus involves risk. Failure, pain and disorientation are all part of the process. Without these, there is no growth, no progress. Peter demonstrates that no one does it right the first try, or the second. He welcomes us into the community of spiritual formation for slow learners! Peter's passion to go to Jesus, to do as he does, is richly rewarded with failure mixed with success. More importantly, it puts him squarely on the path of growth. Peter is a work in progress.

A Window into My Chaos

As a young man, I made a life-shaping decision. It was a response to God in which I see some of the enthusiasm and boldness that must have moved Peter to set his foot on the waters of a stormy sea. Allow me to share the broad lines of that response and a few of its implications as an invitation to you to consider your own life-shaping decisions. As I share my experience, keep in mind that there are many other instances in my life which have been closer to the well-fed disciples on the shore than to Peter. As mentioned above, we should all be able to identify with one of the three positions (on the shore, in the boat, walking to Jesus) at different points in our journey. Also, bear in mind that you do not have to leave your homeland in order to follow Jesus fully. It's reality, not geography! It can happen right in your hometown.

I was seated in a stadium in Champaign, Illinois, surrounded by other university students. It was New Year's Eve, 1979. The world-renowned evangelist, Billy Graham, had just given his message, ending in an invitation to the students to commit their lives to bring the gospel to ethnic groups who had no access to the good news of Jesus Christ. His call corresponded to my dreams. I longed to invest my life in something with ultimate meaning. I wanted to be used of God. As much as I knew myself, that desire was authentic. When Billy Graham gave his invitation, I realized I was not ready to embrace it due to areas of my life that were not aligned with God's purposes. So I didn't stand at first. But thousands of those students did. I wept as I watched them rise, knowing I could not.

Surprisingly, the speaker asked the students to sit down. He felt their response was emotional and his clear call to give our lives in going to unreached peoples had not been understood. He went over it again. During that time, I was expressing my sorrow to God, repenting for areas of my life that I knew were not aligned. When Billy Graham felt he had sufficiently clarified his invitation, he called students to stand again. This time, I was able to join them.

I returned to my small college in North Carolina with a new passion and vision. Those misaligned areas of my life gradually came into alignment. I had a new passion for God's word and a clear vision for his calling on my life. Some short-term ministry opportunities came up in an inner city setting in Newark, New Jersey, and later, in Paris, France. While in Paris, I decided to focus my call on Muslim peoples.

That series of decisions and responses to God's inner promptings set me on a life course of ministry. As I reflect on that period of my life today, I realize how formative it was for all that was to follow. It has been a forty-year journey full of joy and blessing for which I am deeply grateful.

But those formative decisions also led to chaos and confusion for me and for those I love most. It feels almost ungrateful to put these ideas on the screen in front of me. I want to cover all the bad stuff with an easy "count it all joy" and top it off with "all things work together for good." Of course, they do, but we need to see the chaos and understand the rationale behind it. So, I'm inviting you into my chaos, to walk on a stormy sea that doesn't become placid because you stepped out of the boat. Following are some of the broad-brush strokes of my chaos.

Distance from family was a source of pain. The moments I recall most and still feel sadness about were those moments at the airport when we put our arms around our parents' necks for the last time and said good-bye for years to come. It hurt. I recall when our first child was born and there were no grandparents to hold her and share our joy. I recall an anguished call from a father who was struggling with heart failure asking if we could come home soon. My wife returned to the US to see her dad before he passed away, but the rest of us were unable to make the trip.

Our three daughters, all with blond hair and blue eyes, were raised in Islamic settings in the Middle East. As toddlers, their cuteness claimed everyone's attention. However, they longed to be normal kids. The last thing they wanted was to stand out. As they became teenagers they faced flirtation and assumptions about Western girls that were inappropriate and hurtful. If you asked them today, they would have plenty of stories to share.

There was a price to pay for ministering the gospel in a Muslim context. My friends who embraced the gospel paid most dearly and that was a source of pain for me as well. Our ministry was continually three steps forward, two back, or three back. We saw our friends shamed, disowned, imprisoned, tortured and more. We watched many of them flee their homeland. We were accused of having a colonialist or imperialist agenda. I was thought to be a political spy on more than one occasion. I was deported from a country, leaving my wife and children to sell our belongings and move on. Our daughters lost their childhood homeland in that deportation. They felt the chaos even more than my wife and I.

I could mention other financial and health implications, but I think you get the idea. That decision to boldly follow Jesus, as best I could understand it as a young man, brought long-term chaos into my life. The resistance I encountered often took me by surprise. I felt vulnerable and often wondered if the results justified the high price.

My chaos was different from Peter's, and your chaos will likely not be like mine.

Being spiritually formed does not lead to an ideal state of tranquility and serenity. That's an illusion. Jesus said it best, "In the world, you will have tribulation." Get that part! Understand it well. And then remember that he also said, "But take heart; I have overcome the world" (John 16:33). Both parts are true. Affirming the second part, doesn't mean denying the first. Chaos comes as we follow Jesus in a world where the principalities and powers are set against him. He invaded alien territory to bring this world back to himself. We follow in his train and for that reason, we also experience the chaos and disruption of discipleship. In fact, we could say that the chaos we experience is not chaos at all. It is God's order – his intentional means to form us in the image of Jesus.

There is no perfect shalom this side of eternity. We long for it. We work for it. We taste it at given moments. We receive the first fruits through the gift of the Holy Spirit, but it is a life of following. The path of spiritual formation does not lead to perfect wholeness in this life.

Peter's Chaos and Ours

We've observed Peter's spiritual formation through the lens of his walk on the water. I've also revealed aspects of my formation. In both instances, the victory of following Jesus led to disruption, confusion and pain. Now let the searchlight of God's word penetrate your life journey. When have you stepped out of the boat? Did you anticipate a result of wholeness and tranquility? What has the result been? What difference does it make to see those results in light of Peter's walk on the water?

If it was not a bold step of faith like Peter's, perhaps you were in the boat with some other disciples when the storm came up. Did you hope that your following of Jesus would result in serenity? What is your response now, at an emotional and behavioral level, as you review decisions made in your past? How does what you've read here inform your response today?

Take some time to journal your reflections as you overview the implications of following Jesus. Try not to cover your chaos with a platitude, even one from the Bible. The point is to get the chaos out in the open, examining it for what it is. You may have suffered emotionally, relationally, physically, socially, financially, etc. Don't downplay that. Let yourself feel the disappointment and hurt as you express it. This is part of counting the cost of following Jesus. Being objective will help us mature as disciples and pass on the wisdom of our experience to others who are new arrivals on the road of spiritual formation. We become part of the great cloud of witnesses urging them on.

Later in Peter's journey, Jesus will ask him if he wishes to turn back and stop following him. The response is, "Lord, to whom shall we go? You have the words of eternal life" (John 6:68).

The lyrics of Bob Dylan are hauntingly true, "you gotta serve somebody." Falling into line with the spiritual powers that Jesus defeated has some attraction. Following them will secure short-term gains, but that path ends in chaos and destruction. To whom shall we go? Jesus leads us *through the chaos* to his shalom. We await that day.

3

Awakening

A Disciple's Expectation

*The lifelong process of mortifying sin involves a gradual
detection process by which the particular forms in which
sin expresses itself in our lives, our characteristic flesh, are
uncovered to our view. Some of this discovery of sin occurs
early in our Christian lives, but the subtlety of indwelling
sin is such that many of its deeper roots remain under
the surface of consciousness, where they will continue
to distort our lives if they are not uncovered later.*

Richard Lovelace, *Dynamics of Spiritual Life*

*The longer I have worked with people, however,
the more I see that it is cultural and institutional
blindness that keeps most of us from deeper
seeing, and not usually personal bad will.*

Richard Rohr, *Preparing for Christmas: Daily Meditations for Advent*

Now when Jesus came into the district of Caesarea Philippi, he asked his disciples, "Who do people say that the Son of Man is?" And they said, "Some say John the Baptist, others say Elijah, and others Jeremiah or one of the prophets." He said to them, "But who do you say that I am?" Simon Peter replied, "You are the Christ, the Son of the living God." And Jesus answered him, "Blessed are you, Simon Bar-Jonah! For flesh and blood has not revealed this to you, but my Father who is in heaven. And I tell you, you are Peter, and on this rock I will build my church, and the gates of hell shall not prevail against it. I will give you the keys of the kingdom of heaven, and whatever you bind on earth shall be bound in heaven, and whatever you loose on earth shall be loosed in heaven." Then he strictly charged the disciples to tell no one that he was the Christ.

From that time Jesus began to show his disciples that he must go to Jerusalem and suffer many things from the elders and chief priests and scribes and be killed, and on the third day be raised. And Peter took him aside and began to rebuke him, saying, "Far be it from you, Lord! This shall never happen to you." But he turned and said to Peter, "Get behind me, Satan! You are a hindrance to me. For you are not setting your mind on the things of God, but on the things of man."

Then Jesus told his disciples, "If anyone would come after me, let him deny himself and take up his cross and follow me. For whoever would save his life will lose it, but whoever loses his life for my sake will find it. For what will it profit a man if he gains the whole world and forfeits his soul? Or what shall a man give in return for his soul? For the Son of Man is going to come with his angels in the glory of his Father, and then he will repay each person according to what he has done. Truly, I say to you, there are some standing here who will not taste death until they see the Son of Man coming in his kingdom."

That's hard to take . . . stabs me like a knife.

It's not the first time my mouth's gotten me in trouble, but it may be the deepest hole I've ever dug. I guess I had it all wrong.

None of the other guys spoke up but I'm not one to sit on the sidelines.

I mean, he just said I was given the keys of the kingdom . . . that I can bind on earth and it's bound in heaven and if I loose on earth, it's loosed in heaven. That was awesome.

So I thought it was "game on" . . . time to put my best foot forward. I was so excited to be his right-hand man. I thought he was too!

But, boy-oh-boy, did I ever blow it! My head's still spinning . . . not sure how I went from "the rock of the church" to "the play-maker of Satan" . . . from "the keeper of the keys" to holding Jesus back!

And he made sure that Andrew, James, John and all the others heard.

If I could, I'd re-do it. I'm ashamed. I assumed something?! Is that what it was? I thought I knew better . . . better than the others . . . maybe even better than Jesus. Did I think I should lead?

At the moment, it seemed so obvious, but it was hellish to Jesus . . . He made it crystal clear that I was way out of line.

I'm confused. I thought about stopping . . . just walk away from Jesus and the others, insist that I was in my rights and I'm offended.

But I can't. I'm OK with following him on his terms. So I'm not gonna opt out. I'm gonna take it. I still believe what I said – that he is the Son of God, so it has to be his way.

He said that we have to carry a cross. Maybe that's why this hurts so bad.

Re-scripting Expectations

To be formed in the Jesus way requires a rescripting of expectations.

That sounds easy enough, but it is very hard work. It requires examining who we are and why we think, act and feel the way we do. It will test values we were raised with and the culture we've unconsciously soaked up. That requires a courageous honesty and usually results in stripping away our assumptions, long-held core beliefs. Scripture refers to this as "dying to self" and Jesus here refers to it as denying self and taking up the cross.

While that is a life-long journey, there are crisis moments when we realize that beliefs we counted on are shifting sand under our feet. At such times, we feel the full weight of personal change bearing down on us. We are witnessing such a crisis moment in the life of the apostle Peter.

In both Matthew and Mark, it appears that these two events – Jesus's affirmation and rebuke of Peter – occur one right after the other.[1] Mark is thought to be the mouthpiece of Peter, therefore, we may be hearing Peter's version of the events as we read Mark.[2] Whether or not these two events happened in this chronological order is not of primary concern. The fact that these two key witnesses place the two events together means we are meant to consider them together. The two events along with the transfiguration act as an intensive course in Peter's spiritual formation.

The Importance of Place

Both Matthew and Mark state that these things take place in Caesarea Philippi. This picturesque town in the far north of Israel may hold a deep significance for the events we have just read. The Greek name of the city was Paneas, after the Greek god Pan portrayed with the hind quarters and horns of a goat but the torso and face of a man. He was the god of the wild, and the grotto and springs next to Caesarea Philippi were the perfect setting for the cult worship of Pan. He was renowned for his sexual prowess, symbolizing a return to animal-like instincts.

Caesar Augustus gave the city to Herod the Great who reigned at the birth of Jesus. Herod built a lavish marble temple in honor of the Emperor

---

1. Matthew's key phrase "from that time Jesus began" (v. 21) is thought by some commentators to demarcate a new section of the gospel. It is also used in 4:17 as Jesus begins his public ministry. If this is correct, there may have been a time lapse between the two events. Blomberg, *Matthew*.

2. We discuss this further in epilogue 1.

Augustus at the site of the grotto of Paneas. When Herod died, he left the city and surrounding lands to his son, Phillip, who renamed the city in honor of himself and Tiberias Caesar – Caesarea Philippi.

No doubt, the location served as a beautiful setting of retreat and rest for Jesus and the disciples. However, for the disciples, Caesarea Philippi embodied the Greek pagan religious system overlaid by the Roman emperor cult, two spiritual forces that Jesus's kingdom would subvert. The gospel writers place Peter's confession in this location. Matthew and Mark may be indicating that Peter's confession (and the transfiguration which follows) signals the demise of pagan religion as the kingdom of Jesus begins to rise on the foundation of Peter's confession.

Peter's Confession and Keys

The fact that Peter was the first to confess Jesus as the Christ, the Son of the living God, marks him as a man of unique spiritual insight and faith. We are perhaps two or more years into the disciples' following of their master, so Peter's conviction comes as a result of a long journey of relationship with Jesus, observing his authority in both miraculous signs and teaching. Peter's observations have now solidified into conviction which he expresses before his colleagues with full confidence, not being one to understate his conclusions, hedge his bets or temper his enthusiasm. It was radical and risky. To make such an affirmation would surely be costly, as Jesus's subsequent execution proved. So Peter's courage and conviction should not be discounted. His spiritual receptivity is keen as Jesus affirms, "Flesh and blood has not revealed this to you, but my Father who is in heaven" (v. 17).

Jesus the Son directly affirms the Father's revelation to Peter. Jesus's response is uncharacteristic. When he speaks in such glowing terms, we do well to pay attention. As Peter has affirmed Jesus's true identity, Jesus also affirms Peter's: "You are Peter and on this rock I will build my church" (v. 18). Jesus speaks to Peter personally. He becomes the first of the living stones that will comprise the church of Christ. It is Jesus's first reference to the "church" and one of only three in the gospels (the other two are in Matt 18:17).

It is unfortunate that this passage has become the proof text for the Roman Catholic office of the pope and a point of contention between Catholics and non-Catholics. We must set that controversy aside to appreciate what Christ is saying to his chief disciple.

Clearly, Jesus's declaration is directed to Peter, ensuring that he is foundational for the future of the church. Peter's confession and Jesus's affirmation point forward to what God intends to do throughout the whole earth. As the Father reveals this truth concerning the Son to Peter, the church will confess Christ before the watching world and the spiritual powers, represented in Caesarea Philippi through Greek and Roman cults. Peter is the embryo of the church, confessing its faith before the world. As we embrace this confession of faith, we follow in Simon Peter's train.

The keys confer the ability to open and close. Due to the controversy over the papacy, we are pre-conditioned to read this in terms of authority, specifically Peter's authority to bind and loose. "Keys, binding and loosing" are prophetic. They point to the role Peter will play in the unfolding narrative of salvation. Those events play out in the book of Acts. Peter will open the door of the church. Through his agency, the nations of the world will enter. Think of Peter's "key" roles in Pentecost, Samaria, the home of Cornelius, and the Jerusalem Council (Acts 2; 8; 10; 15). We have grown accustomed to the idea that the church includes all ethnicities. For Peter and the disciples, it was unthinkable until it became reality. Peter is given the keys and permitted to bring about a huge change in the identity of God's people as all tribes, tongues and nations are permitted and urged to enter. There will be more to say about this subsequently, but we have Peter to thank that the church has become a family comprised of all nations, tongues and tribes. Simon Peter, chief of the disciples, has *bound* the church together by his confession and *loosed* the bonds that held the nations, inviting them into the people of God.

Jesus's affirmation of Peter is magnificent. It all began at a retreat Jesus took with his disciples and a dialogue about his identity in Caesarea Philippi.

Peter's Expectations

The affirmation sets us up for the stunning rebuke that follows. The gospel writers intend to throw us for a loop, to cause us to shake our heads and ask, "what just happened here?" Jesus affirmed Peter in the most glowing terms imaginable. Yet, there remains serious work to be done, serious internal sculpting, serious heart shaping. That is our concern – how Jesus formed his disciple.

Peter had expectations. Before reading further, pause and take a moment to write Peter's expectations as you imagine them based on this passage. What did he expect to take place as he continued to follow Jesus? What factors in Peter's life might have contributed to his expectations?

Personal Expectations

Peter likely had a mesh of expectations, some of which he would be aware of and able to articulate, others would be indistinct, difficult to articulate but nonetheless present in his mind and shaping his reactions. Let's think of his personal expectations and then his corporate expectations.

Simon Peter had just been named the keeper of the keys, the one whose binding and loosing on earth would carry authority in heaven. In light of Jesus's affirmation, Peter might be excused for thinking of himself as Jesus's right-hand man. Matthew records that Peter took Jesus aside, while Mark says that Peter took Jesus aside *and* began to rebuke him (Mark 8:32). Again, Mark may be transcribing Peter's version of the events so Peter may have that "rebuke" in the forefront of his memory. In both cases, Peter assumes a place of privilege. He supposes that he has been elevated to the role of special counsel to Christ. He presumes that he knows how Jesus should roll out his new kingdom, and suffering and dying have no place in Peter's preconceived plan.

He steps aside from the other disciples for a private word with Jesus to correct his understanding. We see Peter's sense of distinction from the other disciples elsewhere in the gospels (Matt 26:33). Peter is setting up for a private session, "just me and the boss." Jesus will not have it. He turns back to the disciples (Mark 8:33), ensuring they hear the stinging rebuke "get behind me, Satan! For you are not setting your mind on the things of God but the things of man." The words must have struck like lightning in the hearts of the disciples, much more so, Peter.

The point is not to denigrate the lead disciple. In fact, his deep humility must have allowed the record of these events to stand in order to display his faulty presuppositions and assumptions. Naming these assumptions results in words like elitism and privilege. We might respectfully try to imagine where these assumptions came from in Peter's life. We know he led a fishing business in Capernaum and lived in a relatively large house near the synagogue. We might assume he was familiar with influence and enjoyed that privilege in his social circles. He was married and his mother-in-law lived in the house. Like us, Peter brought assumptions to his role of disciple from his previous life-roles of fisherman, community leader, husband, etc.

Alternatively, perhaps Peter always wanted to be a man of influence. His fishing vocation was respectable enough but afforded him no elite status. He has no esteemed role among Israel's religious leaders. He was heavily taxed by the Roman authorities such that amassing personal wealth would have been impossible. He may see his affiliation with the Jesus movement as a means to attain an ambition he had long nurtured – to be a leader, a person of influence.

This aspect of Peter's assumptions highlights the personal aspect of human alienation from God. Our estrangement from God causes us to see ourselves unrealistically. Peter thinks of himself more highly than he should. Sin skews the way we see ourselves in multiple directions. Even those with poor self-esteem are not immune from seeing the self in the most positive light. We are naturally self-justifying. Adam blamed his transgression on Eve. Like Adam, like Peter, we assume we see ourselves aright.

Jesus radically confronts that assumption, refusing to allow it. Following Jesus equates to denying self. Peter's road to discipleship and eventually to leadership must pass through the cross of self-denial.

Corporate Expectations

Peter is living out a script that has been written deeply in his heart, mind and soul over years of life as a Galilean Jew under Roman occupation. He knew the history of his people from Abraham to Ahab, from the exodus to the exile. He and his countrymen languished under foreign occupation. He was aware of attempts to restore Jewish political sovereignty over the past four hundred years. Like all his people, he awaited a deliverer. He now knew John the Baptist to be the forerunner. Jesus was the awaited Messiah, the deliverer of Israel, the new David. Jesus would fix Israel.

In a sense, Peter had it right. His information is correct. The kingdoms of David and Solomon represented the apex of Jewish prominence. Like most Jews of his day, Peter expected something along those lines, only bigger, better, more expansive. We can imagine that Peter's expectations were held almost unconsciously. His mind had absorbed them through a multitude of observations and conversations drawing from his social environment. Nevertheless, this matrix of expectations, which Peter now wed to Jesus's messiahship, did not sync with Jesus's mandate from the Father. Jesus nips it in the bud, abruptly uprooting this Satan-inspired expectation from the heart of his disciple.

The exchange gives us pause for thought. Peter had no inkling that his expectations were off base. He absorbed those expectations from his religious upbringing, from countless discussions with rabbis and fellow Jews, from his knowledge of his people's history, from the Hebrew Scriptures. Peter held these convictions effortlessly and assumed them fully, much like you and I know intuitively that "the early bird gets the worm" or "the squeaky wheel gets the grease."

Jesus's harsh rebuke of Simon Peter rips off the cultural blindfold. The messianic expectation of power, glory, restoration of the Davidic kingdom was the unquestioned collective narrative of the Hebrew people. Peter clearly saw that Jesus had to be the Messiah, the Son of the living God. There could be no other. However, he failed to see what Jesus saw with extreme clarity:

> For Peter, the awaited restoration was national, Hebraic.
>> For Jesus, it was a healing of human alienation affecting all nations.
> For Peter, Israel's enemy was its occupier – Rome.
>> For Jesus, the true enemies were sin and death.
> For Peter, power and acclaim were key to Jesus's leadership.
>> For Jesus, the cross was essential to effect reconciliation.
> For Peter, any diminishment of Jesus's temporal greatness had to be avoided.
>> For Jesus, any distraction from the cross was a strategy of Satan.

The Gospel writers skillfully juxtapose two realities: Peter's errant expectations seen against the backdrop of his unique receptivity of revelation from the Father.

Simon Peter's failure to embrace Jesus's destiny of suffering and death does not negate the fact that he was uniquely favored by the Father in the revelation of Jesus's identity. The two elements co-exist in the soul of the disciple as they do in ours.

Simon Peter's failure to embrace Jesus's destiny of suffering and death does not negate the fact that he was uniquely favored by the Father in the revelation of Jesus's identity. The two elements co-exist in the soul of the disciple as they do in ours.

Aleksandr Solzhenitsyn was imprisoned in a Soviet labor camp. He experienced the reality of oppressive institutional evil. Yet he recognized that the human heart has the capacity for both good and evil to exist simultaneously.

> If only it were all so simple! If only there were evil people somewhere insidiously committing evil deeds, and it were necessary only to separate them from the rest of us and destroy them. But the line dividing good and evil cuts through the heart

of every human being. And who is willing to destroy a piece of his own heart?[3]

Peter was so right and so wrong, at the same time. He had received revelation from the Father that would form the confession of a worldwide church. He was uniquely favored by God. Yet, in his heart, he nurtured expectations that were antithetical to Jesus's purpose and kingdom. Both existed in him at the same time. Jesus set out to extricate the evil from the heart of his disciple while affirming the good. We should expect no less if we are following in the Jesus way.

Our Expectations

The word of God is not given to us merely as a good story or a recitation of the history of our faith. It is inspired of the Holy Spirit and given to shape our lives based on its events and characters.

We are no different from Peter.

Our expectations reflect a skewed view of ourselves as well as the errant assumptions of the culture and context to which we belong. We have absorbed the beliefs and practices of our social environment such that we are unaware, unconscious, of how far off-base they are. We want desperately to exclude ourselves from Solzhenitsyn's verdict on humanity, but we cannot. We must confess that the line between good and evil passes right through our inmost being. This fact, upheld by Peter's example, compels us to dig deep, to search out the nooks and crannies where our alienated expectations hide.

This resident evil in the heart is not done away with by conversion. Peter had been soundly converted to Jesus. He was faithfully following and even receiving revelation from the Father that marked him as a foundational apostle. Yet, his soul-shaping was not done. There remained vast areas of Peter's heart that had to come under the searchlight of submission to the Jesus way.

Many of our expectations must be extricated from our heart through the crucible of life experience under the guidance of the Holy Spirit. Our motivations and expectations must come to light. Often this takes place through relationships. Those who love us can help us discern where our expectations run amuck if we are willing to listen and heed.

---

3. Aleksandr Solzhenitsyn, *The Gulag Archipelago, 1918–1956* (United Kingdom: Collins & Harvill Press, 1974), 28.

Personal Examples

May I briefly share a couple of personal examples of how my expectations have been rescripted while following Jesus? The two examples follow the categories of personal and corporate expectations.

It's a little embarrassing, but I thought I would be asked to fill the role. A ministry I loved and had been active in was conducting a search for a new leader. Some friends had suggested I would be a good fit. I also thought my gifts were suitable to the role. The search process ended and, as far as I know, I was never considered. It stung a bit and I was disappointed. The process caused me to ask those who know me best how they see me, what aspects of my personality deterred this ministry from considering me and how I might use my gifts to greater effect. The eventual outcome was my growth in self-awareness and releasing my hopes for leadership in that ministry.

The second example, which I see as a corporate expectation, is also difficult to talk about because it is an area of contention in our day. It is the subject of male-female relationships. Like many evangelical believers, I was taught male headship in the marriage relationship. The idea comes from Paul's teaching in Ephesians 5:21–33 where the apostle lays out his understanding of family and marriage relationships. The problem was not the biblical teaching, but the cultural assumptions that I brought to my understanding of that passage. Looking back, I now realize that my mental model of "headship" was something along the lines of a coach of a team, a military commander or a project manager – all images I had internalized from my upbringing and held unconsciously. The model I held corresponded perfectly to my cultural assumptions of male leadership, but they were lethal to my marriage and to my personal growth. I thought of myself as a decision maker and my wife as a submissive implementer. Ouch!

Looking back, I smile and shake my head at my skewed vision of the biblical teaching. Of course, the truth was there in plain sight in the Ephesians 5 passage. The husband is to love his wife "as Christ loved the church and gave himself up for her." I eventually realized, through reading and searching my own soul, that Jesus was the *only* model of headship I could embrace. I repudiated my skewed concept of headship. Being the "head" of my wife meant giving myself up for her in love. By the way, that lesson keeps on teaching. I'm still working it out in my marriage.

Societal Effects of Human Alienation

Corporate expectations deal with the societal effects of human alienation from God – sin. Western evangelicals tend to focus on the personal effects of sin resulting in guilt and shame; however, the Bible lays equal emphasis on the corporate effects of sin leading to oppression and injustice. Consider a few more examples of the corporate effects of human alienation from God:

- I grew up as an evangelical from the southern United States. I learned to hold the leaders of my denomination in high esteem. As I progressed through life, I was shocked to learn that my denomination's early leaders defended the institution of slavery and the value of white supremacy from the pulpits of southern churches. They assumed the values of the surrounding society and were unable to prophetically call the church to justice in race relations and economics. Small wonder that the denomination still struggles to achieve racial integration while the nation continues to feel the sting of racial bias.

- Many are aware of Dietrich Bonhoeffer, executed by the Third Reich of Adolf Hitler. His story highlights the fact that the majority of German Lutherans did not resist Hitler. The promised restoration of German greatness was too appealing and the evidence of progress under Hitler's leadership, too evident. The silent acquiescence to Hitler's tyranny made Christians complicit in one of the greatest expressions of injustice of the twentieth century.

- The Trail of Tears is a story of displacement of native American tribes and the occupation of their land by those who came to America in search of religious freedom. It was largely land confiscated from indigenous peoples that became the southern cotton plantations, which, fueled by the slave workforce, made America a world economic power. The irony needs no comment. There were exceptions, but the majority was complicit in this displacement, benefitting from new lands and wealth. The scourge of the removal of native tribes from their lands continues to haunt America, tearing its societal fabric.

Richard Lovelace writes insightfully of the need of "disenculturation" on the road to spiritual maturity in Christ:

> Disenculturation is possible only when we rely fully on Christ for justification and sanctification; it is necessary if we are to be

released from the marriage of religion and culture which prevents our reaching all nations and reflecting the diversity of life in Christ.

Unless new converts are persuaded to stop leaning on their culture and the law and to lean fully on Jesus Christ in every phase of their lifestyle, their spiritual lives and the mission of the church will inevitably be short-circuited by the process of enculturation.[4]

For many evangelicals, the pursuit of social justice has been relegated to "liberal" theology. However, unless we are completely misreading the gospels, Jesus clearly deconstructs the Hebrew cultural expectation of a vanquishing messiah who will restore Israel to political, territorial and military greatness. Peter is at the beginning of the road of deculturation.

For many evangelicals, the pursuit of social justice has been relegated to "liberal" theology. However, unless we are completely misreading the gospels, Jesus clearly deconstructs the Hebrew cultural expectation of a vanquishing messiah who will restore Israel to political, territorial and military greatness. Peter is at the beginning of the road of deculturation.

Future stations of his spiritual formation will demand a more thorough-going deculturation than he could have imagined.

Our corporate or societal expectations are especially destructive, allowing evil to propagate and hold many people in webs of oppression and injustice. It is instructive that, in this context of his affirmation of Peter's discipleship, Jesus declares the "gates of hell will not prevail against his church." Jesus understands his church to be an alternate society where the onslaught of evil will be held in check, and the personal and corporate effects of sin mitigated while his kingdom continues its advance to all nations, tribes and tongues.

Peter's Expectations and Ours

Like Peter, our misplaced expectations become evident through painful confrontations, losses and broken relationships. In response to this chapter,

---

4. Lovelace, *Dynamics of Spiritual Life*, 146, 208.

reflect on a significant painful experience. Recall your emotional response as you faced disappointment. Try to identify assumptions you made that were misplaced and led to perceptions that were off base. While it is possible that we bear no blame in such situations, the reality is that we often contribute to them through our own misplaced expectations. How did you contribute to the breakage? Do you bring similar misplaced expectations to your relationship with Christ? When did you last feel disappointed in your faith? Why? Have you ever reached the point where you considered abandoning the faith? What role did your expectations play? As you identify these expectations, write them out clearly and make notes on the impact they have had on you.

It is also helpful to identify our corporate and cultural expectations. We can begin to pull back the veil on those hurtful ways of thinking by listening empathetically and carefully to those who have been hurt by a dominant cultural narrative. We learn to see the toxin of our cultural assumptions when we encounter individuals from minority or marginalized groups. From my vantage point in the United States, I notice that people of color, indigenous people and immigrants often find it difficult to identify with the narrative of the American dream, largely because they feel it has passed them by. When American Christianity is embedded in the dominant cultural narrative, the results are disastrous for the church as it becomes an implement of oppression and injustice rather than a source of liberation and elevation.

Consider reading the sermons and letters of Martin Luther King Jr. or the writings of contemporary civil rights leaders. King's *Letter from a Birmingham Jail* is a good place to start. Ask if you have been complicit in a cultural narrative that has held some down at the expense of others. A word of caution is that we are typically blind to these areas and, as a result, we must humble ourselves repeatedly to begin to make progress. But don't ask a minority person to "teach" you. Rather, take the initiative yourself to become a learner. Take steps in that direction by careful listening and realize that uprooting our cultural narratives is a long-term process. We'll see much more of that process in the life of Peter.

4

Unveiling

A Disciple Perceives the Father-Son Love

*To be a person is to be in relationship, not for the
sake of influence but for the sake of place sharing,
for the sake of being with and being for.*

Andrew Root, *The Relational Pastor* (loc. 467)

And after six days Jesus took with him Peter and James, and John his brother, and led them up a high mountain by themselves. And he was transfigured before them, and his face shone like the sun, and his clothes became white as light. And behold, there appeared to them Moses and Elijah talking with him. And Peter said to Jesus, "Lord, it is good that we are here. If you wish, I will make three tents here, one for you and one for Moses and one for Elijah." He was still speaking when, behold, a bright cloud overshadowed them, and a voice from the cloud said, "This is my beloved son, with whom I am well pleased; listen to him." When the disciples heard this, they fell on their faces and were terrified. But Jesus came and touched them, saying, "Rise, and have no fear." And when they lifted up their eyes, they saw no one but Jesus only.

I'm still shaking. My feet are unsteady. We were all terrified.

All of a sudden, he was shining like the sun. I couldn't even look at him.

And then, on either side of him . . . Moses and Elijah!! Talking to him, having a conversation, like it's the most normal thing in the world . . . but it was the most incredible thing I've ever seen.

I can't wrap my brain around Jesus. Just when I think I'm tracking with him, he blows me out of the water!!

I didn't know what to think or say. Tents . . . 3 of them.

Yeah, what I said was ridiculous, but nobody else dared open their mouth. We were shaking in our sandals.

That bright cloud . . . It must be the same one that protected our fathers, the same one that filled the tabernacle and temple . . . and it came down right over us. But it wasn't fun. It was more than I could take. How to describe it? Terror. Yeah, we were terrified. We went face down. It was all we could do.

And what we heard! It reminded me of how I answered Jesus's question a week ago. But when I heard it there, it was different. I don't know how to describe it, but it's like I realized Jesus is in the very heart of God. He called him, "his beloved Son, his delight."

And he said, "Listen to him." I'm thinking about my rebuking Jesus just a few days back. For sure, I'll listen to him. I really thought I was listening to him all along, but now I'm seeing it differently. He's all that I thought he was, but he's much more than I ever dreamed.

Emotion and Transformation

The scene on the mountain is punctuated with surprise, fear, even terror. Emotion plays a key role in transformation. In reading the Scripture, it is important to pay attention to expressions of emotion. There are several in this passage as expressed in the three synoptic gospels.

My children sometimes ask me to tell them stories from my childhood. I notice that the scenes I remember best are those that are accompanied by a strong emotion. I remember stories when I was terrified or when I was doubled over laughing or when I was embarrassed and ashamed. Those stories were formative on my character and they come back in vivid tones, making for great entertainment for my kids.

We are pursuing the spiritual formation of Peter in relationship to Jesus. As we saw in the last chapter, the events of Caesarea Philippi constitute an intensive course in his spiritual formation. The revelation of Jesus's glory at the transfiguration is the capstone event of Peter's course. It affords him an opportunity to deepen the lessons learned earlier and apply them as he continues to follow Jesus.

Peter is not the central character of this scene. Jesus is. Nevertheless, as Jesus's protégé, there is much here to glean concerning Peter's spiritual formation. We will focus on those elements. Our observations can be grouped in three broad categories.

- Changing Peter's Orientation: From Project to Person
- Changing Peter's Posture: From Feet to Face
- Changing Peter's Story: From Strength to Weakness

Changing Peter's Orientation: From Project to Person

Transformation occurs as persons indwell one another. Jesus indwells us and we indwell him. "Abide in me, and I in you" (John 15:4). Our spiritual formation is our response to the indwelling Christ, nothing less and nothing more. Jesus invites the three disciples to the mountain to share a holy place, a place where the person of Jesus, and his identity and his relatedness to the Father, are revealed.

Peter has begun well. His confession of Jesus as "the Messiah, the Son of the living God," is the foundation. He is off the starting blocks and appears to be running well. Even Jesus affirms him. However, his immediate rebuke of Jesus in response to the warning of impending suffering and death reveals that something is amiss. Peter's triumphalist expectation reveals that his confession is self-interested. His pursuit of a relationship to the Lord conceals his pursuit of a project, an interest. Peter has an agenda and his words reveal that. On the Mount of Transfiguration, the Father's declaration, though similar to Peter's in form, flows from a relational indwelling – the Father's delight in the Son. On the mountain Peter is invited to hear the Father's statement of Jesus's identity. The core relationship of Father to Son is laid bare to Peter. It is his invitation to move away from his agenda for Jesus and to begin the journey of embracing his own sonship.

> Peter: You are the Christ, the Son of the living God (Matt 16:16).
> Father: This is my beloved Son, with whom I am well pleased;
>   listen to him (Matt 17:5).

The Father's declaration is repeated from Jesus's baptism (Matt 3:17). Its repetition in the gospel narrative indicates it is foundational to Jesus's identity and to a right understanding of the gospel.

The succinct phrase "beloved Son, with whom I am well pleased" reveals the nature of the relationship that binds Father to Son. Simon Peter had viewed the Messiah as a functional leader who would re-establish Israel as a dominant power and liberate her from oppressive Roman rule. His perspective aligned Jesus's mandate with the disciples' background and aspirations, which, not surprisingly, aligned with the Jewish understanding of Messiah. The declaration of the Father on the mount has no triumphalism. It reflects a relational reality that we now know to be a bond of love-unity between persons. We call this the Trinity, but philosophical descriptions we have internalized will not help us access the simple beauty that is stated here and, in fact, may obscure it.[1]

The declaration expresses a unique bond of eternal love between Father and Son. The words "well pleased" connote delight and satisfaction. Our imaginations of a stern or vindictive God must give way before this statement. The Father is delighted. He is effusively happy and this eternal delight flows from a Father-Son relationship that is intimate, personal and fulfilling.

This reality is portrayed clearly in the Gospels, with John's descriptors painting the relational reality in fullest hue. It is a shocking contrast to Yahweh's repeated pleas with his Old Testament people to embrace his love.

---

1. I am referring here to the simple numeric formula "one God and three persons." The declaration serves us well as a caption or descriptive summary of the Trinity interrelations. It abridges the language of the ecumenical councils of Nicea and Chalcedon (AD 325 and 451). However, the underlying reality of the Father-Son-Spirit God is best internalized relationally, not numerically. Though formulas may assist us to simplify the concept, the primary way the interrelations of Father, Son and Spirit is revealed is relationally.

The declaration expresses a unique bond of eternal love between Father and Son. The words "well pleased" connote delight and satisfaction. Our imaginations of a stern or vindictive God must give way before this statement. The Father is delighted. He is effusively happy and this eternal delight flows from a Father-Son relationship that is intimate, personal and fulfilling.

His summons meet only with Israel's betrayal and rejection. There, the tone is somber, brooding.[2] Here the tone is delightful, lyrical.

The revelation of the Father-Son delight embraces the disciples in the sacred space of the mountain. Space is not incidental to the exchange. The disciples are invited here. What they are seeing could only take place as a result of Jesus's invitation to this space and time. Being with him allows them to see him for who he is, which leads to trust. Relational trust is a kind of indwelling. It is our spirit in relationship to another's. Peter and the disciples are invited to trust Jesus and indwell him more fully as a person. As embodied beings we interact in space, in a given place.[3] The mountain is the place of Jesus's welcome of his disciples to his person and, as they listen to him, into the unity that binds Father, Son and Spirit.

Looking to Jesus, the disciple beholds the Father in the person of the Son. The relationship is a spring of eternal joy from which the disciple is invited to drink. The mandate of Jesus is not primarily functional but relational. He has come in response to the pleasure of his Father and the Father responds to us out of his pleasure in his Son as we are united to him in relational trust and faith. The disciple shares in the delight of the Father for the Son. It is a relational security, a foundation of deep personal value flowing from the bond in love of Father and Son.

There is an oblique reference to what Jesus will do in the command "listen to him." The command comes in response to Peter's suggestion of building tents for the prophets and Jesus. It functions as a corrective to Peter's frantic

---

2. God is often depicted as a lover who endures the adulteries of an unfaithful spouse (Jer 2:20–25; 3:1–5; Ezek 16; 23; Hos 2).

3. Thomas Torrance comments that "patristic theology rejected a notion of space as that which receives and contains material bodies, and developed instead a notion of space as the seat of relations or the place of meeting and activity in the interaction between God and the world." Torrance, *Space, Time and Incarnation* (London: T&T Clark, 2005), 24.

proposal and affirms Jesus's recent revelation that he would suffer, die and rise again – the very revelation Peter resisted. The Father's passion that the Son be heard displaces Peter's messiah project with a truer agenda – listening deeply to Jesus. It is an invitation to be with Jesus, setting aside interests that seek to manipulate him. To listen to Jesus, then, is to be with him on his terms, not Peter's. It is the way Jesus is "with" the Father, also expressed in the Son's being "beloved."

Changing Peter's Posture: From Feet to Face

At first blush, Peter's plan to build tents or shelters on the mountain for the three glorified figures, seems nothing more than an emotional outburst, a jumbled outcome of Peter's terror and shock. Luke mentions that the disciples were asleep creating the impression that Peter speaks in a confused, half-awake stupor (Luke 9:32).

Commentators suggest that the idea of "tents" is related either to the feast of booths or to the tabernacle as the dwelling place of God.[4] Trembling at the presence of God on the mount, Simon Peter may be asking for protection from the holiness of God. So we should not see his suggestion as ridiculous.

Peter's posture changes radically as the cloud of the presence overshadows him and the voice of the Father speaks. He goes from his feet to his face. Peter is no longer the man with the plan, the visionary entrepreneur. Only a few days ago, Peter had rebuked Jesus's intention to suffer, die and rise again. He felt sure Jesus would pursue his (Peter's) vision. It was a relationship built around Peter's interest.

"Listen to him" is the divine word. Clear out your agenda! Strip away your interests. Be with him!

Peter's entrepreneurial initiative must die. The overwhelming power of the presence of God forces Peter out of the blur of busyness into a different posture. He is on his face, fearful, realizing that he should not be here, the same realization that once overwhelmed him on the Sea of Galilee. Peter's moment for initiative and action will come, but not yet. It is a moment of surrender. Peter has yet to realize what it all means, but he is on the way.

The question of how *being* relates to *doing* often arises in the journey of faith. Activists call us to get busy for God. Contemplatives urge us to slow down and *be* in his presence. The mountain scene reveals that Jesus's mission flows from his eternal relationship to the Father. We might say that his doing flows

---

4. Card, *Fragile Stone*, 78; Morris, *Gospel According to Matthew*, 439–40.

from being. Peter's error was not that he was too busy. It was that his agenda was misdirected, failing to embrace Jesus's agenda. Jesus would give Peter plenty to do. But his doing would arise from a relationship that was rooted in Jesus's own relational trust and unity with the Father. Doing flows from being.

Changing Peter's Story: From Strength to Weakness

Moses and Elijah appear conversing with Jesus. This dynamic concerns Peter's historic community and the Old Testament story (introduced in ch. 1). Many reasons are suggested as to why these two Old Testament characters appeared: Moses and Elijah represent the law and the prophets which Jesus had come to fulfill;[5] both encountered God on a mountain and descended from it to bring about a great deliverance; both were translated to heaven in a miraculous way.[6]

Seeking how the encounter on the mount impacted Simon Peter and formed him spiritually allows us to arrive at some different conclusions.

We would like to eavesdrop on the conversation between the Hebrew prophets and the Messiah, but the text is cryptic and condensed. How much were Peter, James and John privy to? Did they hear the whole exchange? Our curiosity remains unsatisfied.

The gospel writer mentions these figures, intending that the reader recall their stories. The Bible was a communal library for the Hebrews, not merely a book. The mere mention of "Moses" calls to mind the burning bush, the plagues, the Passover, the Exodus, the wilderness wandering, the covenant, the law, the people's rebellion, Moses's intercession, the revelation of Yahweh's glory, etc. Similarly, the mention of Elijah evokes God's judgment through drought, the confrontation of Ahab, fire from heaven, the routing of Baal and his prophets, the flight from Jezebel, Elijah's despair, etc. In brief, the mention of Moses and Elijah invites the reader to probe their story in light of the Jesus story.

Consider what has just transpired in the gospel narrative. Jesus has recently related to the disciples that suffering, death and resurrection await him. In each of the three Synoptic Gospels, this is the point of transition to the journey to Jerusalem and the events of Passion Week. How do Moses and Elijah relate to this key pivotal moment in the gospel story?

The stories of both prophets conceal the theme of God's strength displayed in weakness. Both prophets experienced crushing defeat on the path to

---

5. Hendriksen, *Gospel of Matthew*, 667.

6. Blomberg, *Matthew*, 263.

stunning victory. Both were resisted and hunted down to be killed by the ruling authorities.[7] Both were falsely accused of leading their people into misery and death.[8] Both interceded for the people when God's justice would have destroyed them.[9] Both experienced deep despair to the point of desiring death.[10] Both died (or left the earth) before seeing a fulfillment of their prophetic visions.[11]

These painful aspects of the ministries of Elijah and Moses were likely not uppermost in the minds of the Jews who celebrated their victories. Like the heroes of our stories, they probably emphasized the bits of their stories that highlighted their triumphs. After all, no one wants to celebrate a depressed prophet, lying under a broom tree, asking his God to take his life (1 Kgs 19:4–5).

The connection was likely not immediate in the minds of the disciples either. We know that because they were taken unaware by Jesus's arrest and trial. Nevertheless, when Jesus reappeared after the resurrection, he would draw heavily on the lives of the prophets to show the divine rationale behind his suffering and death.

The conversation on the mountain is a springboard to Jesus's suffering in Jerusalem. The lesson will remain etched in the memory of the three apostles allowing them to fill in the blanks (as we have done) in the aftermath of Jesus's suffering. In the economy of God, as revealed in Scripture, life comes by way of death. Gain is procured through loss. This is precisely what Jesus taught the disciples, that if anyone would come after him, he must "deny himself, take his cross daily and follow me." It was the story of the prophets. Indeed, it was the story of ancient Israel. It will be the story of her Messiah, only his story will extend beyond suffering and death to resurrection.

Effects of Peter's Discipleship

Peter's stations of spiritual formation will continue to reinforce these experiences with Jesus. His swagger will continue to diminish. His perception of Jesus as the relational delight of the Father will expand. By the time his course is finished, he will have laid aside his drive for self-fulfillment to find his

---

7. See Exodus 14:5–9; 1 Kings 18:7–16; 19:2.

8. Exodus 17:3; 1 Kings 18:17.

9. See Numbers 14:11–19; 1 Kings 18:36–37.

10. Moses asked to be blotted out of the Lord's book if he would not forgive the people (Exod 32:32). He asks to die again due to the crushing burden of providing for the people (Num 11:10–15). After Elijah's defeat of the prophets of Baal, he flees from Jezebel and is overwhelmed by a dark depression. He asks the Lord to take his life (1 Kgs 19:1–8).

11. Deuteronomy 3:23–29; 2 Kings 2.

true identity and significance in his relationship to Jesus. He will re-interpret the collective story of Israel with Jesus as the focal point. He will also come to see that Jesus's suffering defeated the powers of sin and death which estranged humanity from God. He will call the body of Christ to join in that suffering.

The transfiguration is the only event mentioned in the gospels that makes its way into Peter's letters.

> We were eyewitnesses of his majesty. For when he received honor and glory from God the Father, and the voice was borne to him by the Majestic Glory, "This is my beloved Son, with whom I am well pleased," we ourselves heard this very voice borne from heaven, for we were with him on the holy mountain. (2 Pet 1:16b–18)

The experience on the Mount of Transfiguration was deeply etched into Peter's memory. He drew from it on his long journey of spiritual formation as he fulfilled his destiny as a foundational stone of the church and a shepherd of Christ's flock.

Personal Reflections

"We shall be like him, because we shall see him as he is" (1 John 3:2). Someday our transformation will be complete. Still, in his life, we will likely not experience what Peter did on the Mount of Transfiguration. But that does not exclude us from the benefit of his discipleship as the Spirit teaches us the deep things of God.

Allow me to link Peter's journey of spiritual formation to my own. Of course, my experience is not like Peter's, but the lessons I derived were similar. Consider this an invitation to reflect on your own life journey, seeking commonalities with Peter's stations of discipleship.

While in my early thirties I was diagnosed with cancer. Nothing wakes us up like a potential death diagnosis. At the time, I was a young missionary in the Middle East. I was very diligent in language study and was making good progress in ministry. Although I hoped to stay in the Middle East for my cancer treatments, the wisdom of my team leader (and my wife) prevailed and I was promptly sent back to the US for treatment. My convalescence turned into a full year during which time the ministry project I had initiated died.

The combined effects of a serious health issue, displacement and family stress set me up for deep learning. I was struggling emotionally from the effects of chemicals in my body, attacking the cancer. My personal identity as a cross-cultural minister was ripped away. Suddenly I was thrust into a life-transforming moment. My core assumptions were exposed by the reality I faced.

Although difficult to put in words, I realized that I had a preconceived idea of how I would bear fruit. Most things I had accomplished in life had come as a result of diligence and hard work. I attacked my call as a missionary with the same values that had guided my life until that time. Investment brings a return. Cause produces effect. I was a perfect example of the Arabic proverb, *man jadda, wajada*, loosely translated, "The diligent seeker finds" or "Those who work hard prosper" (Prov 13:4).

Being quickly removed from my place of ministry made me feel like a string pulled out of a bucket of water. I had been there, immersed, and yet my extraction left no trace, no impact, no return on my investment. How could I make sense of Jesus's promise that I would bear fruit in light of this loss?

It seemed God was inviting me to change my understanding of bearing fruit. The image of a branch abiding in the vine (John 15) had always been powerful to me, but now it was hammering me. I was getting an inkling of the spiritual reality that Christ's life flowing through me was the foundational reality on which my life should be built. Union with him would have to be the foundation of my identity and the headwaters from which any fruitfulness would flow. *Being* before *doing*. Diligence and discipline had served me well but seeing those values as the key to spiritual fruit would be fatal. I had subtly linked the biblical principle of bearing fruit to a productivity mindset. The reality was that the indwelling Spirit would do his work in and through me in ways beyond my control and plan, beyond my internalized model of investment and return. I had to yield. The experience broke something deep inside me.

The lesson I learned was different from Peter's. I had absorbed different life assumptions from my upbringing and background. But the rescripting, like Peter's, required a serious wake-up call and a willingness to examine core assumptions that controlled my actions and behavior. The experience exposed a shadow-self – values I was living from, somewhat unconsciously, that needed to be broken. My desperate need, unseen until that moment, was to draw my life, identity and significance from my relatedness to Christ, abiding in him as a branch in the vine. I struggle with that lesson to this day, so it's no surprise that my stations of spiritual formation continue to reinforce that lesson.

Go Low, Go Slow

The inter-connectedness of our world allows us to envision our societies as places of rapid change. For many in the West, desires can be obtained almost instantly. Even for those in the Majority World, the steady barrage of information through media gives the false impression that our lives are improving. Self-help manuals explicate steps (7 is a favorite) towards effective leadership, management, thinking, investing, etc. If we know the stuff, we're on the road to change. At least we think we are. Even spiritual growth is often presented in terms of disciplines we practice or programs we follow in order to grow. The disciplines and programs can be helpful, but, in and of themselves, they do little to effect spiritual growth or personal change.[12]

Given this pre-conditioned expectation of self-improvement for many of us, Jesus's discipleship program for Peter is striking. It kept pushing Peter further in his relational trust of Jesus. It could not be reduced to steps or skills, but was a continually deepening relational trust, exposing Peter's shadow-self while inviting him to find his identity in his relatedness to Jesus. The phrase "go low, go slow" can help us remember how Jesus formed Peter spiritually.

Go low. Jesus does not force a lot of material into his training of Peter. It is not "high content," it is "low content." It does not focus on the development of skills. No doubt, Peter learned the skills of ministry as he watched Jesus and embarked on his own ministry. Skills were involved, but Jesus does not equip his disciples with an array of skills as his primary approach to discipleship.

Low also means that Jesus aimed at Peter's foundational values and beliefs. He is laser-focused on the core assumptions that drive Peter's decisions and shape his values. Jesus relentlessly uproots them as Peter actively follows Jesus. Peter was not sitting idly. He was engaged as a disciple following his master. That active following allowed Jesus to operate on Peter's core beliefs including leadership through power, elitism, ethnocentrism, ministry activity, cultural messianic expectations, initiative-taking (outside of Jesus's directives) and a narrow view of Scripture. His intensive course in the region of Caesarea Philippi targeted these core pivotal assumptions in the heart of the disciple. Like a master surgeon, Jesus inserts his scalpel to take away the deadly cancer that will impede the flow of his life through his apprentice.

Jesus aimed low, at the foundational beliefs that governed Peter's values and behavior. By focusing on the core element of the Father-Son relationship, Jesus calls out Peter's shadow-self. He brings his false assumptions to light, forcing his disciple to face those squarely.

---

12. Writers such as Dallas Willard, Richard Foster and, more recently, John Mark Comer have written helpful approaches to the spiritual disciplines. Rightly understood, the disciplines assist us to retrain the body to live aligned with our deepest desires. The disciplines themselves are not the source of those transformed desires. They assist us to retrain our bodies to live them out.

Jesus aimed low, at the foundational beliefs that governed Peter's values and behavior. By focusing on the core element of the Father-Son relationship, Jesus calls out Peter's shadow-self. He brings his false assumptions to light, forcing his disciple to face those squarely.

Go slow. Peter is an archetype (a model of discipleship). His quick responses and emotional engagement reveal common aspects of human personality. In a sense, I am Peter and you are Peter. Even if we don't identify with every aspect of his character, we can identify with his core alienation and the painful realization that he must change. Initially, Peter looked to Jesus to fulfill his personal expectations. Peter's deep need was significance, to be on the winning side, to wield influence. Peter thoroughly expected Jesus to be great, which would, in turn, make Peter great as Jesus's right-hand man. It was an expectation of self-fulfillment. Jesus would have none of it.

In the last chapter, we saw that Jesus affirmed and immediately rebuked Peter, setting the stage for deep personal change. On the Mount, Jesus takes Peter a step further and deeper by revealing his identity (his relatedness with the Father, sharing in his glory) and highlighting the suffering of Peter's collective story through the appearance of Moses and Elijah. The voice of the Father was the death knell to Peter's self-fulfillment expectations. Jesus's agenda flowed from his relational unity with the Father. "Listening to him" meant to be with him in this relational unity, yielding Peter's personal agenda to the greater reality of Jesus's oneness with the Father.

In removing self-fulfillment, Jesus invited Peter to something far more satisfying and real. It was the promise of the fatherly affection of God, extended to Peter through Christ. Peter's quick road to significance and influence came to a dead end. Jesus led him to a road of slow growth through relatedness to himself.

Peter's Formation and Ours

What does Peter's spiritual formation tell us about our own?

Jesus calls us to see ourselves in him in light of his relationship to the Father. He puts his finger on the taproot of our character – the core foundational beliefs that shape our values and behavior. Patiently, slowly, he brings circumstances into our lives to reveal those core beliefs so that we can see their destructive nature and embrace something far better. These realizations are often accompanied by deep emotions, enabling us to recall the moment of crisis and see it as transformational.

Reflect on your life. Consider the pivotal transitions you have experienced. Can you discern how the Spirit of Jesus revealed your shadow-self – the false values and beliefs that shaped your behavior? How did that experience in relation to Christ rescript those core beliefs, transforming them into something more valuable and precious?

Some have lived through those transitions but failed to embrace transformation. The result is usually bitterness and anger, or cynicism and resignation. Our shadow-self may continue to shape our behavior and values. If so, now is the time to review those transitions seeking redemption, embracing relatedness to Jesus as your foundational identity. This is what Jesus meant by calling us to "repentance" – a new way of perceiving ourselves and the world. What was revealed to you in those moments that you still need to embrace? Remember that Peter continues to learn the lessons of the Mount of Transfiguration. He was not able to grasp the full significance of all he saw and heard until later. Jesus was willing to go slow with Peter, but don't miss his invitation through the key moments of transition in your life.

Share the fruit of your reflection with some close friends in your community and invite them to share the same with you.

5

Serendipity

Migrating to a New Identity

*The spiritual journey is not a career or a success story.
It is a series of humiliations of the false self that become
more and more profound. These make room inside us
for the Holy Spirit to come in and heal. What prevents
us from being available to God is gradually evacuated
[as] we keep getting closer and closer to our Center – the
place where God dwells within us as redeemed people.*

Thomas Keating, *The Human Condition*

*Sin is unwillingness to trust that what God
wants for me is only my deepest happiness.*

Attributed to Ignatius of Loyola

When they came to Capernaum, the collectors of the two-drachma tax [the temple tax] went up to Peter and said, "Does your teacher not pay the tax?" He said, "Yes." And when he came into the house, Jesus spoke to him first, saying, "What do you think, Simon? From whom do kings of the earth take toll or tax? From their sons or from others?" And when he said "From others," Jesus said to him, "Then the sons are free. However, not to give offense to them, go to the sea and cast a hook and take the first fish that comes up, and when you open its mouth you will find a shekel. Take that and give it to them for me and for yourself."

He wants me to throw in a hook and a line. It's not my preferred way of fishing, but I've learned to just do what he says.

Those guys were trying to trap me and him. They wanted to catch him, shame him and all of us for not respecting the temple. I can hear it now . . . "the rabbi who is above paying for upkeep of God's house!" They're already afraid he could upset the whole temple business . . . and he could if he wanted.

He wasn't interested in that though.

He took me a little off guard with that question about who the kings collect taxes from. "From their sons or from others?" Strange way to ask the question. A king asking money from his son?! No way a king takes money from his own house to keep up his house!

"Sons?" Same word I heard on the mountain . . . same word I confessed.

Now, I'm supposed to get a shekel for him and for me. "Sons are free but pay the shekel for you and for me."

Huh?! So I'm free too?! Go figure. Coincidence? Nah. He never says anything without purpose.

It's like he said, "Do me this favor Peter . . . You and I are free as sons, but there's no need to give offense, so just go ahead and pay for both of us. Will you do that?"

And I will, gladly. But I want to know how I could be a son? How Simon, son of Jonas could be a free son?

Little Things: Big Impact

Russ was expected to show up in church that day. He was a towering man, both physically and spiritually, known as a gentle giant and a perceptive spiritual leader. He had been diagnosed with cancer and returned to the US for therapy. His health had stabilized allowing him to return to the Middle East to visit friends, but the news was not good. Russ's cancer, barring a miracle, was terminal. Russ was coming back to say good-bye before he died.

I recall only one conversation with him prior to his diagnosis, but it stood out in my memory, confirming what I had heard about him. We spoke only briefly, but he had an uncanny ability to tune in to my thoughts, asking me questions about my hopes and dreams as an aspiring cross-cultural minister. I found myself sharing things with him that some of my best friends didn't know. It was surprising.

When he returned to our church that morning, I knew he would be surrounded. But I hoped, at least, to shake his hand and remind him of our conversation a year before, and tell him how much I appreciated his sincere and selfless questions.

He was surrounded, but when our eyes met, he headed my way. Extending his big hand, he called me by name and, once again, engaged me with striking authenticity, asking about me and where life had taken me since our last conversation. I went home thinking, "I hope I can be like that someday."

A few months later, our church received the news that Russ had died. The total time of our conversation couldn't have been more than ten minutes. In two brief conversations that took place about a year apart, he showed me the heart of a spiritual man – kind, unselfish, perceptive, other-centered. It was a passing encounter, but it had a profound impact, revealing to me the person I wanted to be, the identity I hoped to move toward.

Some of Peter's encounters with Jesus were unplanned – serendipitous – the result of doing life together. The Merriam-Webster dictionary defines serendipity as "the faculty or phenomenon of finding valuable or agreeable things not sought for." If we have ears to hear and eyes to see, our most valuable moments will come to us in the normal course of life. Peter would agree as these passing interactions with Jesus leave an indelible imprint, inviting him to a new identity as a follower of Jesus. In this chapter, we look at three encounters around the theme of Peter's migration to a new identity.

Reshaping Core Identity: An Invitation to Sonship

The Gospels open a window so we can observe personal conversations between Jesus and his protégé. In this first encounter, Jesus questions him concerning who kings collect taxes from: their sons or others? Peter gives the right answer. Sons don't pay, others do. Jesus emphasizes his point, "then the sons are free" (tax-exempt).[1]

Jesus is playing on the word "sons." Peter confessed that Jesus was the Son of the living God and the Father affirmed it on the Mount of Transfiguration: "My beloved Son in whom I am well-pleased." As Peter hears Jesus declare, "the sons are free," we can be sure that he is making the connection.

It is no coincidence that this is a "temple" tax, a voluntary collection from every Jewish adult male of about two-days wages. It supplied the temple with necessary funding to keep it functioning. More importantly, it was God's house on earth. Jesus's question to Peter was about the "kings of this earth," but the temple is not an earthly king's property. It was God's. The tax in question maintains the property of God – the heavenly king. So who should pay this tax? Non-sons, of course, and by implication it means non-sons of God. Jesus is the divine Son and therefore not liable to a tax for his Father's dwelling on earth.

But Jesus isn't asking this question to assert his sonship. Peter already had that lesson, seen and experienced vividly on the Mount of Transfiguration. This is about Peter's sonship. Jesus's inclusion of him in this tax-exempt-son status is intentional.

Spiritual truths are not fully internalized on the first pass. They have to be mulled over, contemplated until they take root in lived experience.

Spiritual truths are not fully internalized on the first pass. They have to be mulled over, contemplated until they take root in lived experience.

Undoubtedly, Peter is still assimilating what he has seen and heard. How easily Jesus's status of divine Son could be used to denigrate Peter, to keep him in a place of inferiority. In Jesus's economy, opposite forces are at work. The

---

1. Some have read this as a contrast between citizens and non-citizens. However, that is not the intent here. Clearly, Jesus contrasts sons of rulers with non-sons. The sons do not pay taxes while those who are not sons, do. See Morris, *Gospel according to Matthew*, 453–54.

weak become strong. The poor are empowered. The orphan becomes a son. The shocking reality is that the status of sonship is open. The Father's embrace extends to Peter, inviting him to a new identity.

"Not to give offense to them, go to the sea and cast a hook . . ." As he takes his hook and line down to the sea, Peter has some time to ponder Jesus's words.

Peter, can you grasp it? Do your eyes see? Do your ears hear? Have you transplanted your identity into a relationship with the Father through the Son? Do you know yourself to be free in his love?

Though free from the tax, Jesus offers no resistance. He accepts to pay what has been asked of Peter, which is even more remarkable given that he will soon prophesy the destruction of the temple (Matt 24:2). The kingdom of Jesus is real, present, now. It is also coming, still to be fulfilled. He invites his disciple into the reality of sonship while, at the same time, living in unfulfilled expectation. It is the reality of "the now and the not yet."

As Son, Jesus is not compelled to assert his rights. One who is secure in his or her identity is most free to forego its outward trappings. By inviting Peter into sonship, he also invites him to live tomorrow's reality today.

Peter's Core Identity and Ours

Jesus's subtle invitation to sonship will become much clearer in the upper room shortly before his death. Being formed in the way of Jesus is not all death and drudgery. It is family, belonging, mutual love and embrace. It is a transplanted identity that is relationally rooted in a Father's love. As the old dies, the new lives. We sense the sunlight breaking through the clouds of Peter's self-understanding.

Identity may not be a familiar term in our discussions on spiritual growth. I only realized how foundational it is to our spiritual life when I walked alongside believers from other religious backgrounds who came to believe in and follow Jesus. We began to realize that as they embraced Jesus, they also shed some of their past identity. Exactly what to shed and what to keep became very important questions.[2]

Working through those questions helps us realize that identity is layered. There is the *core identity* – who we are at the deepest level. Peter's sonship is the core identity he is invited into. Beyond that, there is a *collective identity* –

---

2. If you would like to read more on identity issues for those who follow Christ from other faiths, see Green, "Conversion in the Light of Identity Theories." See also Little, *Effective Discipling in Muslim Communities*, 179–208.

the society we are a part of. It is who we are culturally by virtue of place and upbringing. Between those two is a matrix of social identities – the diverse groups I belong to by associations and relationships (e.g. my family, vocation, education, church and social affiliations, etc.).

Jesus invites Peter to migrate his core identity. I use "migrate" because Peter didn't get there overnight. He was moving in that direction, on a journey of identity transformation. My core identity is how and from where I get my sense of worth. It is what makes me feel valuable. A good way to discern it is to ask, what, if taken from me, would cause me to feel of little or no worth? Warning: for most of us, our first or reflexive answer may be more wishful thinking than truth. Keep probing, with honesty and self-awareness.

The purpose of the question is not to assure me that I'm good, that I'm where I should be. The purpose of the question is to discern my counterfeit identity and face it. If I jump too quickly to the "right answer" (e.g. my core identity is being related to God as a son or daughter), I probably need to rethink my answer. Remember, Peter isn't there yet. His identity is undergoing transformation through a long journey of relational encounters with Jesus. He'll spend the rest of his life getting his core identity aligned with the truth that he is a son of the Father. He still has a long road ahead, as do we.

Now for a second serendipity.

Mark 11:12–14, 20–25

On the following day, when they came from Bethany, he was hungry. And seeing in the distance a fig tree in leaf, he went to see if he could find anything on it. When he came to it, he found nothing but leaves, for it was not the season for figs. And he said to it, "May no one ever eat fruit from you again." And his disciples heard it.

As they passed by in the morning, they saw the fig tree withered away to its roots. And Peter remembered and said to him, "Rabbi, look! The fig tree that you cursed has withered." And Jesus answered them, "Have faith in God. Truly I say to you whoever says to this mountain, 'Be taken up and thrown into the sea' and does not doubt in his heart, but believes that what he says will come to pass, it will be done for him. Therefore I tell you, whatever you ask in prayer, believe that you have received it, and it will be yours. And whenever you stand praying, forgive, if you have anything against anyone, so that your Father also who is in heaven may forgive you your trespasses."

Reshaping a Collective Identity

As I write, my country is in the throes of upheaval due to the unjust murder of George Floyd – a Black man who died under the knee of a White police officer while pleading for breath. The incident, along with a spate of police violence against African Americans, rips open a gaping wound across the nation. It has to do with our collective identity. Who belongs and how does one belong? After a long history of slavery, subjugation, segregation, discrimination and injustice, African Americans, with the support of many other ethnicities, are protesting systemic racism – exclusion from a collective identity. It is a moment for White Americans to face the reality of complicity in injustice and to do the hard work of making space for those perceived as different. Through these events, I am forced to reexamine my collective identity as a White American male and face the reality of exploitation of another ethnicity.

Deconstructing a False Collective Identity

The story of the cursing of the fig tree concerns the collective identity of the disciples and of Israel itself. The fig tree incident, along with the cleansing of the temple, is one step along the journey of redefining Peter's identity. The questions include: To whom do I/we belong? How do I/we belong? What are the visible symbols of my/our belonging? This story alone does not provide a full response. Previously we considered Peter's deculturation as part of his spiritual formation. This is another station along Peter's journey to a new collective identity.

Mark tells the story in two sections. Though the meaning of the parable has been debated, Mark's placing the temple cleansing between the two sections provides a key to the meaning. You recall that Jesus goes to the temple, creates a whip and begins to drive out the money changers, citing Isaiah 56:7: "My house shall be called a house of prayer for all peoples." The event is astonishing because Jesus never resorts to violent means except here. So the cursing of the fig tree is not about figs or even about Jesus's hunger. It is integral to what takes place in the temple. It has bearing on the temple's role in Israel's corporate identity and its leaders, who claim to speak for God and represent him in the temple and its functions. The cursing of the fig tree is an enacted parable.[3]

This is not Solomon's temple which had been destroyed; this is a new temple rebuilt by Herod on a scale equal with his ego. The scope of the sacrificial offerings was overwhelming. Josephus relates that in 66 BC, when the temple was finally completed, 255,600 lambs were slain for the Passover sacrifice.[4] The Sanhedrin (a council of religious elders) oversaw the temple complex and benefited from its illustrious religious commerce. So, in purging the temple, Jesus is confronting the prominent religious symbol of his day. It had profound fiscal and political associations. We know from Jesus's citation from Isaiah that he is enraged by the temple's exclusion of foreigners from its outer precincts. In brief, the temple is a "mountain" of collective religious identity, exclusive and discriminating on the basis of ethnicity and religious pedigree.

The fig tree serves as a parable and prophecy, acted out by Jesus. Though this way of reading Scripture may be strange to us, it is common in the Bible.

---

3. One question that often arises concerns Mark's statement that it was not the season for figs (Mark 11:13). The statement concerns us because it seems Jesus is punishing the fig tree unjustly. When understood as an enacted parable, this criticism loses its force. Jesus was not criticizing a tree, per se, but using that tree to comment on the unfruitful leadership of the temple. It is also plausible that Jesus was looking for the premature figs (known as *paggim*) that would be expected at this season. See Edwards, *Gospel according to Mark*, 340.

4. Edwards, 341.

Ezekiel, for example, acts out many of his prophetic oracles, making them visible messages from God. Jesus is drawing from the playbook of the Old Testament.

Given the horrors of anti-Jewish sentiment in recent history, it is important to underline that the fig tree is not symbolic of the Jewish people, but of a corrupt and mercenary religious leadership which excluded non-Jews from the temple and instigated the proceedings that led to Jesus's execution. Like the leafy fig tree, the religious leaders appeared to be healthy and flourishing. Closer examination, however, reveals fruitlessness. Therefore, the lord of the fig tree will bring it to an end. "No one will ever eat fruit from you again."

Jesus's confrontation with the Jewish leaders is nothing new, but it does suggest finality and an ultimate judgment that cannot be averted. The temple elite are being replaced by a new leadership – the apostles of Jesus. The new "temple," will not be a proud edifice of Jewish nationalism but a welcoming community made up of all nations, tribes and tongues. Peter will play a "key" role in this new collective identity.

Forerunners of a New Collective Identity

The cursing of the fig tree, as an enacted prophecy or parable, paints a stark contrast between the culture Jesus instigates and that of the religious elite of his day. Jesus rejects the symbol which everyone admires – a super temple where powerful people skim profits off religious commerce while they kowtow to political power. Those expressions are rotten to the core and fruitless. Jesus will not countenance them. But what is the alternative? What does Jesus offer Peter in its place?

Jesus's word of power spoken to the fig tree invites Peter and the disciples to a new collective identity with new ways of operating. "Have faith in God." The disciples will become participants with Jesus in removing the mountain of religious fruitlessness, casting it into the sea. Faith in God expressed through prayer will enable the disciples to do their own mountain-moving feats.

In place of the old symbols of religious collective identity, something far better is offered. It is received, not by exploitation and powerplay, but by faith in God. Peter and the disciples are invited to find their collective identity in God through the promise of Jesus. As they do, they will carry forward Jesus's mountain-moving work by faith through prayer.

Jesus addresses an obstacle to the new identity – lack of forgiveness. At the core of the disciple's new identity is a recognition of their need of forgiveness. The contrast with the religious elite of that day could not be starker. Jesus's followers see a perennial need of forgiveness. That posture of humility stands at the heart of their prayers in faith and is the key to their mountain-moving feats.

The chart below draws on this incident as well as Jesus's other confrontations with the religious elite to show the contrast of identity markers he requires for Peter and the disciples – the forerunners of a new collective identity.

	Peter and Jesus's Followers	The Sanhedrin
Source of Authority	Faith: Interior relatedness to God	Position: Exterior trappings of power
Means of Operation	Prayer to move mountains	Exploitation in the name of God
Spiritual Posture	Humility: Forgive others and receive forgiveness	Elitism and superiority
Visible Manifestation	An emerging house of all nations	A grand, but exclusive temple

Before we leave this idea of our collective identity, we drop in on a third serendipitous interaction between Jesus and Peter.

Mark 10:28–31

Peter began to say to him, "See, we have left everything and followed you." Jesus said, "Truly I say to you, there is no one who has left house or brothers or sisters or mother or father or children or lands, for my sake and for the gospel, who will not receive a hundredfold now in this time, houses and brothers and sisters and mothers and children and lands, with persecutions, and in the age to come eternal life. But many who are first will be last, and the last first."

Anticipating a New Collective Identity

In this conversation, a rich young man has just left Jesus saddened because he owned a lot of stuff and Jesus asked him to sell it, distribute it to the poor, and then come and follow him.

Peter has a response to Jesus. We hold our breath, raise our eyebrows, and expect that Jesus may have another stunning rebuke for his protégé as he did when Peter proposed that he circumvent suffering and death. But Jesus does not rebuke Peter. In fact, joy is the dominant note. He seems to be saying, "Trust me. You're gonna love this new life, even with the persecutions." Think of the promise here – one hundred times as much reward in this life and the next. To be clear, Jesus promises Peter and the disciples increased family relations and land holdings – along with persecutions. Interesting.

If we could time travel back to see Peter's life after Jesus's death, I think we would agree that the promise came true. Peter's life was vibrant as he led a new movement of Jesus-followers related to him as brothers and sisters. God worked through him powerfully as he taught, preached and healed. His travels must have allowed him to pass through Galilee from time to time where he enjoyed the warm fellowship of family and friends. He was married and likely had children and other relations in the area of Galilee. We know, of course, that Peter did some prison time and ultimately gave his life in witness to his Lord. So the persecutions came too, but the new collective identity of the body of Christ surrounds Peter as he walks through suffering and then enters death's door and his new life in his master's presence.

Identity in Spiritual Formation

As we follow Jesus, our core and collective identities migrate. We are on a journey in which we learn that, despite all outward appearances, what gives us value and meaning is our relatedness to God the Father through Jesus, our elder brother. We are given the Spirit who pours out the love of God in our hearts. This indwelling sense of being highly valued and pursued by the God of the universe displaces false confidence in our social affiliations and natural abilities. With time, it overwhelms our inadequacies, fears and insecurities.

Our identity is rooted in Jesus, who brings us into the loving embrace of God the Father through the Holy Spirit. Our being and doing are not disjointed. Our actions flow from our being beloved children. We commune with our heavenly Father and exercise faith to bring his love to a world in need, through faith, by prayer. It is the strength of our adoption into God's family that enables us to enter into a new collective identity as peacemakers, reconcilers, salt and light in our societies. Our "new birth" into the family of God generates a whole new social consciousness as we become vessels of God's love outpoured to those who our society views as marginalized and estranged. Our faith-relatedness to Christ is not merely for our spiritual enjoyment. It is for the purpose of communicating God's love and inviting more children into his family.

Our collective identity migrates as our core (personal) identity is transformed. We are not merely the sum of our nationality, ethnicity, family relations, peers and education. On the journey of spiritual formation, those allegiances are held with open hands before Jesus. Some will be refined while others are left behind. Embracing the new collective identity of the body of Christ will eventually eclipse and sometimes enfold much of the rest.

In his prophetic parable, Jesus showed us both his radical inclusiveness and his radical exclusiveness. He himself is the cornerstone of the new temple, the symbol of the collective identity of the people of God. Each stone in that new building is built on him and on his apostles as the foundation. He is the only foundation. The alternate identity markers are cast away – dried from the roots or cast into the sea. That's radical exclusivity! However, those built into the new temple are not triaged by race, social class, gender or education. The family of God, the brothers and sisters of Jesus, do not discriminate based on these externals. In fact, they go the extra mile to ensure that those on the margins are brought in, even if it means destroying old structures so that the new can accommodate the vast variety of his people. It is a radically inclusive family![5]

Peter's brief serendipitous encounters with Jesus appear coincidental but nothing could be further from reality. There is a master plan at work. Jesus is an artist. He knows exactly how to mold the clay, inside and out. He knows when radical change is called for and when gentle re-shaping is required. Peter is still on the journey as are we. Through Peter's evolving identity, we catch a glimpse of how our own identity must change and shift in following Jesus. But that will require intentionality. Some practical steps follow.

Peter's Collective Identity and Ours

Our spiritual formation will not be a mirror image of Peter's. Peter is an archetype, a model of spiritual formation; his experience helps us probe and understand our own spiritual formation. We will not cast the mountain of Jewish nationalist religious leadership into the sea. However, we also engage in the works of Jesus through prayer, by faith. Paul says, "We destroy arguments and every lofty opinion raised up against the knowledge of God." By the way, we do that as a collective – the body. To illustrate, allow me to return to thoughts that opened this section concerning systemic racism.

It is striking that over 150 years after the end of the Civil War, we still do not have racial equity in the United States. I've lived enough places to know that racism is not a uniquely American problem. It exists everywhere, but the US faces unique challenges due to its complex and exploitative history with African Americans, native Americans, Latinos and others.

Jesus reserved his most violent reaction for a temple elite whose actions fenced out the nations (non-Hebrews). He went to battle for a temple that included all ethnicities and ultimately built that "temple" on the foundation of the apostles (Eph 2:20). In the end, he prophesied the destruction of Herod's temple, and it has not been rebuilt to this day. Meanwhile, his all-nations body, continues its global spread.

Much like Simon and the disciples, Christians (in the US and around the world) must ask if their national and ethnic identities supersede their belonging to Jesus's kingdom. Will we ignore the cries of minorities who are telling us

---

5. I am indebted to Tim Keller for this concept of the radical inclusiveness and the radical exclusiveness of the gospel. His sermon titled "The Gospel to the African" is a good example of how he develops this idea. https://www.oneplace.com/ministries/gospel-in-life/listen/the-gospel-to-the-african-881071.html.

they cannot breathe? Or will we engage in acts of faith to destroy the edifice of systemic racism and exclusion so that every ethnicity is welcome. Racist systems are one mountain that must be cast into the sea today. It must begin in Christ's church – a house of prayer for all peoples and nations. If we continue to passively enjoy the fruits of an exploitative system, we have nothing to look forward to except to be dried up from the roots, like the fig tree, or cast into the sea, like the mountain that stands in opposition to Jesus's kingdom. Jesus simply will not have it.

Jesus did something shocking to show his disciples and the temple worshippers that their collective identity was inadequate. Our collective identity concerns our family, social class, political preferences, vocation, gender, religion, military affiliation, etc. Because we rarely question the validity of these elements, we may need a transformative experience – a shock – to see the inadequacy of our collective identity. Previously, we attempted to listen empathetically to someone who has a different understanding of our collective identity. We suggested the sermons or letters of Martin Luther King Jr. as one example of an important outside perspective for White Americans.

This type of rescripting of our collective identity often happens in interracial discussions such as listening circles. It is most effective when it happens through a personal relationship, but media can help. Robert Jones' book *White Too Long* is a social-historical account of racial bias among American Christians. This kind of racial superiority is not unique to the United States, but the history of slavery and white supremacy in the US make this history poignant. It will pain you to read Jones' account, as it underscores how deeply our collective identity is rooted in our hearts and how difficult it is to uproot. Also, consider viewing a documentary (e.g. *13th*) or a film (e.g. *Just Mercy*), or reading an account of injustices suffered by native Americans (e.g. *Neither Wolf nor Dog*) or immigrants. The shock of those conversations and stories can knock the complacency out of us and help us recalibrate our collective identity. *Of Gods and Men* is a French film depicting the martyrdom of seven Trappist monks in Algeria. The film illustrates the challenge and beauty of migrating our identity to include others in a life of prayer. Of course, if you expect to "agree" with everything in these media, you'll be disappointed. Remember that our collective identity likely needs to be disrupted. That only happens if we allow ourselves to see it through the eyes of outsiders. Prayerfully journal what you are learning and share it with others in your community. Are there areas of your current collective identity you should renounce? Are there positive steps you should take towards embracing a new collective identity?

6

The Unmasking

A Disciple's Self-Perception

He who attempts to act and do things for others or for the world without deepening his own self-understanding, freedom, integrity and capacity for love will not have anything to give to others. He will communicate nothing but the contagion of his own obsessions, his aggressiveness, his ego-centred ambitions, his delusions about ends and means, his doctrinaire prejudices and ideas.

Thomas Merton, *Thomas Merton: Spiritual Master*

Now as they were eating, Jesus took bread, and after blessing it broke it and gave it to the disciples and said, "Take, eat; this is my body." And he took a cup, and when he had given thanks he gave it to them, saying, "Drink of it, all of you, for this is my blood of the covenant which is poured out for many for the forgiveness of sins. I tell you I will not drink again of this fruit of the vine until that day when I drink it new with you in my Father's kingdom."

And when they had sung a hymn, they went out to the Mount of Olives. Then Jesus said to them, "You will all fall away because of me this night. For it is written, 'I will strike the shepherd and the sheep of the flock will be scattered.' But after I am raised up, I will go before you to Galilee." Peter answered him, "Though they all fall away because of you, I will never fall away." Jesus said to him, "Truly I tell you, this very night, before the rooster crows, you will deny me three times." Peter said to him, "Even if I must die with you, I will not deny you!" And all the disciples said the same.

I'm all in. That's the one thing I know for certain.

These three years with Jesus have been a crazy ride, but I'd never seen or heard or felt the things I have since he said "follow me" that day in my boat. My whole life has turned upside down and there's no going back.

I know the Sanhedrin is scheming to get him. The way he takes them on . . . Listening to the things he says makes me shake my head. I've never heard boldness like his . . . totally secure in who he is. Only the Messiah could do that. They have to know that too.

The people know it. They were calling out, "Save us, Son of David!" as they threw their cloaks and branches on the ground in front of him. He feeds the hungry and heals the sick. He even raises the dead!

No doubt in my mind . . . I'm all in. It's Jesus or nothing for me.

I've told him that too. I told him that even if all the other guys leave, I won't. He can count on me. He mentioned denying him, but I made it clear that's not happening . . . even if I have to die with him.

I'm all in!

The Danger of Self-Assurance

We were gathering both house churches for the first time. The meeting place was set for a small house outside our city. You might anticipate that there would be a joyful expectation around such a gathering, that the believers would be looking forward to it. In a sense they were, but there was also a cloud of suspicion that hung over the meeting. The house churches were small, each one hosting a circle of believers who knew and trusted one another. Today, for the first time, the two circles would intersect. Believers who did not know each other were to meet. That was the rub.

Some of the believers that gathered that day had been imprisoned for their confession of Christ, but most had not. An active network of underground police and informants were the constant nemesis to the church in that Middle Eastern city. Cell phones were tapped, churches were infiltrated. Converting to a new faith was seen as a threat to the religious stability of the country. The charge of "sectarian sedition" was easily invoked and sufficient to lock away new believers for months at a time during which physical and mental torture wreaked havoc and wrecked lives.

In such an atmosphere, the normal joy of bringing believers together takes a back seat to the stark reality that there may be an informant among the "unknowns," a traitor. That particular day, unfortunately, there was. The young man showed up for the meeting, but fell strangely ill shortly after he arrived. He quickly excused himself to return home. We all wished him well. Later that morning, an unmarked car showed up outside. We noticed. How could we not notice? The officer inside had a video camera and was recording the license plates of all vehicles and anyone who went in or out of the house.

The meeting proceeded, but now with a dark awareness that there would be ramifications.

The young man who left the meetings would never have considered himself a traitor. He loved the Lord and his people. But something broke him. Knowing the tactics of the authorities in that country, it was likely a threat, not to himself, but to a family member. If he failed to produce accurate information, his loved ones who knew of his faith but strongly disapproved, would be the ones to suffer. The pressure caused him to divulge information.

Rarely are we forced to face such stark and menacing circumstances. In his weakness, this young man must have learned something about himself that was painful and yet essential. He was not nearly as strong as he fancied himself to be, not nearly as reliable as he wanted to be, not nearly as true as he should be.

Peter was about to learn that lesson as well.

Peter's Progress

Only John records a significant event that took place in that upper room, probably only a short time before Peter's claim to be willing to die with Jesus. It is his final act of service to his disciples (John 13:1–7). Jesus will soon undergo jeers and taunts, scourging and nails. He is intent on leaving his disciples with this last lesson – enacted poignantly, unforgettably. What happened in that upper room sets the stage for the unmasking of Peter's pseudo-devotion.

Allow your familiarity with the scene to paint the details in your imagination. The master takes off his outer garment and wraps a towel around his waist. He grasps the clay vessel filled with water. There were no other volunteers. He begins to move around the outer circle of those disciples, now reclined on their sides around the low table with feet extended outward. The water does its work as the grime from hours of walking trickles off and away from tired feet. He comes to Peter.

"No, Lord! You shall never wash my feet!"

"If I do not wash you, you have no share with me."

That statement must have been enough for Peter. His initial rejection of Jesus taking a servant's menial role appeared unbending. His Rabbi and Lord should not do this. It would be shameful, unbecoming. However, knowing that if he remains unwashed, he can have no part with Jesus, obliterates his objection.

"Lord, not my feet only but also my hands and my head."

We should pause and hear Peter well. This is his version of "I surrender all." Inasmuch as he knows himself, Peter wants Jesus to have his way with him. He is all in. We know that the tragic denial is only hours away. Jesus knows that as well. To Peter, the denial is unthinkable at this stage. All he knows is that he wants Jesus to wash him, to purify him, to change him. He's learned that Jesus's ways are unconventional so he's willing to go counterculture, to allow the divine Son, the object of the Father's delight, to wash him.

Peter is making progress. He is learning to temper his impetuous zeal in response to Jesus's counterintuitive directives. Something is happening inside him. He knows that his reflex may land him in deep mud so he stops to place himself in the flow of Jesus's cleansing. That's a good spiritual reflex and it will appear again in Peter's reactions.

Considering the deep valley that Peter is about to pass through as he denies his Lord, this is a reference point.

Peter expresses his desire that Jesus do with him all that is needed. Jesus accepts it at face value, knowing full well that his protégé is under a delusion of pseudo-spirituality. He is willing to let Peter walk through the experience, knowing it will be a life-giving remedy.

Peter expresses his desire that Jesus do with him all that is needed. Jesus accepts it at face value, knowing full well that his protégé is under a delusion of pseudo-spirituality. He is willing to let Peter walk through the experience, knowing it will be a life-giving remedy.

Seeing the Self

Peter categorically denied that he would deny. I wonder if you, like me, have ever shaken your head in disbelief that Peter could be so fickle, so unreliable. The way the story is told invites us, does it not, to ask ourselves, "but how could he have been so wrong? How could he have thought so highly of himself when it was so contrary to reality?"

Dear, dear Peter! What a disappointment he was to himself, to the disciples and to Jesus.

At the end of our discussion, we will conclude that Peter simply did not know himself. He was not self-aware. That's an easy diagnosis, too easy. Discerning the ingredients of his self-deception may serve us well if we hope to avoid a fall like Peter's. We'll look at three of those ingredients: comparison, pseudo-devotion and denial.

Comparison

The first ingredient is comparison. Peter's words reveal his heart and that is why he is such a valuable archetype to us. Perhaps, like me, you've lived long enough and eaten your words enough times that you now know how to avoid costly self-revelation. Peter comes right out with his thoughts. They challenge us, or at least they should, to self-examination.

"Though they all fall away because of you, I will never fall away."

Peter was a leader. Jesus had affirmed it. He styled himself as a pacesetter, the one leading the charge, waving the banner as the troops fall in line behind. It is striking though, that right there in the hearing of the other disciples, Peter has the gall to compare himself to the others claiming that he would not be weak like them, that he would stand aloft when they fall away. His words unveil his sense of superiority – a bravado that he can and will do what others cannot.

I suppose Jesus saw this as a teachable moment. He was a master, after all. So he must have determined that he would not leave Peter, the keeper of the kingdom keys, vulnerable to the death trap of comparison. He would oblige Peter to see himself, not as superior, not as he longed to be, but as he really was. That's the topic of the next chapter.

For us, the lesson is too valuable to pass up. The disciple must stand with other believers, not over against them.

We live in a society that longs for heroes, likely because they are so hard to find. Feats of great bravery and self-sacrifice form the themes of our cultural stories. Perhaps we too long for that moment of greatness, when we stand above the masses, our nobility evident to all.

It seems that Jesus would have Peter stand alone first. Peter must come to terms with who he is. He must face himself before he is ready for noble feats. The sting of his comparison will come back to bite him at a later point. Jesus will drive the lesson home, but for now, I observe this comparative tendency and turn the searchlight into the crevices of my own soul. Does superiority lurk there? Do I fancy myself as better than others, more dependable, more deserving? That tendency is antithetical to spiritual formation in the Jesus way. It simply cannot persist.

Pseudo-Devotion

The second ingredient to Peter's tragic self-deception is pseudo-devotion. It's obvious, isn't it? Peter thought of himself as the super devoted disciple. The fact that he wasn't must have come as a rude awakening, but a necessary one.

The layers of Peter's personality cannot be easily categorized. Internal motivations are nuanced in many shades between black and white. Make no mistake – Peter is devoted to Jesus. Three years have proven that. He had many opportunities to turn away. He never did. He could have opted for material rewards. But he didn't. We should not miss that. If we do, we fail to learn the lesson of this encounter. Peter's commitment to Jesus is profound and life-altering. We should feel a little ill at ease as we contemplate the fact that Peter is probably far ahead of us in his devotion to Jesus and yet he misjudges himself, over-estimating his own level of devotion to his Lord. As we read about Peter, we must not allow ourselves to objectify him or treat him merely as a study. Peter is a person as are you and I. His failings and reactions could very well be ours, and they often are. To benefit from Peter's spiritual formation, I must enter into it. Matthew informs us that Peter is not alone. All the disciples said the same thing (Matt 26:35).

There was a pseudo-devotion lurking in Peter's soul. "Pseudo" suggests a devotion in name only. It presents as the real thing, looks very authentic to all outward appearances, and yet, where the rubber meets the road, Peter is deceived. His willingness to go to death with Jesus, even when others abandon him, is pseudo. It's fake. It won't stand the test.

My friends who have experienced torture have often told me that if you think you can't be broken, you are deceived. One told me that he could easily be broken such that he would say anything his captors desired even though they never laid a hand on him. All they had to do was deprive him of sleep. This was easily done in a way that left no scars, no marks, and yet it was a full proof means to extract information. A person who has experienced such trauma might know himself or herself more deeply than most of us. They walk in humility, much like Jacob did with the limp that forever marked him. They know how limited they are, how far they fall from their ideals. They have faced themselves.

I hope that you never have to endure torture to face yourself. Peter's example, if taken to heart, can help us avoid some of the pitfalls which he endured. He is there to serve us and lead us into authentic spiritual formation.

If we scan the horizon of contemporary spirituality, there is no escape from the fact that pseudo-devotion is prolific. It offers an easy road to respect in religious circles. Following are a few examples of how pseudo-devotion has reared its ugly head in my journey. Feel free to add your own examples.

Worship music often declares the willingness of the worshipper to enter the sufferings of Jesus or to give him thorough devotion. "All to Jesus I surrender. All to him I freely give. I will ever love and trust him, in his presence daily live. I surrender all." When understood as an expression of longing, lyrics like these can be valuable, urging us on to more faithful living. However, they also threaten us with pseudo-devotion as we declare something that may be beyond our ability to understand. Peter shows us that we do not know the degree of our surrender to God. Perhaps it would be best to confess that reality as we declare our longing to surrender to him more fully.

The tendency to put our spiritual depth on display is a continual temptation. There is something about the corporate nature of the church that goads us to show ourselves as more than we are, much like Peter's spiritual bravado before Jesus and the disciples. We want to look good in front of others. We put on our best face. In terms of spiritual formation, that reflex is deadly. It is all about appearance and has little to do with reality. Peter warns us not to externalize what we have not internalized.

The call to global mission to unreached peoples has figured large in my spiritual formation. In fact, as I lived in the Middle East and was exposed to monasticism for the first time, it dawned on me that mission among evangelicals acts as monasticism did among the early and medieval Christians. It draws passionate hearts to profound and life-changing commitment. As I review my formative years in mission, I must admit that self-deception was at play. The messages I heard moved me profoundly calling me to give my life to reach those with least access to the gospel. I "laid my life on the altar" more than once, committing myself to that ministry. My mistake was in thinking that once my life was laid on the altar, it would stay there. The sacrifice did not die easily and was prone to crawl off the altar! In fact, it still dodges the sacrificial knife, feigning shock that the old life persists. Along the way I realized that embittered relationships, spiritual pride, secret addictions and a host of other forces kept the blood of the old life pumping through my spiritual veins. It was not a "one and done deal." The journey to an authentic self remains a long one. Peter shows us that and he will continue to do so even after his greatest victories.

Denial: Failure to Heed Jesus's Words

It is stunning that Peter, after all we've watched him endure, is content to cast doubt on Jesus's words. We looked at length at Peter's rebuke of Jesus and his attempt to deter him from suffering and death. After that abrupt rebuke, we might think Peter would be able to keep his thoughts to himself. Shouldn't he know better by now? Jesus said Peter would deny him. Peter's response: "Never! Even if they all fall away, not me!" Peter is in denial of his capacity to deny Jesus.

Peter, the last time you contradicted Jesus, it didn't work out too well for you!

We are trying to keep the perspective that Peter's impetuous nature is for our benefit. He serves as a model to help us identify areas we should be addressing to conform to Jesus's pattern for spiritual formation. Nevertheless, it defies belief that Peter counters Jesus's words. What are we to make of that?

The two sources of spiritual transformation are the word and Spirit. Those are best accessed in and through the community of Christ's followers – the church. I realize other means exist such as disciplines, sacraments, relationships, etc., nevertheless, none of those yields spiritual growth if not empowered by the Spirit and inspired by the word of God.

Peter has just received yet another hard word from Jesus: "You will deny me three times." Would you want to hear that from your master and teacher for the past three years? Neither did Peter. And yet, that's exactly what he heard and rejected. "Can't be true! You're wrong this time, Jesus."

What can we learn from this? The word of God confronted Peter with his reality, but he was not able to hear it. The word of Christ is brought to us by the Spirit of Christ and it can come to us through the words of Scripture or a brother or sister or some other means. It often happens in conflict or some disagreeable confrontation, exactly as we see here with Peter. His immediate reflex was to defend himself. Denying Jesus was unconscionable, too painful to accept. If we pay attention, we will notice that some things people tell us evoke the same kind of pain. We deny it reflexively. "It may be true for some people, but not me. No, you misunderstand my intentions. You're not seeing the whole picture, let me spell it out for you."

When the urge to defend ourselves arises within us, stop. Could it be a word from the Spirit? Why the need to defend? What is going on in the deep self?

When the urge to defend ourselves arises within us, stop. Could it be a word from the Spirit? Why the need to defend? What is going on in the deep self?

Jesus is setting Peter up for the deepest confrontation with the self that he will ever experience. It will be excruciating. No doubt, Jesus knew that. Still, he didn't spare his mentee. In fact, it is intentional on his part. He is designing this path of spiritual formation, custom-made for Peter. Jesus is determined that Peter face his shadow-self. That should tell us how important it is that we do the same. We're no better than Peter. How tragic if we rise to our own defense when, in fact, we are hearing a word from the Spirit, if we have ears to hear.

This story is not only about Peter. It is about the nature of humanity. The self, alienated from God, is a master deceiver. Our denial must be exposed to the design of the master discipler and spiritual mentor. If we fend off that exposure, if we reject the Spirit's inspired word, we will not make progress. Continuing to nurture our alienated self, we will not lay hold of the good things that Christ has ordained for us.

Christ's word to Cain comes to mind.[1] "Sin is crouching at the door. Its desire is contrary to you, but you must rule over it" (Gen 4:7). Cain, like Peter, presumed that he was good, that he was further down the road of spiritual formation than he thought. Christ confronts him with a hard word which he was unable to hear. In the end, he murders his brother. The next word Cain hears from Christ is that his brother's blood is crying to God from the ground.

Failure to hear that Spirit-given word is disastrous.

It seems Peter is unable to hear the word. Are we on the verge of losing Peter as a model of spiritual formation? Will he persist in his denial and end up a spiritual train wreck? Or will he come through? Jesus prays for Peter (Luke 22:31–32) and, in the end, he receives the Spirit-given word. He owns his alienated self and from that point of ownership, begins to move to a more authentic self.

Peter's Self-deception and Ours

Thomas Keating tells of a panel discussion he attended in which the panelists were Holocaust survivors. One woman's story struck him. Her parents had been killed in the Holocaust. In response, she founded a humanitarian organization to prevent such atrocities. In the conversation she mentioned casually, "You know, I couldn't have started that organization unless I knew that, with the situation just a little different, I could have done the same things that the Nazis did to my parents and the others in the concentration camps." Keating felt this woman possessed true humility – "the knowledge of one's self that clearly perceives that with just a little change of circumstances, one is capable of any evil."[2]

Is Keating right? Could I really engage in Holocaust atrocities?

The Spirit speaks through Peter to indicate that we disciples do not fully know ourselves. We do not grasp how tentative are our desires for righteousness nor how effectively circumstances preclude our passion. It's not fun to consider such things. Couldn't we just forego all that demanding internal work? Isn't that why we pray, "lead me not into temptation?"

---

1. It may be unfamiliar to think of Christ speaking to Cain in the pages of Genesis. I speak that way intentionally for two reasons. One, the persons of the Trinity are always present with one another, working in concert. So it would be incorrect to think of this as one of the persons of the Trinity without the others. Second, Jesus consistently taught that he was the central topic of the Old Testament and that Moses wrote about him (see John 5:39, 46; 8:56–58; Luke 24:27, 44–45; Acts 10:43).

2. Keating, *Human Condition*, loc. 271–77.

Jesus apparently wanted Peter to face himself. If Peter is our archetype follower of Jesus, that means we should face ourselves too. There's something here for us – what Keating calls "true humility." Awareness of our shadow-self will come in different, albeit similar, ways than it did for Peter. We will experience some pain as we confront who we really are and how far our reality is from our desire.

We've already mentioned that listening to Spirit-given words from others can be one source for facing our shadow selves. We desperately need the outside perspective of those who love us or who care enough to speak hard words to us. Even if those words wound us, they carry enough of the truth that we would do well to examine them for elements of truth.

I recall attending a meeting in the Middle East where it was suggested that my Western perspective could be motivated by a colonial attitude towards the East. The background of that accusation needs explanation. Suffice to say that Christian ministries that came from the West are sometimes viewed as exploitative by Middle Easterners. Their concern has to do with financial management and control of ministry activities. I was quite upset that my colleagues felt my words indicated a latent colonialist attitude. In my mind, there was no Westerner who was more attuned and sensitive to the dangers of colonialism than myself (shades of Peter, "I would never do that!"). You can imagine that hearing that accusation was painful. Though it felt like an unconscionable accusation, it led to my thinking through my involvement in ministries in the Middle East, scrutinizing the roles I played for any exploitative elements. So listening to criticism, especially when it stings, is important.

You may never have been accused of colonialism, like me, or told that you would deny Christ, like Peter. But what stinging criticisms have you heard? Why did they hurt so badly? Have you been confronted with a reality that was terribly hard to face? What could the Spirit be saying through that?

Another level is simply listening to the Holy Spirit. Some helpful disciplines have been developed to help Jesus followers engage in listening to the Spirit. Keating's "centering prayer" is one such discipline. Another is the Examen prayer of the Jesuits. Both disciplines help us become quiet and attentive to the Spirit's voice through the memory of actions and emotions.

I have found it helpful to repeat short phrases from the Psalms, such as, "you delight in truth in the inward being" (Ps 51:6a), "the Lord is my Shepherd" (Ps 23:1a), "unite my heart to fear your name" (Ps 86:11b), "lead me in your truth and teach me" (Ps 25:5a), "my soul thirsts for God" (Ps 42:2a), or "to you, O LORD, I lift up my soul" (Ps 25:1). I need only a few words, sometimes the fewer the better. As I repeat them prayerfully while inhaling and exhaling slowly, I am better able to listen to emotions, and then listen through them to the voice of the Spirit. Though it is slow work, I sometimes leave those prayers with a better sense of who I am and who I am not. Emotions such as anger, fear, jealousy, cynicism and insecurity tend to bubble up. With a little patience, the underlying shadow-self comes to light.

I'm inviting you to engage in these ways of identifying the shadow-self. Involve your community by sharing your experience with a few friends. Remember Peter, of course. His passion was to be all in for Jesus and he was sure his soul was up to it, but it wasn't. He was deceived. Jesus had a plan to let Peter see his deception and ultimately to rid him of it. He has a similar plan for me and you, even if our paths are a little different than Peter's.

7

The Sifting

A Disciple's Dark Night of the Soul

If I can trust that what comes to me is for me and not against me . . . Pain breaks my idols, it breaks my isolation, it challenges my independence and does all kinds of things that I would not choose for myself but that are good for me spiritually and emotionally.

Barbara Brown Taylor

My own pain in life has taught me that the first step to healing is not a step away from the pain, but a step toward it.

Henri Nouwen, *Life of the Beloved*

"Simon, Simon, behold Satan demanded to have you, that he might sift you like wheat, but I have prayed for you that your faith may not fail. And when you have turned again, strengthen your brothers." Peter said to him, "Lord, I am ready to go with you both to prison and to death." Jesus said, "I tell you, Peter, the rooster will not crow this day, until you deny three times that you know me."

Then they seized him and led him away, bringing him into the high priest's house, and Peter was following at a distance. And when they had kindled a fire in the middle of the courtyard and sat down together, Peter sat down among them. Then a servant girl, seeing him as he sat in the light and looking closely at him, said, "This man also was with him." But he denied it, saying "Woman, I do not know him." And a little later someone else saw him and said, "You also are one of them." But Peter said, "Man, I am not." And after an interval of about an hour still another insisted, saying, "Certainly this man also was with him, for he too is a Galilean." But Peter said, "Man, I do not know what you are talking about." And immediately, while he was still speaking, the rooster crowed. And the Lord turned and looked at Peter. And Peter remembered the saying of the Lord, how he had said to him, "Before the rooster crows today, you will deny me three times." And he went out and wept bitterly.

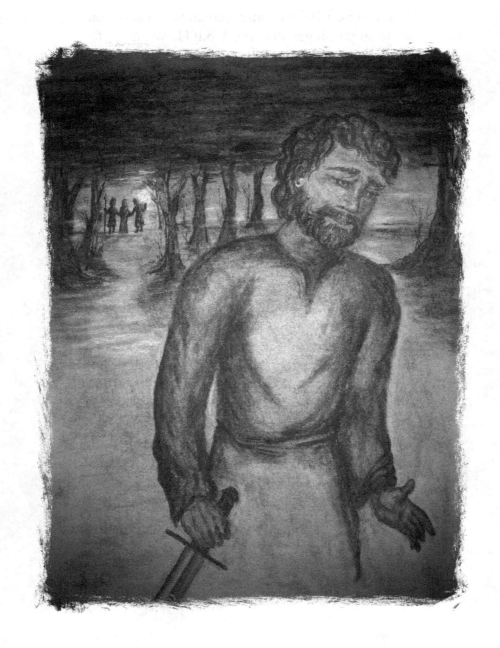

What's that noise?! Who's coming? It's a mob and they're coming toward us. Wait, who's that? It's Judas! What does he think he's doing? . . . Why, that conniving son of a . . .!

[PETER STEPS BETWEEN JESUS AND THE SOLDIERS]

If you take him, it'll be over my dead body!

[PETER SWIPES HIS SWORD FRANTICALLY . . . JESUS RESPONDS, HEALING THE SERVANT'S EAR]

You can't just give yourself up! You said to bring swords and we did! Do something! I'm ready to defend you but I can't do it all myself. You've gotta stand with me, Jesus. You've gotta fight! I need a little help here!

[JESUS IS LED AWAY]

He controlled every situation . . . always knew what to do. I never saw him taken off guard, unprepared. What's up with this? Why did he go? Where is he going? Do I follow? Do I run? The others are. I promised and I was good for it. He saw that. But he put a stop to it. Why?

[OUTSIDE THE COURT OF CAIAPHAS]

What now? John knew somebody, so he got in. If he comes out for me, how do I play this? This girl out here already asked me if I was a disciple of his. I fended that one off, but I've been by his side everywhere he went and there are a lot of people here . . . And he's walked right into the lion's den! What does he expect? . . . We can't all let ourselves be led off in chains to God knows what awful end?

So if I get in there, shrewdness is the name of game. I'm not gonna be an easy target for this mob. Bide your time, Simon. Give yourself space to figure this out.

[INSIDE THE COURTYARD]

OK, I see him there just opposite us.

Just as I thought. Someone recognized me. Man, pressure is on, but I gotta hold them off as long as I can. Who knows where all this ends?

[A FEW HOURS LATER]

That guy keeps looking at me. It all happened so fast back there in the garden, but I think he was part of the group that took Jesus. It's like he's studying my face, listening to the way I talk. Just keep the dogs off. The last place I wanna be is where Jesus is now. I'd be of no use there.

"Damn it! How many times do I have to say it? I swear to God, I don't know the man. Now get off my case!"

[A ROOSTER CROWS . . . JESUS RAISES HIS HEAD, GLANCING TOWARD PETER]

Oh . . . but . . . I didn't think he knew I was here. Could he have heard?

Please tell me that didn't happen . . . that it's a bad dream. I couldn't see it. I was just biding my time . . . All I wanted was to keep our dream from ending.

[PETER RUNS OUT THE GATE AND FALLS TO THE GROUND, SOBBING]

How could I? What have I done? John heard me. They all heard me. Jesus must have heard me . . . he looked right at me . . . for the first time all night, he looked right at me. Oh God!

He said I would do that. He even said I would do it before the rooster crowed. Oh Jesus . . . how could I?

When Followers Get Lost

Some events in life are so devastating that one wonders if normal life can go on in their aftermath. It is difficult to admit, but many followers of Jesus find that faith in God feels absurd in such circumstances.

I should warn you that this chapter discusses such an event in Peter's life. As such, it is a dark chapter. We have been digging deep into Peter's shadow-self, but what happened in Caiaphas's courtyard takes us to the very bottom. It will be hard going, but do persevere. After we hit the bottom in this chapter, our friend Peter will begin to ascend. Things will get better. But we must pass through this station to get to the next ones. There's no avoiding it.

Let's set the tone for this station of Peter's spiritual formation with the lyrics of a song by Andrew Peterson. One of my daughters once presented me a book with her artistic impressions of these lyrics. I was going through a tough transition at that point. She knew I loved this song and I believe she wanted to help me come to terms with my struggle. As you read these words, prepare your heart and mind to enter Peter's experience. In fact, I suggest you listen to a recording of "The Silence of God" as you read the lyrics.[1]

> It's enough to drive a man crazy, it'll break a man's faith
> It's enough to make him wonder, if he's ever been sane
> When he's bleating for comfort from Thy staff and Thy rod
> And the Heaven's only answer is the silence of God
>
> It'll shake a man's timbers when he loses his heart
> When he has to remember what broke him apart
> This yoke may be easy but this burden is not
> When the crying fields are frozen by the silence of God
>
> And if a man has got to listen to the voices of the mob
> Who are reeling in the throes of all the happiness they've got
> When they tell you all their troubles
> Have been nailed up to that cross
> Then what about the times when even followers get lost?
> 'Cause we all get lost sometimes
>
> There's a statue of Jesus on a monastery knoll
> In the hills of Kentucky, all quiet and cold
> And He's kneeling in the garden, as silent as a Stone

All His friends are sleeping and He's weeping all alone

And the man of all sorrows, he never forgot
What sorrow is carried by the hearts that he bought
So when the questions dissolve into the silence of God
The aching may remain but the breaking does not
The aching may remain but the breaking does not
In the holy, lonesome echo of the silence of God

We are looking at the event in which Peter's perception of Jesus and himself crashes on the rocks. It is hard to overstate how pivotal and critical this moment is in Peter's spiritual formation. Peter provides us with a case study, if we are up to it, of when "followers get lost" or how "questions dissolve into the silence of God." I suspect some degree of aching remained, though the breaking did not.

Last Gasps of a Dying Vision

To this point, we've observed that Peter's understanding of Jesus is misguided. This bubbles up to the surface from time to time in their interactions: Peter rebukes Jesus for suggesting that suffering awaits him; he refuses to have Jesus wash his feet, etc. Now another striking revelation takes place in the garden scene as Peter, awaking from sleep and stunned by the arrival of Jesus's captors, draws the sword in defense of Jesus.

As with most of Peter's impetuous actions, we may find ourselves sympathizing, even admiring the man. Had Jesus not suggested that swords were necessary? Had not the disciples responded that two were on hand and Jesus replied that was enough (Luke 22:35–38)?

Given there were two swords but only one was drawn when Jesus's captors came, can we not infer that Peter's courage was exemplary? He was ready to fight against odds that were, frankly, impossible. The little band of disciples with two blades were hardly a match for the well-armed Roman soldiers that accompanied the religious leaders to apprehend Jesus. Peter really was prepared to die, it seems, in defense of his Lord.

At the same time, the gospel writers do not paint a rosy picture of Peter. It was Jesus's final hour. He had taken the three who formed his inner circle, exposing his deep sorrow to them, sorrow even to the point of death. They were to keep "watch," to stay awake (Matt 26:38). It was an interesting choice of words. Jesus may be recalling Passover eve. On that night the Lord kept watch in preparation for his deliverance of his people. Subsequently, the nation kept watch on that night as a remembrance of the Lord's salvation (Exod 12:40–42).

The disciples' failure to watch and pray looks back in time to ancient Israel's failure to keep alive the memory of God's salvation. Now the Lord of the Old Testament is incarnate on earth, keeping watch, calling his new community of disciples to keep watch with him.

Jesus knew that Judas would lead his captors to this place. It fell to Peter and the sons of Zebedee to alert Jesus to any advance of the enemy. Their assignment was to pray, but also to keep watch. As in the Exodus story, the night of watching was the Lord's watching, his preparation for the great salvation that was about to take place. Would the disciples join their Lord in his night of watching? No. They slept.

Jesus enters the struggle of his final moments of communion with his Father, asking that this cup of suffering might pass if it were possible. To borrow the phrase that later Christians will lay hold of, it was his "dark night of the soul." When he returns to find the three sleeping, he turns to Peter with a final plea: "Watch and pray that you may not enter into temptation." Even the rebuke is accompanied by Jesus's recognition that Peter, James and John are simply unable to do what they want to do: "The spirit indeed is willing, but the flesh is weak" (Matt 26:41).

When the captors arrived, Peter sprang into action. It must have been a confusing and disorienting turn of events. John recalls that the band of soldiers and their leaders "drew back and fell to the ground" as Jesus declares, "I am he" (18:6). Peter, apparently realizing the gravity of the moment, swipes with his sword at Malchus. What happens in the next instant is critical. Will Jesus endorse Peter's action? "At-a-boy Rocky! Now you're getting it!" Peter expected that from Jesus, I believe. We would have too had we not been pre-conditioned by our knowledge of this story and our general perception of Jesus as "meek and mild." Of course, the opposite happens. Luke recounts that Jesus healed Malchus's ear with a touch. Jesus commands that the sword be sheathed: "Shall I not drink the cup that the Father has given me?" (John 18:11). Those words must have fallen on Peter's ears like a nuclear bomb. They turned his world completely upside down, upending all his expectations and leaving him lost and alone.

Jesus did not resist his captors, but allowed himself to be taken into custody. He will continue to be led as a sheep to the slaughter until he hangs, limbs outstretched, nailed to a cross outside Jerusalem.

As we've walked through the stations of Peter's spiritual formation, we've seen that Jesus was constantly challenging Peter's expectations and assumptions, calling his core beliefs into question. Peter may have been hard-pressed to articulate those beliefs, nevertheless they form the worldview out of which he operates. Like a leech they have embedded themselves in Peter's soul to suck the lifeblood from his spirit. Jesus is determined to do the hard work of extracting that leech. Until this moment, Peter's basic understanding of Jesus's role as Messiah is still more or less intact. As the soldiers led Jesus away, we imagine Peter standing confused and disoriented, still holding a sword dripping with Malchus's blood, shaking his head in disbelief. How can it end this way? Is this the end of the messianic dream?

It is not only Peter's vision of Jesus as the Messiah that will undergo radical transformation. Along with it, Peter's vision of himself is upended. His show of force is futile. He cannot defend Jesus, and Jesus would not allow it anyway. He is reduced to powerlessness and vulnerability. All Peter's determination that Jesus will not suffer, dissipates like sand that passes through the fingers of a clinched fist. He can no longer cling to the vision. It is dead. Jesus is gone, subject to the judgment of religious and political tyrants. Peter can do nothing. Peter was unable to keep awake with Jesus as he entered his "dark night of the soul." Now Peter enters, for different reasons and to a different end, his darkest moment.

The Invisible Villain

We leave Peter there for a moment to consider one other aspect of this eventful night. In his mercy, Jesus reveals a reality to Peter that, for all we know, never occurred to him. It suggests a new dimension of Peter's spiritual formation, one that we should not overlook.

"Simon, Simon, behold Satan demanded to have you, that he might sift you like wheat, but I have prayed for you that your faith may not fail. And when you have turned again, strengthen your brothers" (Luke 22:31–32).

Luke allows us to peek behind the curtain that separates material and spiritual realities. We learn that the struggle extends beyond Peter's gradual awakening to his shadow-self. There is another party, an adversary, an accuser (see Rev 12:10). Although the word "demand" appears only here in the New Testament, Satan takes a similar approach in his accusation of Job. His desire is to put the righteous man's vulnerability on display. In so doing, he ridicules faithfulness, undermines testimony, and subjects the faithful to absurdity and disillusionment. His name is the adversary or accuser, and his accusations are not merely clever arguments. They find leverage in the shadow-self, exposing its ignorance and egocentrism. Satan delights to display the worst of the shadow-self, building his case that humankind cannot re-enter relationship with the Creator. He passionately demands to maintain his strangle hold on humanity.

Jesus's words are carefully chosen to reveal that Satan will pounce upon the community of the disciples and that Simon Peter, after his repentance, will play a key role in strengthening their faith. "Satan demanded to have you [plural, i.e. the disciples], that he might sift you [plural] . . . but I have prayed for you [singular, i.e. Simon] that your faith may not fail." And when Simon has turned again, he is to strengthen his brothers. Jesus certainly prayed for all the disciples, even that night. But here, he stipulates that he has prayed for Simon Peter.

The image Jesus chooses deserves our attention. Sifting wheat through a sieve to separate the grain from the chaff was a common practice. The mental picture it evoked was a rapid shaking and shifting from side to side, tossing the contents up and shaking the sieve yet again as the wheat fell back. The image gives us an idea of the violent contortions that would assault the disciples' faith in the ensuing hours.

Though Jesus's body would be flailed and nailed to the Roman crossbeams, the disciples' interior world would be shattered, shaken to the point of crumbling.

Though Jesus's body would be flailed and nailed to the Roman crossbeams, the disciples' interior world would be shattered, shaken to the point of crumbling.

Sifting is the perfect image, given that it was one of the twelve, a companion and friend, who led the mob to Jesus and betrayed him with a kiss. The disciples scattered, with only Peter and John making their way to the courtyard of Caiaphas to watch the One they had seen in radiant light on the Mount of Transfiguration, bloodied and mocked by crude warriors. He will be led to Golgotha, too weakened to carry the implement of his execution. A crown of thorns bloodied his head and face. His back ripped to shreds. Naked. Sifting.

We rarely see through that veil to the spiritual reality of Satan's pursuit of God's people. Nevertheless, Peter's denial must have been a gleeful victory for the accuser during those days before Jesus's appearance to his disciples. Peter the Rock was little more than a clod. The shaking had dissipated his devotion and revealed his self-preserving treachery.

Yet, it was a mercy to Peter that Jesus told him there was an accuser, that what he would experience was not only the result of his internal weakness. He was hunted. His words "when you have turned again, strengthen your brothers," must have resonated through Peter's darkest hours. He knew that the Master had both known of his fall and reserved a role for him, assured of his return. It was a pin prick of hope on a horizon of despair.

Michael Card has pointed out that when Peter declared that he did not know Jesus, it is more than a mere denial of relationship.

> Peter's Messiah would have slaves washing his feet, not the other way around. His Messiah would command the legions of angels to destroy his enemies. His Messiah would have drawn his own sword as well. Peter understood a king who would take up arms to kill his enemies. Never in his wildest dreams could he imagine a king who would die to save his enemies. The despair that settles over his heart will be so complete that even when he sees the empty tomb and the grave clothes lying in their folds, Peter will walk away "wondering what had happened" (Luke 24:12).[2]

Peter had never internalized Jesus's warnings of imminent persecution and death. The mental image of a politically and militarily victorious Messiah clung stubbornly to his mind. His last stand with a sword in the garden was proof of his willingness to die for the Messiah he envisioned. Jesus's refusal to live up to Peter's vision was the straw that broke the back of Peter's idealism. His only hope for Messiah was being led away, captive to Jewish religious authorities under the thumb of oppressive Roman rule. The scene dashed Peter's hopes on the rocks of reality. His dream dissipated into the silence of God. His disavowal of Jesus, then, was both a denial of his relationship and a reflection of his disillusion. He truly did not know this Jesus.

Peter's state between the denial and Jesus's appearances is revealed to us in sparse words:

> "He went out
>   and wept
>   bitterly."

The scene commands our silence, not our commentary.

Peter's journey of spiritual formation has brought him to the end of himself. Some describe the journey of spiritual formation as a transition from the first half of life to the second half. It has nothing to do with the passing of time and everything to do with how we respond internally to life's disillusionment. Peter

---

2. Card, *Fragile Stone*, 109.

is at the lowest point of his journey. Those ensuing hours of bitter weeping may be his rite of passage. No doubt, we anticipate his response because we know the story so well. But, let us resist the urge to move ahead quickly. Let us sit with Simon as he weeps bitterly. His grip is loosening. His loyalties are exposed. His heart is acquiring a tenderness; his mind, an openness; his will, a sensitivity.

Peter probably lived with the ache of this moment for years. "The aching remains, but the breaking does not." I doubt he ever fully lost his regret that he denied his Lord. On the contrary, he fully owned it. If the tradition is correct, that Mark's gospel represents Peter's memory of events, we learn something important. Mark records Peter's curse and invoking an oath as he denies his relationship to Jesus. Mark's telling of the events was likely a source for Matthew and perhaps Luke. Apparently, Peter had no interest in preserving his honor. He wanted the truth to be known, read and discussed as part of the apostolic witness to Jesus's life, death and resurrection.

That suggests that Peter bore the wound of his denial permanently and willingly. He made no attempt to embellish the image. If anything, he wanted it exposed in all its repugnance.

That suggests that Peter bore the wound of his denial permanently
and willingly. He made no attempt to embellish the image.
If anything, he wanted it exposed in all its repugnance.

The event broke the old Simon and from the breakage emerged a new phase of his journey. He wore it humbly as his personalized rite of passage to a new Peter.

Peter's Dark Night and Ours

The film *Unbroken* relates the story of Louis Zamperini, an Olympic athlete turned fighter pilot. He was captured during World War II, and the horrendous suffering he endured in Japanese prisoner camps was indescribable. Zamperini carried scars of soul and body as he left that prisoner of war camp. His suffering, however, came to hold a deeper meaning both for him and the people he fought to defend. He embodied the tenacious hope of a nation as well as the absurdity and sacrifice of war. The book and film are, in some ways, hard to countenance. The cruelty of a prisoner of war camp sends shock waves to our comfort zone. Yet Zamperini's story became a badge of honor for him and for countless others.

If what we have suggested is true, that Peter intentionally entered his denial in the public record of the early Christians, the implications are stunning. On the walls of our homes and offices we display images of loved ones, or perhaps photos of ourselves with dignitaries, or our diplomas to showcase our life accomplishments. They are the tokens of our history, our journey. Simon wanted to hang the portrait of his denial in the hall of the apostolic church. It was his "break-out-of-the-cocoon" moment – the occasion of his breaking free of the first half of life and emerging into a new life. He wanted it etched in perpetuity in the collective memory of the church. There was something there he wanted us to take hold of. More importantly, the Holy Spirit who inspired this story wants us to see it clearly.

What is it, Peter? What should I take away?

When Jesus announced his kingdom, he called his followers to "repent." The word literally means to change one's mind, to enter a new way of thinking, to do a complete reversal moving from the kingdom of the world and the enthronement of self to follow him. In much of our Christian experience, the full meaning of that word has been reduced to a single confession of sin, a "sinner's prayer," a "born again" experience. For most of us it was a moment of profound transformation and shining newness when we entered the life of Christ by faith. I've no desire to minimize that; however, it was never intended to be a one-time transformation – an instantaneous change. It was intended to be a journey of continually changing our mind, of progressive transformation through ever-deepening levels of personal and spiritual formation. Jesus called the world to repent and for those who did, he said "follow me."

Peter's path of following Jesus has been thrilling, eventful, brimming with life and possibility. Yet it has also led him to the end of himself – to a full reckoning of repentance – a transformed vision of Jesus and the self. Peter had to experience a profound disillusionment to eradicate his shadow-self. Actually, it still isn't fully eradicated, but Peter, from this point on, is fully awake to his shadow-self. He knows it is there, and he has learned to distrust it. His spirit is now recalibrated to recognize the shadow-self and reflexively take a posture of suspicion towards it. He still has some stations of his spiritual journey to pass through, but his orientation, from this point forward, has changed profoundly.

But we still need to take the lessons Peter learned and apply them to ourselves. How do we do that?

I am thinking this morning of a friend in a Middle Eastern country. He was a student at the seminary where I taught, but he was not able to continue his studies because of the age of his children. The residential seminary was unable to accommodate small children at that stage. So he returned to his homeland, no doubt, disappointed. This week we heard the tragic news that his wife gave birth to their third child and, within days, passed into glory. She died of COVID-19, leaving her husband with three young children in a society beset by poverty, raging with contagion, often boiling with religious militancy. I wonder what that young Middle Eastern man is thinking and feeling today. Is it his "dark night of the soul?"

We don't like to go there. There are no easy answers, yet I wager that every person reading these lines has felt at some point that God has forgotten them. The psalmist lets us know that these feelings of distance from God are not confined to our era of secularism.

> O LORD, God of my salvation;
>> I cry out day and night before you.
> Let my prayer come before you;
>> incline your ear to my cry!
> For my soul is full of troubles,
>> and my life draws near to Sheol.
> I am counted among those who go down to the pit;
>> I am a man who has no strength,
> like one set loose among the dead,
>> like the slain that lie in the grave,
> like those whom you remember no more,
>> for they are cut off from your hand.
> You have put me in the depths of the pit,
>> in the regions dark and deep.
> Your wrath lies heavy upon me,
>> and you overwhelm me with all your waves. *Selah.*
>> (Ps 88:1–7)

I have faced a few moments like this. Inevitably, when I look back on them now, they were not as desperate as I thought at the time. Nevertheless, I recognize that they were pivotal moments of spiritual formation. For instance, I recall a moment when I saw my ministry as absolute futility. The small flock I was attempting to nurture was ripped apart by conflict. After a painful confrontation with a known leader, I was accused of power mongering. There were hidden evils in our fellowship of which I had recently become aware. I realize now, in light of Jesus's instruction to Peter, that an accuser was working secretly, quietly, to expose the inadequacy of my shadow-self. I was, in some way, being sifted. However, at that moment, all I felt was despair and uselessness. I recall laying my forehead against the steering wheel of our family car and weeping.

I'm not alone.

Most of us have passed through some dark night of the soul, when our prayers, if we could pray, seemed to stop as soon as they left our lips. These are moments when life seems utterly absurd, when we've come to an end of ourselves, when our will to live is wilted and the spring has left our step.

Most of us have passed through some dark night of the soul, when our prayers, if we could pray, seemed to stop as soon as they left our lips. These are moments when life seems utterly absurd, when we've come to an end of ourselves, when our will to live is wilted and the spring has left our step.

It's very difficult to share these moments with those around us. We don't want to discourage them and, frankly, they seem to be "reeling in the throes of all the happiness they've got."

Assuming you are not in that place of your journey right now, could you go there in your memory and ask how your shadow-self was exposed? Ask yourself how your expectations were rescripted by that event. Ask how the limp you walk with now, as a result of that experience, has changed you. I suspect you'll find it difficult to put into words. I do. Silence may be the best response, but in that silence, let your soul open to the Father's love. "Though I walk through the valley of the shadow of death, I will fear no evil, for you are with me; your rod and your staff, they comfort me" (Ps 23:4). Feeling his rod on our back is not nice, yet it is necessary if we are to keep following him on the journey. If you can have a conversation with a spiritual friend or mentor about your "dark night," do that in response to this chapter.

Peter put his "dark night" on display through the writers of the Gospels. He did not hide from it. He made no attempt to explain it or justify it. For him, it was a pivotal moment of his spiritual formation.

It may be difficult to see our "dark night of the soul" in such positive terms, as the place where we came to an end of ourselves and emerged into a new way of life. I am convinced that happened in Peter's life and that it was the result of Jesus's intentional design for Peter's spiritual formation. From Peter, we learn not to tuck away the painful chapters of our journey, fearful to bring them out and examine them. Peter's example invites us to take another look, to realize that pain can be remedial, that our experience of absurdity need not render the verdict of our entire life.

8

The Pursuit

A Disciple's Restoration

In a futile attempt to erase our past, we deprive the community of our healing gift. If we conceal our wounds out of fear and shame, our inner darkness can neither be illuminated nor become a light for others. In Love's service, only wounded soldiers can serve.

Brennan Manning, *Abba's Child*

After this Jesus revealed himself again to the disciples by the Sea of Tiberias, and he revealed himself in this way. Simon Peter, Thomas (called the Twin), Nathanael of Cana in Galilee, the sons of Zebedee, and the two others of his disciples were together. Simon Peter said to them, "I am going fishing." They said to him, "We will go with you." They went out and got into the boat, but that night they caught nothing.

Just as day was breaking, Jesus stood on the shore; yet the disciples did not know that it was Jesus. Jesus said to them, "Children, do you have any fish?" They answered him, "No." He said to them, "Cast the net on the right side of the boat, and you will find some." So they cast it, and now they were not able to haul it in, because of the quantity of fish. That disciple whom Jesus loved therefore said to Peter, "It is the Lord!" When Simon Peter heard that it was the Lord, he put on his outer garment, for he was stripped for work, and threw himself into the sea. The other disciples came in the boat dragging the net full of fish for they were not far from the land, but about a hundred yards off.

When they got out on land, they saw a charcoal fire in place, with fish laid out on it, and bread. Jesus said to them, "Bring some of the fish that you have just caught." So Simon Peter went aboard and hauled the net ashore, full of large fish, 153 of them. And although there were so many, the net was not torn. Jesus said to them, "Come and have breakfast." Now none of the disciples dared ask him, "Who are you?" They knew it was the Lord. Jesus came and took the bread and gave it to them, and so with the fish. This was now the third time that Jesus was revealed to the disciples after he was raised from the dead.

When they had finished breakfast, Jesus said to Simon Peter, "Simon, son of John, do you love me more than these?" He said to him, "Yes, Lord; you know that I love you." He said to him, "Feed my lambs." He said to him a second time, "Simon, son of John, do you love me?" He said to him, "Yes, Lord; you know that I love you." He said to him, "Tend my sheep." He said to him the third time, "Simon, son of John, do you love me?" Peter was grieved because he said to him the third time, "Do you love me?" and he said to him, "Lord, you know everything; you know that I love you." Jesus said to him, "Feed my sheep. Truly, truly, I say to you, when you were young, you used to dress yourself and walk wherever you wanted, but when you are old, you will stretch out your hands and another will dress you and carry you where you do not want to go." (This he said to show by what kind of death he was to glorify God.) And after saying this he said to him, "Follow me."

Peter turned and saw the disciple whom Jesus loved following them, the one who also had leaned back against him during the supper and had said, "Lord, who is it that is going to betray you?" When Peter saw him, he said to Jesus, "Lord what about this man?" Jesus said to him, "If it is my will that he remain until I come, what is that to you? You follow me!" So the saying spread abroad among the brothers that this disciple was not to die; yet Jesus did not say to him that he was not to die, but, "If it is my will that he remain until I come, what is that to you?"

This is the disciple who is bearing witness about these things, and who has written these things, and we know that his testimony is true.

After a three-year whirlwind I just want to get back to sea with my buddies – I need some space, a return to normal.

I feel so confused, and sad, and ashamed. Out here, all of that melts away. We don't have to talk, I don't want to anyway, we just know what to do.

Cast the net, pull it in. Again, and again. It's back to the old normal. Even the disappointment of the empty haul . . . the reality that we'll go hungry today . . . that there's nothing to pay our debtors . . . we remember all of it. The familiar is comfortable, but I don't want to stay here.

Am I right back to where I was three years ago . . . when he said, "Follow me and I'll make you fish for people?" Was it all a dream?! Did I just hear what I wanted to hear?

No. No way I could have made it all up.

But why couldn't I just stand up for him . . . keep my word that I would never abandon him? How could I let a little girl get to me?

And now that we've seen him, what does it all mean?

Man, do I miss him. I miss our life together when every day was an adventure. How do I "follow him" when he shows up and then he's gone?! We all saw him . . . I was shell-shocked . . . couldn't even speak. Every time he shows up, I keep waiting, hoping he'll have something for me . . . knowing I don't deserve anything but his scorn.

Who knows when we'll see him again?

And would I even be welcome to follow? After what I said there? After what he said I would say? Does he still want me?

I guess one of the guys in this boat will take my place. He and John always had something special between them.

Come back to earth, Simon! Enough is enough. We gave it a good try but it's one of those nights when we go home with nothing. If the nets come in empty again, we're gonna call it a night. Yep. Let's pack it in.

"Boys, have you got anything to eat?"

Ha. An early riser come to tell us how to do our job.

"Cast on the right side of the boat," he says. I'll never forget the last time someone said that to me! Who is that guy? Too dark . . . can't quite make him out.

One more cast of the net . . . OK. What do we have to lose?

John's starboard. He'll know. We both see it. Just like it happened before . . .

[THE SURFACE OF THE WATER COMES TO LIFE AS A NET FULL OF FRENZIED FISH IS PULLED UP]

John looks at me and says what we both know: "It is the Lord."

That instant, I realized that only he would be here . . . at this place . . . at this time . . . and only he would do what I just saw. I hit the water. All I want is to get to him . . . to see him . . . to hear him say something to me . . . to hear him call me "the Rock" one more time. I've no right to go to him. I should be swimming the other direction.

Yet, he's here and I'm here and I know he knows how bad this hurts and how much I want to keep going. So I've got to get to him.

Revisiting the Starting Point

Luke tells the story of Peter's original call by Jesus. Beautiful in simplicity, profound in impact, Jesus sat on Peter's boat, directing him where to fish.

John places this event on the same Sea of Galilee with Peter in a fishing boat with his brothers and friends. Just like before, they are coming home empty. Just like before, Jesus suggests casting the net one more time and, just like before, they haul in a fabulous catch.

So much happens in this encounter that we may miss the significance of place. Reading the two stories side by side (Luke 5 and John 21), it is impossible to see it as a fluke. Luke and John "just happen" to tell a very similar story at the beginning and end of Peter's journey with Jesus? No, Jesus is re-creating a scene from Peter's past. He's taking him back to the very beginning. John recognizes that and tells us the story so that we can't miss the fact that these two events form a parenthesis around Peter's discipleship journey. They form the introduction and conclusion of a rich story of the Jesus–Peter friendship.

It's an invitation to us as readers to contemplate, to enter the story through the door of imagination. In Luke 5, Jesus called Peter to a vocation of fishing for people. As a result of Peter's denial, he had sunk deeply in despair. Is Jesus saying, "Come back with me, Peter. What I said to you then is still your true north. You will bring a multitude of people into the net of my kingdom?"

No doubt, the confusing events of Jesus's crucifixion had caused a deep haze to descend on Peter's soul. His return to his previous vocation may be an indicator that he is looking for a mooring, something solid to hold to in the midst of his confusion.

Jesus, the master of spiritual formation, chooses to remind Peter of his original call. He recreates a scene of experiential learning. It is a participatory review of his initial discipleship lesson – "follow me and I will make you catch people!" Without saying a word, Jesus is renewing the discipleship agreement. Peter has never left. He lapsed and denied, yes, but he did not leave. Now is his time to show that.

We may picture Peter doing a belly-flop on to the water of the Sea of Galilee. Or maybe we imagine him gingerly stepping off the boat, although that doesn't seem like Peter at all. Peter most likely grabbed his cloak, tied it around him, and with both hands over his head, went head first into the water. I imagine a smile creeping over Jesus's face as he watched his protégé flailing the water, desperate to get as close as he could, as fast as he could. Yep. That's Peter.

Why the Leap?

One of the most striking elements of the resurrection story is that none of the disciples expected it. We seldom think about that. Jesus foretold that he would suffer, die and come back to life. The gospel writers record that, but we must remember that they wrote their accounts years after the fact. They understood it in hindsight. We tend to think of the peoples of that time as "unscientific" or "superstitious" such that it was easier for them to believe in miracles and resurrections. That's our "chronological snobbery."[1] The people of that time lived with death. There were no funeral homes, hospitals or sterilized methods of dealing with dead bodies. Families and loved ones anointed bodies, covering them with spices, laid them in family tombs with their ancestors and then visited the tomb weekly.

Resurrection simply was not a category that existed in the disciples' minds. They struggled with it as much as you and I, probably more, and the Gospels don't hide that fact from us. In fact, when the women first reported the empty tomb, the disciples thought their words were nonsense (Luke 24:11). Peter sees the empty tomb and the folded graveclothes, and then goes away "wondering" or "marveling" at what had happened (Luke 24:12). He was not mentally or emotionally prepared for Jesus to rise from the dead. Resurrection was not plausible. He didn't know what to do with it.

By the time of this fishing trip, however, Peter has seen Jesus alive. He appeared to the disciples at least a few times. Jesus has a physical body. He eats and invites examination of the wounds in his hands and side. Nevertheless, the disciples must have had some difficulty recognizing him. It begins with Mary who mistakes him for the gardener (John 20:15). The two on the road to Emmaus only recognized him as he broke bread (Luke 24:30–31). He assures the disciples that it is he himself and not a ghost (Luke 24:39). He appears without coming through a door (Luke 24:36; John 20:26). There is an appearance to Peter specifically about which we know nothing. Luke's account mentions it (Luke 24:34) as does Paul (1 Cor 15:5). We may surmise that because Jesus knew of Peter's despair, he desired to bring him hope. As it was one of the first appearances of Jesus, and we have no record of any dialogue between them, we cannot know if Peter's denial was the topic of conversation. Whatever was said in that meeting remains between Peter and Jesus. However, the conversation we know, happens here, on the shore of the Sea of Galilee.

---

1. C. S. Lewis defines "chronological snobbery as, "the uncritical acceptance of the intellectual climate common to our own age and the assumption that whatever has gone out of date is on that account discredited." Lewis, "Surprised by Joy," 114.

Peter hopes to end the misery and guilt resulting from his denial. That's why he leaps from the boat.

His pre-dawn dip was the opposite of Peter's initial reaction to Jesus three years earlier, when he had asked Jesus to get out of his boat. The days preceding that event had blown Peter's mind. He knew Jesus was no normal rabbi and he was deeply aware of his own sin and unworthiness to be in Jesus's presence. Now, his response is the opposite. He is desperate to get to Jesus, to be in his presence, to hear something from his lips.

Perhaps Peter is concerned that Jesus will suddenly disappear, that he will live forever haunted by the specter of his own denial. He is overcome with a desire to make it right with Jesus, to return to the friendship they once enjoyed. Perhaps this would be the moment. Peter is driven by relationship.

This reflexive leap into the Sea of Galilee is not about his status or his future apostleship. He sees Jesus and one last opportunity to affirm that he loves him and deeply desires to follow him, whatever that will mean.

This reflexive leap into the Sea of Galilee is not about his status or his future apostleship. He sees Jesus and one last opportunity to affirm that he loves him and deeply desires to follow him, whatever that will mean.

He is driven by a painful longing to restore his friendship with Jesus. He knows he has caused the breach. Peter, never short on action, is once again "all in" to right his wrong.

Relational Restoration

This story of Peter's restoration is familiar. You've probably read it many times and heard many sermons about it. Still, let's try to get a fresh understanding of this restoration scene. The first question of Jesus is, "Simon, son of John, do you love me more than these?"

Peter has held himself up as a stalwart, one whose love and faithfulness would never fail, even if all the others abandoned Jesus. But he failed. Jesus's first question, in the company of his brothers, is an invitation to Peter to reconsider his self-evaluation. "With the wisdom of hindsight, Peter, looking back on the events of the past days, do you still hold yourself as superior to these in your love for me? Are you better than they? Do you really love me more than these love me?" It is a gentle corrective.

I have occasionally been asked which of my three daughters I love most. Ha! The question is unthinkable. Jesus uses the first question to set the tone of familial love among his brothers and sisters. Comparison betrays the very nature of that familial love. Peter must no longer see himself in comparison to the other disciples. Though Peter answers the question affirmatively, his response refers only to his love of Jesus, avoiding the comparison. Later in the chapter, Peter wonders to Jesus about the other disciple, John, the one whom Jesus loved. "What about him?" Jesus again hammers the nail of comparison, beating it back into the woodwork. Get rid of that, Peter. It's of no use to you!

So the corrective moves in two directions. First, Peter's self-assessment is simply wrong. He is not superior to others in commitment, faithfulness and love for Jesus. Second, the nature of love among the community of disciples is not a commodity. It doesn't lend itself to measurements and comparison. Love, among Jesus's friends, cannot be quantified to establish a pecking order. It is a family love, unquantified, freely given, received, shared.

I wonder if Peter knew where this was leading when he heard the question the second time. John uses a different Greek word for love, the same one that Peter used in his response to the first question. I mention that because we have heard it in sermons and books that discuss this passage. Actually, John uses the two words interchangeably throughout his Gospel leading to the conclusion that the second question is substantially the same as the first, except that the idea of comparison is no longer the issue: "Simon, son of John, do you love me?" The change in words from *agapao* to *phileo* may be nothing more than a stylistic flare, common in John's writings.[2]

Posing the question a second time moves Peter beyond the comparative thinking that once enveloped his understanding of love for Jesus. We're getting closer to the heart of the matter. Jesus knows that Peter's love is not "more than" – he wants Peter to struggle with what it means to declare his love for Jesus. What does it mean to love Jesus? What will this imply for his present and his future?

Peter's response expresses his hope. Jesus, the Lord, knows all. He knows of Peter's love and Peter will rest there. It is the ultimate resting place of a disciple. Peter's own abilities have failed him, betraying his love. Peter knows

---

2. For a summary of the various views on John's use of *agapao* and *phileo*, see Carson, *Gospel according to John*, 677.

his denial was a lapse, not a defection. He confides in the one who knows all for his vindication.

When Jesus asks the question a third time, Peter is grieved. It is painfully obvious, is it not, that Jesus's three-fold repetition mirrors Peter's three denials. It is an example of the rebuke of a friend that brings healing. Jesus plainly intends to recall the three-fold denial. He wants to get at the cause of Peter's grief, and he wants to bring it out here in plain view of all the other disciples. This means it is unlikely that Jesus dealt with the denials in his first encounter with Peter, which was private (Luke 24:34; 1 Cor 15:5). Though intensely painful, there is something restorative about revealing our defects before our friends, family and loved ones. Odds are, they already know anyway. Certainly, Peter's friends were well-aware of what had transpired. Jesus makes the recall of Peter's denial brief, penetrating and restorative.

It is *brief*, in that Jesus makes only an indirect reference to Peter's denial, but it was certainly foremost in Peter's mind and it must have been a looming question in the minds of the other disciples. Had he avoided it, Jesus may have consigned Peter to a place of perennial wondering and the constant mental and verbal bombardment of critics who would remember him as the "denier," much as Judas would forever be the "traitor." It was a mercy of Jesus to bring the unspoken self-accusation of Peter to the surface, to get it out there so it could be dealt with.

Though brief, it was *penetrating*. Peter's denial was not functional or positional. Jesus was not concerned about "company loyalty" or fidelity to the brand. It was personal, deeply personal. Peter knew that. Jesus's entire approach to discipleship was "come and see." He took the disciples with him. He explained his public teaching to the twelve in private. They took their meals together. Their home became his. His friends became theirs. It was a communal affair that was rooted deeply in the soil of personal trust and friendship. By denying that he knew Jesus, Peter had deserted him at his point of greatest need. That was first and foremost; but Peter had also betrayed the community of Jesus's followers including the twelve and the band of women. That's why the question was so penetrating. Think about it. Jesus could easily have asked, "Peter, why did you deny that you knew me?" He did not. He could have asked, "Why did you enter Caiaphas's courtyard if you knew you were going to deny me?" He could have asked at least a dozen other questions, but none of them would have gotten to the heart of the matter: "Peter, do you love me?" That's the only question that would resolve all the other secondary matters by resolving the one primary matter. The crux of the issue was the relationship. Jesus gave Peter the chance to reaffirm that before the disciples, and he did affirm it.

It was brief, it was poignant and it was *restorative*. If there was a three-fold repetition of the question, there was also a three-fold repetition of Peter's new commission. John uses different words to express the same idea: "feed my lambs, tend my sheep, feed my sheep."

Three years prior, Peter received his first discipleship invitation: "Follow me and I will make you a fisher of people." Peter did that and did it well. Now the metaphor shifts slightly. It's not that Peter will no longer bring people into Jesus's kingdom. He certainly will. In fact, his best people-fishing days lay ahead of him. But another commission is now in view. Peter is to shepherd, to tend, to feed the sheep of Jesus's pasture. It was a well-known image among the Jews, steeped as they were in the Old Testament. From David's pastoral imagery of the Lord as the good shepherd to Ezekiel's stunning rebuke of the shepherds of Israel who fed themselves rather than the flock of God, the evocative image of the shepherd stood as a reminder of the tender love and care of the Lord for his people. Peter's new mandate invites him to be the vessel of that shepherding love. More importantly, Jesus had used the image of himself as the "good shepherd" who lays down his life for the sheep. The chief shepherd now appoints his under-shepherd. As Peter had observed Jesus seek and care for the lost sheep, so now he would love and care for the sheep of his Lord.

Though the crux of the matter is Peter's relationship, the vocation also comes into focus. The spiritual formation to which Jesus calls Peter does not separate "being" from "doing." One flows from the other.

Being is primary. Without it, all *doing* is wood, hay and stubble.

Being *is primary. Without it, all*
doing *is wood, hay and stubble.*

It is expressed in Jesus's piercing question and Peter's deferential response, "You know all things. You know that I love you." Jesus's acceptance of the affirmation is evidenced by his appointment of Peter. His vocation issues from the relationship. "Because you love me, Peter, you are fit to tend my sheep. Indeed, you are my choice to tend my sheep."

The other disciples were there. They heard it. Perhaps this is the reason that we never hear again of Peter's denials. It is not an issue in the early church. Jesus himself had set the record straight. It might be instructive that it is the apostle John who records this whole exchange. If anyone would have been a candidate to take Peter's place after the tragedy of denial, it would be John. He was the intimate friend of Jesus whose contemplative and relational traits stood in contrast to Peter's vociferous activism. Apparently, John realizes that Peter's gifts are essential for Jesus's flock and he includes Peter's restoration in his gospel, preserving it for posterity.

Peter's Restoration and Ours
A Place of Pilgrimage

As a young boy, I often wandered in the woods near our family home. I recall one occasion when, after hiking to the top of a mountain, I felt the presence of God. In the joy of that energy, I ran all the way down the mountain, thinking of myself as Elijah running before the chariots of Ahab. Perhaps it was just a boy's overly active imagination. Many years later, I returned to the top of that mountain with my dad, only this time, his four-wheel drive truck hauled us to the top. Though I was still a young man, my body had been ravaged by cancer and chemotherapy. My hair was gone and my energy was at a low ebb. As I stood on top of that mountain, I recalled my boyhood scamper down those hills and into the valley below. Honestly, I can't describe what happened in my soul at that moment. All I know is that I remembered. But maybe that was enough. The youth and vigor of my boyhood was no longer at my disposal, but just being there, reminded me that I had a long history with God's Spirit. The wind still blew atop that mountain. The sun still warmed my face. I knew that I would live and find strength to run again.

Place is not incidental in our spiritual journey. The earth is our home, created as a temple for us to commune with our Father. We should expect certain places to hold spiritual significance. For Peter, the shallow waters and shores of the Sea of Galilee provided the setting for life-altering events. I wonder if he made his way back there from time to time when he needed to renew his vision.

Pilgrimage is an Old Testament practice that we rarely think about in our mobile era. Returning to significant places has a way of renewing the faith we started with. We realize our journey isn't a mistake. We return to reconnect. What is your special place(s)? A room in your home where you first knelt and prayed? An assembly hall where you made a commitment? A retreat center? Can you get back there to confess again your love for the Lord, renewing your relationship? If you cannot, try imagining that place while journaling or sharing the memory with a friend.

Grounded in Transparency

"I would never burden them with the weight of my soul's depravity." Admittedly, this pastor was old-school in his unwillingness to share his sinful tendencies with his congregation. While his awareness of his deficiency was admirable, his staunch privacy in soul matters fell short of the apostolic example. By contrast, among post-moderns, it's "cool" to showcase your struggles. How else would you connect with your listeners? In a recent podcast, I was somewhat surprised when every speaker on the panel made reference to the advice of their therapist! These were all Christian leaders of the up-and-coming generation. It wasn't shocking that they found therapy helpful. What surprised me was their freedom to talk about a private therapy session in such a public forum.

So, which is the better way? Is it the old-school that keeps their cards close to the chest, or the post-modern tendency towards reveal-all, therapeutic spirituality?

We've discussed Peter's revelation of his slow uptake on spiritual truths, assuming that he is relating his story through the Gospel of Mark. Here, let's take a different tack. John records this entire scene for posterity, and Peter's restoration becomes a well-worn, sub-narrative of the Christian gospel. John must have recorded it with the church in view. It is a story that relates a profound spiritual reality. Peter is the keeper of the keys. He is one of Jesus's most inner circle of three disciples. He is the one who, when he is restored, will strengthen his brothers. The Gospels provide ample context, down to the detail that Satan has desired to sift the disciples like wheat. Peter's role of honor among the twelve does not provide immunity to spiritual lapses brought on by his own false assumptions as well as the enemy's assault. The twelve were privy to the whole grueling affair and through the Gospels they invite future generations of Jesus-followers to watch, listen and learn.

In the family of Jesus-followers, there is no hierarchy of moral merit. Peter is given a gift to shepherd God's people. That gift is an honor, but it is not based on Peter's impeccable behavior. Peter failed miserably as do we. The twelve knew that, and yet Jesus's careful restoration of his protégé allowed Peter to fulfill his role despite his failure. It is notable that John and James and the others did not hold an executive session to render their verdict concerning Peter. They knew his faults, intimately and fully. I suspect they even felt his pain that night on the shores of the Sea of Galilee. They had abandoned Jesus too. Yet, they were content to honor Peter's leadership role. Jesus's word settled the matter.

In summary, following Peter's example, our spiritual life should be an open book to a few colleagues and friends. The wider the scope of our gifting, the more the walls that hide our defects from our brothers and sisters should come down. It seems especially effective when someone else is relating our shortcomings as John related Peter's. We tend to relate our own faults selectively. The story urges us to remove every hint of a spiritual meritocracy. Jesus's kingdom simply does not work on the principle of merit. It thrives on grace and humility. Peter held the keys of the kingdom and yet all the world knows of his tragic lapse. All the world also knows of his humble pursuit of Jesus and his restoration. It is the passion of relationship with Jesus that moves us to transparency. To move forward with the Lord, we either go forward with authenticity or we go backward. If we fake it, we lose. That's why Jesus was so dismissive of the Pharisees. He saw them as white-washed tombs, cups that were new and shiny on the outside but filthy on the inside. Peter is a total contrast. For him, filth shows on the outside where everyone can see it, but he is eager to keep the inside under the flow of God's pure and Holy Spirit.

Absolving Shame

We conclude our contemplation of Peter's restoration by looking forward. Peter has just suffered a tragic fall, denying his Lord at his most needful hour. Given such a horrific lapse, it is striking that Jesus does not require penance of Peter. He doesn't set him up in a rehabilitation program or put him on probation or under surveillance. There's no sense that Peter now has two strikes. One more, and he's out! Peter moves forward free and uninhibited. No one is looking over his shoulder, ready to pounce on him should he fail again. He is absolved of shame.

Put yourself in Peter's shoes for a moment. If you had denied Jesus at that crucial moment, how would you recover?

Scripture reveals no sense of surprise at Peter's fall. Rather, the whole event is taken in stride. Once it happens, it is dealt with, but there is no long and arduous healing process for the apostle. Peter rebounds immediately. He's right there in the upper room with the disciples choosing Judas's replacement, praying and waiting for the promised Holy Spirit. And when the Holy Spirit comes, guess who will emerge as the fearless preacher of Pentecost.

Let that sink in for a minute.

Perennial grief and remorse over our failings are antithetical to grace, contrary to the way God deals with us.

Perennial grief and remorse over our failings are antithetical to grace, contrary to the way God deals with us.

Like the Father of the prodigal, he wants to hug us and throw a big party. Forget the rehearsed repentance speech when the son asks if he can be treated as a servant. That's not what the Father wants! He simply delights that his son has returned home. So it is with Peter. He immediately occupies his place as apostle, preacher and shepherd. He doesn't sit on the sidelines, not even for a moment.

We can take heart. This is our God and this is the way he rolls. Wallowing in our sin and weakness serves no purpose whatsoever. God knows we are dust, weak, frail, sinners. Get up. Get back in the game. He's calling you . . . and me.

Are your past failures haunting your present journey like a dark cloud? Do you find yourself saying, "If only I had not done that, said that . . ." Let this station of Peter's journey inspire an embrace of exactly who you are, now re-centered in God's profuse favor and grace in Christ. Hear Jesus's key question: "Do you love me?" He's more aware of your failures than you are. Yet today is your chance to affirm that it was a lapse, not a defection, and that you still want to follow him.

> He does not deal with us according to our sins,
>> nor repay us according to our iniquities.
> For as high as the heavens are above the earth,
>> so great is his steadfast love toward those who fear him;
> as far as the east is from the west,
>> so far does he remove our transgressions from us.
> As a father shows compassion to his children,
>> so the LORD shows compassion to those who fear him.
> For he knows our frame;
>> he remembers that we are dust (Ps 103:10–14)

It's past time to give up the idea of a spiritual meritocracy.

9

Spiritual Reflexes: Part 1

A Disciple's Maturity

From the moment we claim the truth of being the Beloved, we are faced with the call to become who we are.

Henri Nouwen, *Life of the Beloved*

When we have found our rest in God we can do nothing other than minister. God's rest will be visible wherever we go and whoever we meet. And before we speak any words, the Spirit of God, praying in us, will make his presence known and gather people into a new body, the body of Christ himself.

Henri Nouwen, *The Way of the Heart*

Then Peter, filled with the Holy Spirit, said to them, "Rulers of the people and elders, if we are being examined today concerning a good deed done to a crippled man, by what means this man has been healed, let it be known to all of you and to all the people of Israel that by the name of Jesus Christ of Nazareth, whom you crucified, whom God raised from the dead – by him this man is standing before you well. This Jesus is the stone that was rejected by you, the builders, which has become the cornerstone. And there is salvation in no one else, for there is no other name under heaven given among men by which we must be saved."

Now when they saw the boldness of Peter and John, and perceived that they were uneducated, common men, they were astonished. And they recognized that they had been with Jesus. But seeing the man who was healed standing beside them, they had nothing to say in opposition.

We wanted to know if now was the time . . . the time for the kingdom to come? Ha! Jesus's answers always just bring more questions! All he said was we were to be witnesses.

But he was right. In just a few days we told the Pentecost crowds in Jerusalem, and then all the temple leaders. I couldn't believe the words coming out of my mouth. Was that really me??!! What's even more amazing is how many are coming.

Our leaders just don't get it. Jesus pointed it out to us right there in the Psalms. They "gathered together against the Lord and against his anointed." Why couldn't I see that before? It's like God planned the whole thing . . . every last detail and spoke it through the prophets!

I remember he said the temple wouldn't last . . . "not one stone will stay on top of another." I was shocked! "No temple" meant the end of everything . . . our people . . . our purpose . . . everything! We didn't get it.

But from the time he breathed on us and said, "Receive the Holy Spirit," our eyes opened. We began to understand it differently.

So when the time came . . . well, it was undeniable. We spoke languages . . . different dialects. Boldness too! People healed . . . just like when Jesus was with us.

He's gone but his Spirit is here with us. That's what he said . . . that he and his Father would come and dwell in us. He's working through us. . . . Of course! That's why he said we would do his works and even greater.

So now I see it's not about the stones of the temple. Jesus said he is the cornerstone – the whole building rests on him. And he called me a rock too . . . said he would build his church on me. That's it. He's building a new house. That's why he called me a rock!

What's next? Jesus said, "Go into all the world." Yeah. He wants a different kind of house . . . a living, breathing, witnessing house. No wonder he said the temple wouldn't last. He's the foundation and the rest of us are being built into the house of his presence . . . a family of priests. He's here . . . with us . . . in us. He moves with us, goes where we go.

Why couldn't I see it before? But now I am beginning to see!

The "End" of Spiritual Formation

A musician begins his journey to mastery of his instrument with the most basic lessons, how to hold the bow or place fingers on piano keys. The hands respond awkwardly at first. Simple melodies are followed by scales and then more complicated chord formations and harmonies. All of this takes place under the mentorship of a skilled musician who has walked this path ahead of the student. After many years, the student will be able to play a complex piece of music with relative ease if they practice regularly. Nothing is more beautiful and inspiring than a skilled musician performing at the highest level. They have achieved mastery – the goal of their musical training.

Jesus said that when disciples are fully trained, they will be like their teacher (Luke 6:40). That's the "end" of spiritual formation – its *telos* – a word that means "goal." That doesn't mean that spiritual formation stops, but we reach a goal which is to respond to situations in the same way Jesus himself responds. It sounds a little intimidating, but it will help us to remember that Peter didn't do it alone. He did it with other people, as part of a body.

We don't arrive at that goal by good intentions. Like the musician, we have to go through the rigors of training. Peter has done that. He has walked with Jesus for three years, observing every movement and developing skills through ministry assignments. In the early chapters of the book of Acts we watch Peter come into his own as a disciple, reflexively doing what he saw Jesus do. He leads the new community of Jesus followers into the kinds of ministry he observed in Jesus with amazing effectiveness. His mastery of life in the Spirit bursts into full bloom in the early chapters of Acts.

In this chapter, we observe the fruit of Peter's spiritual formation. His actions mirror his mentor who spent years rescripting Peter's expectations. His entire worldview has been the object of Jesus's relentless bombardment. Now, for the first time, Peter emerges from the fog. He's beginning to see clearly and it is beautiful to watch.

Before we look at Peter's spiritual reflexes, we should pause to think about the role of the Holy Spirit in Peter's transformation.

The Holy Spirit and Peter's Transformation

We've heard sermons about Peter's amazing transformation, from denying Jesus to "we cannot but speak of what we have seen and heard" (Acts 4:20). Peter's 180-degree turnaround is stunning, even staggering. But there is an explanation. It's the Holy Spirit. The Spirit came as Jesus promised and Simon the coward became Peter the apostle of Pentecost.

We owe it to Peter to dive a little deeper into his transformation. Recall that Peter was not "cowardly" in the garden of Gethsemane when Judas led the soldiers and temple leaders to take Jesus into custody. He was there with sword drawn, swinging away in the direction of Malchus's head. The reason for Peter's denial is not cowardice primarily. Rather it lies in his complete disillusionment with Jesus's allowing himself to be arrested. Peter simply could not conceive of a Messiah who died on a cross. For him, Jesus's arrest, suffering and crucifixion were the end of a dream – a dream in which he had invested three years of his life. He didn't deny Jesus because he was a coward. He denied Jesus because his world had just imploded. Confused and disillusioned, he truly did not know *this* Jesus.

Disillusion. An illusion is something that's not real. To be dis-illusioned, then, is to release the false, the fake, for the purpose of latching onto what is real and authentic.

Disillusion. An illusion is something that's not real. To be dis-illusioned, then, is to release the false, the fake, for the purpose of latching onto what is real and authentic.

Jesus strips Peter of his illusions in order to form him into an authentic son.[1]

With that perspective, we are in a better place to understand the role of the Spirit in Peter's transformation. We usually think that the Spirit was given at Pentecost, but John's version of events casts the reception of the Spirit in a new light. Jesus breathed on his disciples and said "receive the Holy Spirit" before he ascended into heaven (John 20:22). In fact, according to John, this happened on Sunday evening – the day of the resurrection. That is almost fifty days prior to Pentecost. Furthermore, Luke informs us that Jesus appeared to them "during forty days and speaking about the kingdom of God" (Acts 1:3). Peter along with the other disciples were undergoing a massive paradigm shift – a change in their basic assumptions. Their "kingdom seminar" with Jesus was reorienting their understanding of the Messiah and his role. Now they were putting things together. The things Jesus said to them before his death began to make sense.

---

1. I'm indebted to Jeff Kuhn for this idea, shared with me through our conversations and correspondence.

This is not to minimize the role of the Spirit in Peter's boldness. In fact, as John relates it, the Spirit was present in the disciples, renewing their minds, helping them understand the words of Jesus. The transformation took place before Pentecost. Pentecost was a dynamic outpouring of the Spirit's power that shook Jerusalem and established the new community of Jesus's people. But the Spirit was already present, reminding them of Jesus's words, leading them into all truth, just as Jesus had promised.

So Peter's transformation from cowardice to courage was just the surface. What happened went much deeper. His transformation radically changed his mind, will and emotions. He began to understand Jesus as the cosmic Savior of the world – the fulfillment of all the Old Testament promises – and not merely a temporal renewal of Israel's monarchy. Peter probably never lacked courage, but he needed insight into the bigger picture of God's purposes. This transformation began between Jesus's resurrection and the outpouring of the Spirit at Pentecost. As Jesus departed, the Holy Spirit was given to carry on Jesus's pursuit of holistic transformation in Peter's (and the apostles') heart and mind. He was given by the breath and word of Christ on the evening of his resurrection. The point is that it was not merely a transformation on the emotional level – from cowardice to courage. It was the beginning of a full-orbed transformation – intellectual, emotional and behavioral. That's the deep work of the Holy Spirit in Peter and the apostles.

Reflexes of Spiritual Maturity

The early chapters of the book of Acts are brimming with examples of Peter's transformation. Our man shines here. We'll consider events described in the first five chapters of Acts as well as chapters 7 and 8. Peter's training as a disciple under Jesus is now bearing fruit in the mature actions of an apostle. His mind is renewed in truth, bringing his devotion to Jesus, at the emotional level, to fuller fruition. Transformed actions follow as a natural result. In this chapter, we look at Peter's personal reflexes of grace and communal reflexes towards the body of Christ. In the following chapter we observe leadership reflexes of truth and integrity and scriptural reflexes of rootedness.

Personal Reflexes: Spirit-Filled Courage

An all-time favorite hymn is "Alas and Did My Savior Bleed" by Isaac Watts. One line of that classic is, "Would he devote that sacred head for such a worm as I?" Some of us were brought up in a spiritual atmosphere that kept the reality of our total depravity constantly before our eyes. Let's call it "worm spirituality." Seen as the antidote to spiritual pride, this vision of the self is a constant reminder of our unworthiness. It was Peter's first station of spiritual formation: "Get out of my boat, Lord, for I am a sinful man." Peter needed a deep awareness of his sin. He didn't lose that awareness but he moved on, refusing to allow it to dominate his mind and heart. So must we. The contemporary hymn has it right: "Two wonders here that I confess: my worth and my unworthiness."[2]

We ended the previous chapter with the observation that Peter didn't stay down long. His denial was abhorrent, and by all human measures, he would have been excluded from apostolic leadership. But that did not happen. Peter got right back in the game.

The early chapters of Acts refer to Peter "standing." He *stands* among the apostles prescribing how they should go about replacing Judas (Acts 1:15). Then he *stands* with the apostles to preach his fiery Pentecost sermon (Acts 2:14). As I listen to him describe Judas, I find myself wanting to say, "Hold on a minute Peter! You're forgetting something. Judas betrayed but you denied! How can you be so hard on Judas?" Then, preaching to his fellow Jews, he castigates them, placing the verdict of Jesus's death on their shoulders: "This Jesus, delivered up according to the definite plan and foreknowledge of God, you crucified and killed by the hands of lawless men" (2:23). Again, I find myself thinking, "A little humility would go a long way. You do remember, Peter, that this plan God was working out was beyond your ability to comprehend as well. You were completely blindsided by Jesus's crucifixion!"

The story of Peter's intrepid leadership is so well-known that it no longer surprises us. To get the full effect, let it surprise you again. This guy should have been down for the count. How did he get back up? What's more, how is it that he's operating with full conviction, without a hint of his dark moment of defeat only a few weeks ago?

Peter has left behind "worm spirituality" for a holy boldness. How did he do it? I think part of the explanation is Peter's self-awareness. That's a well-used term in our day, referring to someone who is "self-actualized" or fully alive to their potential. That's the contemporary sense, but it doesn't capture Peter's self-understanding. Peter is aware that he is created and called for a purpose. It is a self-awareness in relation to God's purpose for him as his son. It's the furthest thing from individualism or self-absorption as it sees the self's value in relation to God's purpose and call. Those have become crystal clear in

---

2. Keith Getty, Kristyn Getty, and Graham Kendrick, "My Worth Is Not in What I Own (At the Cross)," Getty Music Publishing, 2014.

Peter's mind over the past fifty days as he saw the risen Christ and heard him expound the Scriptures, enlightened by the indwelling Spirit.

Peter is no longer living in the conscience-binding guilt of his denial. He is absolved of shame. He has not forgotten what happened. He is aware of his ability to deny his Lord. In fact, his future spiritual growth bears out that awareness. Nor is this newfound confidence expressed in the same vein of Peter's former assumptions about leadership and notoriety. He has internalized the lesson of a disciple who follows a cross-bearing Lord.

Peter is no longer Peter's central concern; he is not absorbed in his own issues. First, he knows himself to be loved by Christ, having been fully embraced in Jesus's love and brotherhood in the presence of his fellow disciples (John 21). Having received the Spirit of adoption, he is freed from self-absorption to enjoy his position as beloved son of the Father and brother of Jesus. Second, he has a purpose to serve, a call to fulfill. To focus on his downfall would only deter him from the relational reality of his being beloved and God's purpose for him. He moves forward in full confidence, knowing that Jesus has pardoned him and re-commissioned him.

What looms large for Peter is his assurance of pardon from Jesus as well as his re-commissioning before his friends. Together, they become a taproot from which he will draw life and bear fruit. To dwell in a tortured conscience would only sabotage the call of Christ on his life. Simon lays aside the shame of his former life and boldly, confidently, steps fully into his new identity as Peter.

I recall a pastor friend who was excluded from ministry for a time due to a moral failure. Years later, he sought to restore his pastoral status. It meant a much smaller role for him and a public examination that recalled the pain of his downfall. In private conversation he told me he was still "paying for his sins" (he meant, experiencing sins' consequences). Yet, when he stood to preach, he felt no need to grovel. He knew he was forgiven and that he had a call to fulfill.

At the end of the last chapter we said that if you are wondering if your past sin disqualifies you for a present or future role in Jesus's kingdom, stop it. He knows your frame. He remembers you are dust. Rather than wallow in the failures of the past, stand in the love of God displayed in Jesus. Receive the Holy Spirit. Then move forward to future victories.

God is more willing to restore us than we are to receive it. After all, he created us to be his image-bearers. There's nothing that gives him more pleasure than to see us doing exactly that.

Permanently mourning our sinfulness only serves to deter us from that purpose.

God is more willing to restore us than we are to receive it. After all, he created us to be his image-bearers. There's nothing that gives him more pleasure than to see us doing exactly that.

Now I must qualify that statement. There are some addictive behaviors that so overpower and domineer the will, that they disqualify from public roles of ministry. I am thinking of pedophilia or other forms of sexual deviancy, or ongoing anger that leads to a pattern of verbal and physical abuse. These harmful behaviors clearly disqualify an individual from public trust and from public ministry in Christ's body. Peter's failure is of a different nature. While serious, it is neither patterned nor destructive to others. His return to leadership is instigated by Jesus and received by the collective body of apostles and early followers. A new Peter is on the scene – confident in God, bold in his calling.

Communal Reflexes of the Body of Christ: Mutuality and Interdependence

Peter's embrace by a community of people saw him through the denial of Jesus to a fruitful and powerful ministry post Pentecost. That sentence was easy to read, but think about it. Simon would have never been Peter without John and James and Mary and Siloam and John Mark and all the others.

I live in the most individualistic society the world has ever known. The United States was founded on the concept of individual freedoms (e.g. life, liberty and the pursuit of happiness). I never realized that I carried that cultural value over into my spiritual life until I lived among a more collective people. I viewed my spiritual life as *my* relationship with God. I think Peter must have understood that Christ's Spirit filled the community of the early believers and that he was embraced by that community as an integral thread of its tapestry. He could not be removed from it nor would he ever consider that possibility. As the community fared, so fared Peter. His growth was wed to his community.

This sense of community was modelled by Jesus and his traveling band of disciples (both men and women). The first question the disciples asked Jesus was, "Where are you staying?" And his reply was, "Come and you will see" (John 1:38–39). Jesus formed his disciples by inviting them into his life. They got to see him up close and personal. They watched him pray, observing each reaction and relationship.

So it isn't surprising that after Jesus ascended to heaven and they made their way back to Jerusalem, they "went to the upper room, where they were staying." There, they "devoted themselves to prayer." It was the eleven disciples along with "the women and Mary the mother of Jesus, and his brothers" (Acts 1:13–14).

Has it ever struck you that when Jesus left the earth, he did not leave anything in writing? Nothing. Of course, he left words, but those were etched in the memory of his disciples. Nor did he leave an institution or a building. What Jesus brought into being and left in place was a community – people in relationship with one another. Luke tells us that it was approximately 120 people (Acts 1:15). It seems like such a precarious little group, does it not? That early community of Jesus-followers was nothing more than a loose network of brothers, cousins, mothers, sisters, relatives, acquaintances, all of whom had first-hand experience with Jesus and with one another. That's what Jesus left on earth – a community.

What were the odds that the little community would survive 2,000 years until today? Likely, a million to one against it! But it has survived. The little community received a communal outpouring of God's Spirit, forming it into the "body of Christ." In that way, the life of the community was assured by Jesus who had ascended to the right hand of God the Father. The people he left on earth would continue what he had begun, pouring out the love of God for the world through themselves.

With Jesus as the cornerstone, Peter was also the foundational rock on whom the little community was built. Further on, we will consider his role as spokesman and leader. For now, consider the relational nature of the life they shared. There was an awe-inspiring mutuality and interdependence. As you read the description from Acts, remember that Peter is the solid-rock on which this is built.

> And they devoted themselves to the apostles' teaching and the fellowship, to the breaking of bread and the prayers. And awe came upon every soul, and many wonders and signs were being done through the apostles. And all who believed were together and had all things in common. And they were selling their possessions and belongings and distributing the proceeds to all, as any had need. And day by day, attending the temple together and breaking bread in their homes, they received their food with glad and generous hearts, praising God and having favor with all the people. And

the Lord added to their number day by day those who were being saved. (Acts 2:42–47)

The community of early Jesus-followers existed within the greater Jewish society of Jerusalem. It was not an exclusive community, but an open and inviting one. The sense of care for one another was not mere words, but action as they sold their possessions to provide for those in need.

After Peter heals a man lame from birth, Peter and John are taken into custody and then released. After their release, they "went to their friends and reported what the chief priests and elders had said to them" (Acts 4:23). The community became the base and the spiritual heart from which the apostles operated. That community lifted its prayer, asking God, not for protection, but that they would continue to speak with boldness as God stretched out his hand to heal and perform signs and wonders (Acts 4:30). The Spirit comes and fills them yet again, shaking the place where they are gathered.

Peter's spiritual life was nurtured and bore fruit in a community of disciples. They continued the prayers of the temple and they certainly would have prayed the words that Jesus taught his disciples. They nurtured one another from the apostles' teaching and broke bread together according to Jesus's example. Their common experience of following Jesus united them in a communal life of faith and prayer from which flowed powerful acts of service, liberation and enlightenment to the surrounding society. As we conclude this chapter, we will return to ask how the example of the early believers can nurture our spiritual formation as they did Peter's.

Peter's Spiritual Reflexes and Ours
Personal Reflexes of Grace

Shame is a shackle. It is a pain of conscience that infiltrates all we are and do. For some, it can be a lifelong impediment to growth. Peter's shameful denial was, apparently, well-known to all in the early Christian community. Odd to say this, but it was for Peter's good. He couldn't hide. His denial was heard by many, certainly by John and those gathered in Caiaphas's courtyard. Then it was recorded by the gospel writers for posterity. Remember, the Gospel of Mark was likely Peter's own telling of the story indicating that Peter owned his shame. He had to face himself and probe the reasons why he acted in the way he did.

I would like to tell you there is a quick cure for shame, but that would be a lie. In the life of the Spirit, shame is never fully eradicated. It stays, ever calling to our minds its sting, lethal to body and spirit. So what do we do? There is a positive way to deal with our shame which Peter models for us.

I think Peter held two forces in dynamic tension in his soul and mind. He knew both how wrong he was, and how loved and accepted he was. He must have gotten over the shock of his own denial. As he looked back, he must have realized that, contrary to his former way of thinking, he was a good candidate for denial. Jesus had seen it when Peter could not. But now, Peter could see it in the rearview mirror. He knew himself far better now. He could look back on that lapse and accept it as the fruit of who he was then, without staying there. His restoration included forgiveness and recommissioning, allowing him to move beyond the pain of the denial and accept himself. Finally, he embraced his given status as beloved brother, apostle, rock, preacher, leader of the community, as Jesus's gift of acceptance acted as a continual balm to Peter's memory of failures.

As I review my past failures, I realize they were the outworking of who I was, how I thought, how I viewed the world and myself. I had to pass through those stations to know myself more fully. Those failures are like the stones in the stream of my journey. They served me, allowing me to cross over to where I am now. They still sting a bit (I think Peter's failures did as well), but I view them in the rearview mirror, not on the horizon of vision.

In response, take some time to review your areas of shame. Only you know them. As you see Peter "standing" to take his place among the apostles in the early community, realize that your own shame can also be overcome. Peter's shame was absolved as it was dealt with in the presence of his friends. We can defang the serpent of shame as we seek out someone to share it with. Realize that as Jesus was present in the telling of Peter's shame, he is also present in yours. This is not asking you to confess your sin (though that may be part of it) but to name and own your shame. To identify clearly what is causing you to hide. Though it stings, realize you had to pass through those stations. Doing so allows you to know yourself far better and that results in deeper trust of his love and care. Follow Peter. Don't allow the shame to shackle you. As you let it be known, you can cast it off. View it in the rearview mirror, where it belongs. Carry Peter's example in your heart and move forward to stand in Jesus's calling and acceptance.

Peter's shame was known. He didn't have to live under the false pressure of being a spiritual giant. If our shame is known, at least to a few, it will help us leave it where it belongs – in the past.

The Community of Jesus's People

Concerning Peter's Christian community, perhaps, like me, you read the amazing stories of the early Christians and bemoan the impossibility of finding such life-giving community today. On the one hand, we should not dismiss that disappointment too quickly. Let us sit with it for a while, inviting the same Spirit to do his work within us. While we may not replicate all that took place among the early community of Jesus-followers, we must engage that story, inviting it to impact and inform our story. The communal life and miraculous phenomena that accompanied the initial outpouring of the Holy Spirit have not been the consistent experience of believers throughout history, although aspects of it have reappeared from time to time. When I consider these things, I recall Jesus's exhortation to Thomas: "Blessed are those who have not seen and yet have believed" (John 20:29).

Rather than grieve our lack of community, let's ask where are the signs of life in our present community? For the early Christians, those signs included sharing their goods and resources. Their mutual life resulted in reconciliation, meeting the needs of the poor and healing the sick. If we see some signs of life, we should not be too harsh in our judgment. Let us join in with the same spirit of mutuality, asking the Spirit to blow the embers into flame. Peter's maturation took place among his brothers and sisters. We will not reach the goal of our spiritual life apart from the community of God's people.

The Spirit's Role in Transformation

As we think about Peter's transformation in relation to our own, we have to ask ourselves about the role of the Holy Spirit. Peter's transformation was not merely emotional (from cowardice to courage); there were deep intellectual and behavioral underpinnings that brought about a holistic transformation in the apostle. It was mind (intellect), heart (emotions), and will (behavior and actions). If we are to be transformed by Jesus, it will only happen as his Spirit comes to teach, comfort and lead. How do you see the Holy Spirit? Is the Spirit welcomed by your prayers, anticipated, invited? Do you listen attentively for his promptings? Or does the Spirit confuse you, scare you?

It is unfortunate that divergent views of the Spirit's work have been the cause of division in the contemporary church. Some who claim gifts and manifestations of the Spirit raise serious questions in the minds of thoughtful followers.

The ancient leaders of the church thought of the Holy Spirit as the love of the Father breathed out toward the Son and then from the Son back to the Father.

The ancient leaders of the church thought of the Holy Spirit as the love of the Father breathed out toward the Son and then from the Son back to the Father.

It is helpful to think of the Spirit as the Father's loving embrace of the Son that has now extended to include us. We are held in the Father's embrace of the Son by the Holy Spirit. Understanding the Spirit in this way will rid us of intimidation, fear and cynicism. Simply ask that you and your community be renewed by the presence, purity and power of the Spirit of the Son and Father (Luke 11:13).

Although she is rarely mentioned in the book of Acts, Mary the mother of Jesus was a central figure of that early community. The ancient church viewed her as a role model of response to the Spirit. Her words "let it be to me according to your word" (Luke 1:38) express the receptive and submissive heart of unrestrained devotion. Remembering Mary, let us look for the Spirit's work in unexpected people and places. He is still bringing down the mighty and exalting the humble (Luke 1:52). The Spirit's life is still manifested in "small" people who are putting themselves in God's hands with utter devotion. Perhaps looking for the work of the Spirit among the humble will help us discern anew the beauty of Jesus's community.

10

Spiritual Reflexes: Part 2

A Disciple's Impact

The glory of God is man fully alive.

Irenaeus of Lyons, *Against Heresies* (Book 4, Chapter 20:7)

Prepare your minds for action.

The Apostle Peter (1 Pet 1:13)

Now there was in Joppa a disciple named Tabitha, which, translated, means Dorcas. She was full of good works and acts of charity. In those days she became ill and died, and when they had washed her, they laid her in an upper room. Since Lydda was near Joppa, the disciples, hearing that Peter was there, sent two men to him, urging him, "Please come to us without delay." So Peter rose and went with them. And when he arrived, they took him to the upper room. All the widows stood beside him weeping and showing tunics and other garments that Dorcas made while she was with them. But Peter put them all outside and knelt down and prayed; and turning to the body he said, "Tabitha, arise." And she opened her eyes, and when she saw Peter she sat up. And he gave her his hand and raised her up. Then, calling the saints and widows, he presented her alive. And it became known throughout all Joppa, and many believed in the Lord. And he stayed in Joppa for many days with one Simon, a tanner.

It's been good to get out of Jerusalem. Getting out in the country reminds me of our travel with Jesus. Then, we were preparing for his arrival. Now, he's with us, or maybe he's there ahead of us.

Seeing Aeneas lying there, for eight long years, it was obvious that I should do what Jesus did. So I spoke just the way I heard him speak: "Jesus heals you, man! Get up and make your bed!" I could almost hear Jesus saying it, so I said it that way. Today, Aeneas walks!

Was I surprised? Not really. These healings are happening regularly now. With each one, my sense that he is here only grows deeper.

News travels fast. Some of the brothers and sisters in Joppa heard about Aeneas and immediately sent for me. The two brothers who came informed me that Tabitha (Dorcas) had died and asked me to come. I went with them right away. The scene was familiar. Her lady friends reminded me of my mother . . . showing off the dresses Tabitha had made, between their sighs and wails.

I took it all in for a moment. It was like I was right back in the house with Jairus's daughter. Sometimes I wonder if Jesus did all of that because he knew I would be doing what I am now. He sent everybody out of the room, except me and James and John. I did that too. He took the little girl by the hand and said, "Get up." I knew he was there, so I knelt beside her. The words, "Tabitha, qumi" came out of my mouth. Now, I shake my head, because it's almost exactly what Jesus said "Talitha, qumi." And she did. The dead came to life.

I was the one to give Tabitha back to them. "Overwhelmed," would be an understatement.

I've stayed on here in Joppa for a few days. What happened with Aeneas, and with Tabitha, has opened hearts. So many of my fellow Jews are turning to Jesus. He said we would be witnesses and he said we would receive power. I'm here to tell you, it's happening, just like he said!

The Miraculous

Before we continue discussing Peter's spiritual reflexes, there's a question we should face squarely. Peter is our model of spiritual formation. So, what do we do with these miracles? If he's our model, is that what we are to do too? Should I be healing people and raising them from the dead? Didn't Jesus promise that his followers would do the same works he did and even greater? At the outset, I confess that I have often struggled with the lack of the miraculous as I attempt to follow the model of the apostles and prophets. Is my lack of faith the problem? Are miracles for certain epochs? Are some uniquely gifted to do miraculous signs? These are difficult questions.

A simple and helpful definition of a miracle is "a less common kind of God's activity in which he arouses people's awe and wonder and bears witness to himself."[1] I've spent nearly three decades of my adult life as a witness to Jesus among peoples of other cultures, specifically Islamic peoples. I am not alone in noticing that the majority of those who come to Christ from an Islamic worldview have experienced dreams, visions, healings, etc. It seems to happen naturally, without fanfare or spotlights, often without human intermediary. The misconception is that the sign or miracle leads an individual to faith in Christ. Not true. Often the sign leads to a believer who speaks the gospel, which opens the individual's heart to faith in Jesus. The miracle or sign opens the mind, creating plausibility for a new way of thinking. The gospel, explained and often demonstrated through a person, opens the heart.

Peter and the apostles are in a similar situation. They operate in a society which has rejected the claims of Christ. Their task is to establish the church in their Jewish society and beyond, continuing the work Jesus began, proclaiming and demonstrating the kingdom of Jesus. Miraculous signs play an important role in establishing Jesus's kingdom where it is unknown and considered to be implausible.

The Bible may appear to be replete with miracles but there are many instances where we expect or hope for miracles that do not take place. For instance, it is noteworthy that miracles of deliverance and healing rarely take place among the community of the apostles. The exception, of course, is the release of Peter from prison in Acts 12. But note carefully that James, the brother of John, was executed, giving such pleasure to his adversaries that Herod intended to continue killing Christian leaders (Acts 12:2–3), which

---

1. Grudem, *Systematic Theology*, 355. Professor Grudem notes that the definition is adapted from unpublished lectures by John Frame, professor of systematic theology at Westminster Theological Seminary.

is why he imprisoned Peter. We recall the amazing account of Peter's release, but we must not forget the martyrdom of James, also a prominent and early disciple.

We have brief mentions of illnesses the apostles dealt with. Paul had a thorn in the flesh for which he asked deliverance on three separate occasions. The Lord's answer was "my grace is sufficient for you, for my power is made perfect in weakness" (2 Cor 12:9). Timothy was instructed to take a little wine due to his frequent illnesses (1 Tim 5:23). Paul's litany of sufferings (2 Cor 11:23–29) leaves the reader with the impression that miraculous interventions were not the norm: Paul left Trophimus sick in Miletus (2 Tim 4:20); John suffered exile on the island of Patmos. Though Scripture tells us virtually nothing of Peter's life after the Jerusalem Council, the traditions of the early Christians record that he was crucified near Rome. Indeed, nearly all the apostles died as martyrs. A miraculous escape was not always provided. In fact, it was the exception rather than the rule.

As we read the accounts of Peter's miracles, we should recall that miracles are for a purpose – to bear witness to God's presence, creating plausibility for the gospel among those who observe or experience them. Miracles serve to open minds, allowing the gospel to penetrate hearts that were previously closed. Peter's unique apostolic role was establishing the church where it did not exist before. The apostles do not summon miracles for their personal benefit. It would be unthinkable.

Yet not all miracles fit neatly into this category of "establishing" the church at the hands of the apostles. Some miracles are gifts of God, expressing his love and concern. The churches of Corinth and Galatia experienced miraculous occurrences (1 Cor 12:4–11; Gal 3:5). Miracles were a known feature of church life and did not depend on the presence of apostles. The metaphor used for the church in the New Testament is the "body of Christ." The church's "members" are the hands, feet, eyes and ears of Jesus in the world. The body draws life from its head – Jesus Christ – being joined to him through the Holy Spirit. Jesus has not left the world. His Spirit animates the body of Christ, the church.

I believe this is how to account for Jesus's words that those who follow him will do the works that he does and even greater works. The church's presence worldwide continues its ministry of witness to Jesus through word and demonstration of the Spirit's power. So while my own ministry does not display the apostolic miracles of Peter, I am part of a global body through which the "less common activity of God continues to arouse awe and wonder." As Peter moved the focus of interest in his miracles away from himself to Christ, so I must make Christ's presence my focus. The church, at its best, does the same. The glory belongs to God alone who still acts in uncommon ways to call people to himself.

In summary, miracles were prominent in the ministry of Jesus and the apostles as they established the community of Jesus followers. Miracles continue to occur in and through the church collectively as a witness to the presence and power of God caring for and working through his people. Following Peter's example, let us recall that all miracles are the work of Jesus through his Spirit among his people. They are not a source of spiritual privilege, used by a special class of highly "spiritual" people. Conversely, a lack of miracles must not be attributed to a lack of faith. However, let us banish fear and believe God will work in and through us. Peter had to act in faith as he told the lame to "get up" or called Tabitha to arise. Let us also anoint the sick and pray, laying on hands. Let us cast out the demons of our society and serve as peacemakers in our conflict-laden world. The Spirit of Father and Son is still at work through "less common" means to arouse awe and wonder as he calls the nations to himself.

Reflexes of Spiritual Maturity

Now, back to our discussion of Peter's spiritual reflexes from the previous chapter.

Leadership Reflexes of Courage, Knowledge, Integrity and Passion

In previous chapters we noted Peter's authenticity. His lack of duplicity revealed the raw material of a leader of Jesus's people. In the early chapters of Acts, Peter's authenticity flows beautifully into leadership reflexes that appear spontaneously throughout the Acts narrative.

His remarkable courage which we saw in the previous chapter, once again arrests our attention. He looks the Sadducees (the temple elite) in the eyes and tells them they crucified the Lord of glory. He calls them to repent and has the audacity to expound the Old Testament before them. Peter had cowered before a servant girl when he denied Jesus, but now he held his ground to defeat the religious elite of his day and demonstrate the truth of the resurrection in Jerusalem. He wins a stunning victory for the apostles and the new community.

Consider Peter's impressive display of knowledge. If we translate Peter's confrontation with the temple elite to our day, it would be like a rural carpenter or farmer in direct confrontation with renowned academic theologians. No doubt, we would root for the country man and admire him, but could we really expect him to possess a wide-ranging knowledge of the Scriptures and history that would set his more educated opponents on their heels. How does that happen? They knew how. He had been with Jesus!

Peter's penetrating commitment to truth and integrity sets a high bar for the newly formed body of believers. After healing a lame beggar, Peter is called before the temple officials. Guess who was in attendance? "Their rulers and elders and scribes gathered together in Jerusalem, with Annas the high priest and Caiaphas and John and Alexander, and all who were of the high-priestly family" (Acts 4:5–6). Luke's mention of these names clues us in that this is a moment of sweet vindication for Peter. It was the courtyard of Caiaphas where Peter denied and fled. Jesus himself was interrogated only weeks previously by this same group of somber, robed and crowned religious leaders, while Peter, fearful and confused, looked on. Now, with the whole entourage of the temple elite present, Peter is "filled with the Holy Spirit" (4:8). It makes you want to stand up and yell, "Go, Peter!" And he does.

Peter's declaration is unflinching. Void of self-promotion, he turns the attention of the entire assembly to Jesus Christ whose power has healed this man. Peter did the miracle, but he reflexively moves himself out of the limelight and puts Jesus front and center. It is the Jesus you crucified, whom God raised from the dead. Though rejected by the builders (the temple leadership), he has become the cornerstone. Furthermore, there is salvation in no one else. By the way, Peter is citing Psalm 118 which Jesus also quoted, relating it to himself after a conflict with the temple elite (see Luke 20:17).

The uneducated fisherman leaves them shaking in their boots. "What can we do? Everyone can see that an amazing sign has been performed" (see Acts 4:16). It's a classic example of position versus authority. The religious leaders held the position of leadership empty of spiritual authority. Jesus had given it to Peter and the apostles, and it was obvious to all. Peter's authenticity burns away the fog of religiosity.

Luke must have a flair for humor as he relates the story of the apostles' arrest in Acts 5:17–42. The high priest and his Sadducee accomplices have the disciples imprisoned. The "angel of the Lord" releases them and tells them to return to the temple and teach. When the arrogant temple elite gather the next day, they send for the apostles to interrogate them. Poor guys! They can't find their detainees until someone comes in to let them know that, "hey, they're in the temple teaching!" – exactly what they were told *not* to do, and what the priests and Sadducees *should* be doing! Now the temple elite are really worried because the apostles intend "to bring this man's blood upon us." They command the apostles to shut up and Peter responds, "We must obey God rather than men" (Acts 5:29).

Peter has become unflappable, undeterrable. He's zealous to be the witness Jesus told him to be, and no amount of human intimidation will shut him up. He has spiritual authority even though he's been given no position or role among the religious leaders of his day. Peter is amazing us now.

In another scene, Ananias and Sapphira are caught up in the fervor of the new community. The spiritual life of the community must have been intoxicating and the spiritual peer pressure to conform caught up with them. Everyone was bringing their goods to the apostles so they could be distributed according to the needs of the community. This couple wanted a piece of the action, but not really. So they lied about the price of land they sold and brought only a portion to the apostles. Peter was in no mood to hear excuses for deceit in the body of Christ. Like a hound on a scent, he stares them down: "Why has Satan filled your heart to lie to the Holy Spirit? . . . You have not lied to man but to God" (Acts 5:3–4).

Peter's soul is aflame with truth. His abhorrence of duplicity and passion for integrity is injected into the DNA of the community. "And great fear came upon all who heard of it" (Acts 5:5, 11). The church is being built on Peter, the rock! Luke's conclusion has a strange juxtaposition of ideas. "None of the rest dared join them, but the people held them in high esteem," and "more than ever believers were added to the Lord, multitudes of both men and women" (Acts 5:13–14). Peter's holy intrepidity and the Spirit's power manifested through the apostles marked Jesus's church as a radically new society, animated by the presence of God, that attracted many but also evoked fear and respect.

A final example: Peter and John often act in tandem in the book of Acts. The outpouring of the Spirit is now spilling over into the non-Jewish community. Philip witnesses in Samaria and it seems that the whole city is embracing the new faith. Luke's account calls to mind Jesus's words in Samaria – that he had sent them to reap where they had not sown. That promise of John 4 is fulfilled in Acts 8. Peter and John go up for a pastoral visit, lay their hands on the believers and pray for them. The Holy Spirit comes on them, just as he did on the apostles, shocking everyone!

In the midst of it all, another Simon, who was renowned as a magician, makes the mistake of offering Peter money if he can only have the apostolic power to give the Spirit by laying on hands. Here's a guy who has spent his whole life trying to make people believe he has spiritual power. He couldn't resist the chance to cash in. You know what's coming, right? Peter will not tolerate compromise and "Mr. Celebrity Convert" of Samaria is soundly called on the carpet. When Peter and John left, the church in Samaria had no doubt about the source of spiritual power and how to get it. It came as a gift of Jesus Christ, through his apostles. It was not for sale.

Time and again, Peter's passion for authentic spiritual life, devoid of duplicity and hypocrisy, comes through.

For Peter, it was authenticity or nothing at all. He would not fake it and as a result the church would become a community of authenticity.

For Peter, it was authenticity or nothing at all.
He would not fake it and as a result the church
would become a community of authenticity.

We have Peter to thank for that standard even if we fail to live up to it.

Scriptural Reflexes of Rootedness

We see Peter's scriptural rootedness with stunning clarity in the early chapters of Acts. Peter becomes the mouthpiece of the community to the Jewish world that surrounds them. He belongs neither to the temple-elite Sadducees nor the Torah-proficient Pharisees, and yet he skillfully explains the meaning of recent events concerning Jesus, relating them to a wide array of Old Testament prophecies and Psalms. He interprets the strange phenomenon of tongues of fire and foreign languages based on the prophet Joel. He explains the resurrection was declared beforehand in Psalm 16 as God did not "abandon his soul to Sheol or allow his Holy One to see corruption." David, Peter contends, could not have been writing about himself as his tomb is with us to this day. Peter's daring conclusion is that David was writing about his descendant and his words had just been fulfilled here in this city. Surprisingly, Peter even confidently states that Jesus has been received into heaven until the time for restoring all things which the Prophets spoke about long ago (Acts 3:21). Peter stands before these experts in prophecy and declares that everything written is fulfilled in Jesus Christ. The proposition is nothing less than a complete overhaul of the Jewish understanding of their Scriptures – quite an undertaking for a Galilean fisherman!

Peter's understanding had come to a full flowering. He has seen and is now able to articulate that Jesus is the fulfillment of the story of the Jewish people. He fulfills the Old Testament images and prophecies, bringing them to their culmination. Jesus's death was not the end of his story as Peter once thought, but the initiation of a new epoch of salvation for all who believe.

As we've seen, Luke wryly recounts the conclusion of the Jewish leaders who noted that these uneducated, common men had "been with Jesus" (Acts 4:13). It was their sole credential and yet it was more than sufficient. Had not Jesus taught that Moses wrote about him (John 5:46)? Had he not faced down the Pharisees with his declaration that Abraham had seen his day and rejoiced? That "before Abraham was, I am?" (John 8:56, 58) Did not the hearts of the Emmaus road disciples burn within them as Jesus opened to them the Scriptures (Luke 24:32)? Did he not open the minds of the disciples to see that everything written about him in the Law of Moses and the Prophets and the Psalms had to be fulfilled (Luke 24:44–45)?

It is no overstatement to say that somewhere between Peter's denial and the day of Pentecost, he had an epiphany – an awakening that brought the disparate pieces of his understanding together. Peter reflexively knew that his story was the story of his people, but now he knew that Jesus was the objective of that story. This new understanding equipped Peter with a new lens to read the Hebrew Scriptures. He found that Christ fulfilled them. After all, Jesus inspired them as Peter said in 1 Peter 1:10–11: "Concerning this salvation, the prophets who prophesied about the grace that was to be yours searched and inquired carefully, inquiring what person or time *the Spirit of Christ in them* was indicating when he predicted the sufferings of Christ and the subsequent glories" (emphasis added). This knowledge formed the heart of the apostolic message and the identity of the community of Jesus followers – the church.

Unless we sink roots deeply into the whole story of the Bible, our spiritual formation cannot be well-rooted. Peter shows us this. Every time he speaks in the book of Acts – a total of eight speeches – he digs into the soil of the Old Testament prophets to demonstrate the centrality of Jesus to all of life. We will consider below how this transforms our vision of Jesus.

Peter's Spiritual Reflexes and Ours
Truth and Integrity

The demise of Ananias and Sapphira speaks volumes. One would think that true spiritual desires would be immune to peer pressure and the desire to please others. Alas, it is the downfall of many. Peter, at least in this story, is the counterpoint. He is the person of authenticity. But remember that Peter had to pass through the fire to get here. He blew it on numerous occasions but still stuck with Jesus and engaged in the hard work of changing his expectations and shedding the shadow-self. Perhaps that's why Peter is adept at discerning inauthenticity in Ananias and Sapphira. He knows it when he sees it.

The problem with our shadow-self is not only that it is fake, but that it tries to convince us that it is authentic and sincere.

The problem with our shadow-self is not only that it is fake,
but that it tries to convince us that it is authentic and sincere.

No doubt, Ananias, had he had the chance, would have justified himself, pointing out that he had given a large gift to the community. I tend to blame outside influences for my lack of integrity and then justify myself. Oddly enough, the people closest to me – my parents, my wife, my work associates, get the brunt of it. "If only so-and-so gave me more of this, then I wouldn't be like that!" It goes all the way back to Eden. Adam blamed Eve, justifying himself, which meant he was blaming God, who gave him Eve. It's a vicious cycle that leads us down the black hole of addiction, blame and death.

Peter doesn't tolerate it in the community that is built on his confession. And you and I will do well if we refuse to tolerate it in our souls. Inauthenticity is the death knell of spiritual formation. It hides in our souls like a snake in the grass. To find it, I ask myself whose admiration I desire and why? That's likely the taproot – our desire to please others, to appear good (self-justification), like Ananias and Sapphira. Exposing my desire for the admiration of others is a significant step in spiritual formation. Once I've found the taproot, I'll need to dig it out, either withdrawing from my false parade of self or possibly exposing my true self to those whose rejection I fear.

Scriptural Rootedness

Unlike Peter, you and I have multiple narratives (stories) that vie for our attention. They lay claim to our lives and compel us to consider them as the overarching story that contains our small story. We hear them in scientific materialism, in philosophical nihilism, capitalism, consumerism, hedonism and materialism. Religious narratives such as Protestantism, Catholicism, Orthodoxy, Judaism or Islam also attempt to claim our allegiance. For some, the story of our denomination or faith hero (e.g. Aquinas, Calvin, Luther, Wesley) forms our over-arching narrative. Our love of country may lead us to see our national narrative and history as the great story that contains our personal story. We affiliate with narratives of the armed forces, our vocation, our sports team or even a political ideology. All of these stories clutter our minds with debris that must be cleared away if we are to lay hold of the central story of the world which Jesus culminates and fulfills. That story is related through the simple and yet profound experiences of the Old Testament people of God.

In its fascination with the Bible, the post-enlightenment era has attempted to dissect it through various means. The Bible is subject to debates over its scientific and historic reliability or over a literal versus a metaphoric reading. The academic critique of biblical sources and the history of its reception across time and cultures receive ample scholarly attention. All these areas may be helpful to study and discuss. Nevertheless, we need a "true north" in our understanding of Scripture, a unifying direction that brings focus to our reading and application of the Bible's story. Jesus provides that. His post-resurrection appearances and the Spirit's enlightenment opened the disciples' minds to see the story of Scripture moving toward its fulfillment in Jesus's person and work. As a result, the apostles become masters of the Old Testament in the Jesus way. The New Testament can be understood as a sequel to the Old Testament, explaining it in terms of who Jesus is and what he did. Peter's collective story remained in the orbit of the Old Testament prophets, but its gravitational center became the Messiah.

You and I were not privy to Jesus's forty days with the apostles. What we have is bits and pieces of what he shared with them, preserved in the New Testament. We will revisit this question in epilogue 1, but consider for a moment how you think of Jesus. We must ask ourselves, where is our starting point in thinking about him? If we start with the manger in Bethlehem, or the call of the disciples or the Sermon on the Mount, we have a truncated Savior, a half-Christ. John has a flare for simple and profound truth: "In the beginning was the Word, and the Word was with God, and the Word was God" (John 1:1). If we begin to see Jesus as the eternal Son, beloved of the Father, effecting creation, judging through the flood, calling Abraham, leading the children of Israel, inspiring the prophets, etc., our vision of him will expand vastly. He moves from being "my savior" (true but incomplete) to the Creator and Redeemer of the cosmos. Our understanding of Jesus's role will also shift from saving those who believe in him (again, true but incomplete) to effecting the reconciliation of all things. Getting the big view of Jesus will change how we think, what we care about, talk about and ultimately, how we act.

The ancients linked depth of soul with a vision of Jesus. They didn't mean a literal vision, but the way he is perceived in our minds and hearts. Many think of Jesus as waiting behind the curtain of the biblical drama until his name is called to make his first appearance in the Bethlehem manger. To that shrunken idea of Christ, Peter replies that his Spirit inspired the prophets. Paul retorts that by him and through him and for him all things were created and in him all things hold together (see Col 1:16–17). John responds that he was in the beginning with God. If we are not encountering Christ in Eden's question, "Adam, where are you?" or in Abraham's deliberations with the angel of Yahweh, or with Moses on the mount, or in the laments of the Psalms, then our Jesus is truncated, less than the real Jesus.

Peter has made huge strides, but his journey isn't over. In the next chapter we see that Peter, even in maturity, continues to grow, embracing change in core areas of his assumptions and actions.

Internalizing Spiritual Reflexes Modeled by Peter

As we attempt to bring our lives in line with Peter, it is important to probe our integrity. The word integrity derives from the Latin *integer*, meaning "whole or complete." It is the opposite of duplicity. It is a consistency of character from our hidden thoughts to our audible words and visible behavior. For the Christ-follower, having integrity implies that we accept Scripture's assessment of our heart as incurably duplicitous. Now that sounds like a contradiction, but it is the reality modeled by Peter, who allowed himself to be continually corrected and redirected at the heart level through his journey with Jesus. How do we do that? Try discussing the following points openly with a small group of like-minded companions.

First, let us search our hearts for blame. Do we blame others (spouse, parents, society) for our current attitudes and behavior? If so, now is the time to own our responsibility and seek help to change.

Second, we must not deceive ourselves that our hearts are "pre-loaded" with integrity. We are infected with a human condition called sin, alienating us from what is true, good and beautiful. Like Peter, we need the watchful, caring and empathetic eye of a community to help us walk the path of Jesus. That means we seek out accountability and never run away from it. It means we share our proclivities to financial, sexual and social deceit. We are no longer surprised that duplicity lurks in our heart and therefore, we no longer hide it from ourselves and others. In the present day, it means holding to some form of screen accountability including social media.

Finally, the scriptural rootedness of discerning Christ's presence in the whole biblical story is critical to forward progress in our journey. As our perception of Christ's glory and majesty grows, we will naturally be drawn deeper into him, increasing in knowledge and passion in the light of his overwhelming grace and beauty. Epilogue 1 in this book addresses this topic, but as an introduction, read again Jesus's interaction with the Jewish leaders in John 5:30–47 and John 8:31–59. In reference to John 5:46 and 8:56, ask yourself what Jesus is saying about Moses and Abraham and their relationship to him. Are they merely pointing to the future birth of Jesus or did they actually interact with Jesus as Old Testament prophets? Try to take a fresh look at precisely what Jesus said, and ask the Spirit to enlighten your mind by what he meant.

11

The Reorientation

A Disciple's Realization

*To be chosen as the beloved of God, . . . instead of excluding
others, includes others. Instead of rejecting others as
less valuable, it accepts others in their own uniqueness.
It is not a competitive but a compassionate choice.*

Henri Nouwen, *Life of the Beloved*

Show hospitality to one another without grumbling.

The Apostle Peter (1 Pet 4:9)

The next day, as they were on their journey and approaching the city, Peter went up on the housetop about the sixth hour to pray. And he became hungry and wanted something to eat, but while they were preparing it, he fell into a trance and saw the heavens opened and something like a great sheet descending, being let down by its four corners upon the earth. In it were all kinds of animals and reptiles and birds of the air. And there came a voice to him: "Rise, Peter; kill and eat." But Peter said, "By no means Lord; for I have never eaten anything that is common or unclean." And the voice came to him a second time, "What God has made clean, do not call common." This happened three times, and the thing was taken up at once to heaven.

Now while Peter was inwardly perplexed as to what the vision that he had seen might mean, behold, the men who were sent by Cornelius, having made inquiry for Simon's house, stood at the gate and called out to ask whether Simon who was called Peter was lodging there. And while Peter was pondering the vision, the Spirit said to him, "Behold, three men are looking for you. Rise and go down and accompany them without hesitation, for I have sent them." And Peter went down to the men and said, "I am the one you are looking for. What is the reason for your coming?" And they said, "Cornelius, a centurion, an upright and God-fearing man, who is well spoken of by the whole Jewish nation, was directed by a holy angel to send for you to come to his house and to hear what you have to say." So he invited them to be his guests.

I'm dying for something to eat! The smell of that food downstairs is making me crazy!

But what was that all about? "Get up, use the knife and take your meat of choice." No way! It was Gentile food.

I can't go against Moses and the fathers. No matter how hungry, I can't break kosher!

Three times he said it. "What God has made clean . . ."

Three times . . . hmm. Just like that morning by the Sea . . .

"What God has made clean, do not call unclean."

So, are unclean animals really clean?! Does he want me to eat with Gentiles?

I've gotta think about that. I'd be on the outs with the whole Jewish nation! It would compromise everything!

[LATER, AFTER PETER RECEIVES THE VISITORS FROM CAESAREA]

He let me know.

One of the three was a Roman soldier . . . Now he's eating and sleeping with us!!

Samaria . . . that was unbelievable . . . what John and I saw there! He knew what we didn't – that we would be his witnesses in Samaria.

That Roman Centurion . . . Jesus healed his servant.

He surprised us just about every day we were with him. Every Jew knows Rome is like a cancer to Israel! Jesus was immune to that. In fact, he said he had not seen faith like that in Israel!

He saw everything differently . . .

Hmm . . . witnesses in Jerusalem and Samaria and to the ends of the earth.

Not what goes in your mouth, but what comes out . . . envy and hatred . . . that makes you unclean.

It's not about food. It's about people.

Growing up I called them "dogs." Now, we're eating with them . . . welcoming them into our house.

It could mean trouble back in Jerusalem, but Jesus praised a Centurion, and if what they say about Cornelius is true, who am I to turn him away?

Fierce and Merciful

C. S. Lewis' delightful children's fantasy, *The Chronicles of Narnia*, probes our imagination and entertains. The stories convey deep spiritual realities in disarmingly simple prose. In the fifth Chronicle, *The Voyage of the Dawn Treader*, Lucy and Edmund are swept into their Narnia adventure with their cousin Eustace – a perfectly insolent little twerp. Eustace spends his days aboard ship furiously complaining to his journal about the horrid conditions on board and threatening to report the whole sordid affair to the nearest British consulate. Reepicheep, the gallant rat, keeps Eustace in his place with his trusty sword. When the *Dawn Treader* finally drops anchor in the enclave of a deserted island, the crew busily makes reparations to the ship. Predictably, Eustace, realizing he can escape the chores, spends a leisurely day touring the island. He loses his way and a torrential rain causes him to take shelter in a cave – a dragon's cave. Eustace looks on as the dragon breathes his last and then proceeds to help himself to the dragon's treasures of gold, silver and diamonds. Exhausted, Eustace falls asleep on his pile of loot, awaiting the end of the storm. When he awakens, he notices a dragon's claw extending into the air above his head and to the left. Two streams of smoke float above his head. He sees another claw to his right side. Convinced he is surrounded by two dragons, he makes a run for it. Just before he dives into a pool of water to escape, he notices his own reflection staring back at him. Eustace has become a dragon. His desires for the dragon's treasure transformed him into a dragon.

It's such a good story that I had to retell it; but the important part, the part that concerns us, is how Eustace was turned back into a boy. The majestic lion, Aslan, finds Eustace in the dark of night and instructs him to follow him. He leads Eustace to a garden surrounding a wondrously clear pool of water. As Eustace the dragon enters the pool, Aslan tells him to undress. Eustace realizes that, as a dragon, he is able to shed his skin, as does a snake. He repeats the process three times. Each time, the dragon scales are easily laid aside, but each time Eustace looks over his body, he is dismayed to find he is still a dragon. Aslan determines to do the work himself. He will have to undress Eustace. The dragon, now desperate, lies on his back as Aslan's claws cut to his very heart, disrobing him of his dragon skin and laying it aside. When his work is done, Aslan throws Eustace into the pool of water. Having just endured the deep wounds of Aslan's claws, the plunge is painful, but only for a moment. He emerges from the water as Eustace, the boy. His dragon scales now completely removed by Aslan's fierce, but merciful claws.

The image of Eustace's "descaling" may help us understand Peter. We have observed Peter's struggle to cast off his shadow-self – the deeply held assumptions and beliefs that prevent him from seeing himself, the world and God the way Jesus does. Jesus's journey with Peter was a deep-heart surgery – an excision of the shadow-self. Peter did not become perfect. Rather, he became aware of the shadow-self and his need to continually disrobe. Peter's encounter with Cornelius reveals a transformed man – an apostle who is now beginning to see himself and others as Jesus does. Aware of the danger of his shadow-self, he now responds quickly to the Spirit's promptings, uniting harmoniously with Jesus's purposes.

Before diving into that story, pause with me a moment. A question that often comes to my mind as I contemplate the path of spiritual growth is, "Is all this necessary?" Must I really pursue transformation in areas I'm hardly aware of? Is conformity to Jesus this all-consuming? The reader can likely guess my answers to those questions. Rather than answer them explicitly, I ask you to ask yourself those questions. How deep am I willing to let Aslan's claw cut? How close to my heart? Am I desperate enough to lie on my back while he performs surgery?

How deep am I willing to let Aslan's claw cut?
How close to my heart? Am I desperate enough to
lie on my back while he performs surgery?

Peter and the Early Christians as Jews

Contemporary Christianity is so thoroughly Gentile (all ethnicities) that we easily overlook the deeply Jewish nature of the first Christian community. When we read our Bibles carefully, it shows up in ways that surprise us. Think of the apostles who regularly observed the hourly prayers of the temple. They saw no need to divert from their Jewish practices.

When Paul makes his way back to Jerusalem, the apostles are anxious to share that thousands of Jews have come to the faith and all are zealous for the law! Because of rumors that Paul is teaching the Gentiles to break the law, the apostles exhort him to demonstrate his loyalty to the law by taking a vow, shaving his head and performing various rituals outlined in the Old Testament (Acts 21:20–26). And Paul did it! He felt it important to prove to all the Jerusalem believers that he kept the law of Moses and the customs of the Jews.

Peter's vision is another key indicator of how deeply the roots of the Christian faith are planted in Jewish soil. The vision is of "all kinds of animals." There must be both clean and unclean animals there – those allowed by Jewish law and those prohibited. Somehow, Peter knew that he was being asked to kill and eat meat that was not kosher. He finds the suggestion appalling. "By no means, Lord; for I have never eaten anything that is common or unclean!"

Dietary restrictions of a religious nature are unfamiliar to most of us. I got a lesson in their importance to religious people as I interacted with Muslims. Often, before accepting an invitation to my home, they would ask if my wife ever served or cooked anything with pork. I quickly learned that my answer determined their response to my invitation. They were unwilling to accept an offer of hospitality if it meant defiling themselves through eating forbidden meat.

Peter had been on the road with Jesus for three years. In the Gospels Jesus declares all foods clean. Right? It's in Mark 7:19. So we might envision Jesus and Peter enjoying a ham and cheese sandwich by the Sea of Galilee. Not! The Gospels were written several decades after Jesus's death. They had the advantage of hindsight. Peter and the apostles are still working it all out. The fact that Peter had never eaten non-kosher food tells us he is a staunchly committed Jew, deeply loyal to the law and customs of the Jewish people. The vision is asking him to break with a lifelong communal discipline of eating kosher – an ordinance given by God to Moses. Peter cannot fathom it.

Let that sink in a minute. The lead apostle is required to release much of his cultural upbringing. It is another layer of "deculturation" in which the confines of one's own culture are released to make room for the values and traditions of another. The fact that Peter has to return to this station of his formation again and again may show us that it's more important than we have understood. If we fail to grasp the depth of transformation asked of Peter, we will be taken unaware when it is asked of us.

The lead apostle is required to release much of his cultural upbringing. It is another layer of "deculturation" in which the confines of one's own culture are released to make room for the values and traditions of another.

It was a vision. Acts calls it an *ekstasis* – Peter experienced it as though it were real, but he never does what is asked of him. He never "kills and eats."

The vision of the four-cornered sheet (possibly representing the four points of the compass) is taken up three times leaving Peter to wonder what it means.

Try to forget that you already know what it means. Put yourself in Peter's shoes. Here's a guy who has had almost all his presuppositions rescripted over the course of a three-year journey with Jesus. He has developed a reflex, thanks to the stark wake-up call of his own denial of Jesus. He has begun to suspect his own beliefs, the ideas that he assumes are right. He knows that Jesus tends to push him out of his comfort zone into new ventures of faith and obedience. This vision is clearly Jesus speaking to him. But what is he saying? What does he want? Peter is ready, but he can't quite put it together. Until he overhears the men who have just arrived from Caesarea.

Peter is travelling beyond Jerusalem, strengthening the small communities of Jesus-followers. Joppa and Lydda are Jewish communities, but Caesarea, the capital of the Roman province, is teaming with Gentile pagans. It is not coincidental that Peter is in Joppa, which is the place where Jonah started his flight from God to Tarshish (Jonah 1:3). The author of Acts (Luke, the Gentile) may be signaling God's extravagant compassion for "the nations" – a theme which dominates Jonah's story. Note also that Peter is sometimes referred to as the Son of Jonah (Matt 16:17).

Can you imagine Peter peering off the roof of Simon the Tanner's house? He's delirious with hunger, confused by a vision, and he sees three men, one of whom is a uniformed Roman soldier. At that moment, the Spirit says to Peter: "Check it out! Three men are looking for you." Say no more. Peter gets it immediately. He knows what that vision means. He realizes that to be obedient to the vision, he will have to break with long-standing customs of his people. Remarkably, he does so with no hesitation, no argument with God, no excuse that he's famished and it wouldn't be good to make a big decision now. The three men become his guests. That in itself is a violation of Jewish customs. But Peter recalls that Jesus was fond of eating with sinners, of staying in the home of Samaritans. Peter is on the way to a new station of spiritual formation – a new venture in obedience and soul-forming discipleship. He's dropping his cultural guardrails and, in the process, opening the gate of Jesus's kingdom to the nations. It's beautiful to watch.

Curious Cornelius

How does Cornelius happen? Seriously, how can you explain the phenomenon of Cornelius? He's a captain of an elite Roman division of soldiers. He's entrusted with protecting the Roman governor in his embattled occupation of Israel. He must have shrewdly navigated the politics of the empire. He must have enjoyed a lifestyle of wealth and power. He would have been able to isolate himself behind the walls of the imperial Roman community, avoiding contact with the locals. Yet, he is a God-fearer – the title applied to those who worship the God of Israel but have not yet embraced a Jewish identity through circumcision. Even more impressive, his family is reputed for the same God-fearing qualities. He's not quiet about it either. At least two of the marks of Jewish piety are attributed to him. He gives generously to the poor and he prays. In fact, he is praying at the normal time of Jewish ritual prayers (3:00 in the afternoon) when he is also given a vision. Somehow, unknown to us, God is working in Cornelius's heart, preparing him. Then God also prepares a messenger – the right apostle (literally, "sent one") – to help Cornelius into the kingdom.

Cornelius intrigues me. He joins many other non-Jews strewn through the story of Scripture who are uniquely prepared by God. On a personal level, he provokes some introspection as I review my career of witness to Jesus in places where he is little known. In the early years, I spent a great deal of time in personal evangelism, trying to persuade people to believe in Jesus. After some time, I realized that there were dozens of people, if not hundreds, making their way to churches, websites, media outlets, etc., asking to be taught the truths of the gospel – to be discipled. My frustration at the minimal response to my evangelism opened my eyes to recognize that God has his own ways of reaching people. I still believe in evangelism, but it began to make a lot more sense for me to follow up with those who had already experienced something of God's call and grace and were looking for more. That's Cornelius. He's still present in our world, still asking questions, still hoping some of us "mature" folks will spend some time with him and help him along the journey of spiritual formation.

I love that Cornelius bows down to Peter to worship him when he enters his house. That's not there by accident. It gives Peter the chance to brandish his spiritual integrity as a foundation stone in the early Gentile Christian community – "Get up! I'm a man too!"

It's in Cornelius's house that we get Peter's new understanding of the vision: "God has shown me that I should not call any person common or unclean." I suppose Peter never broke his kosher code, although we don't know. We do know that he never considered any person unclean and that was the lesson he took from the vision.

Peter doesn't conceal his Jewishness. He's true to who he is. The way he expresses it seems abrupt, even rude, to our ears. "You yourselves know how unlawful it is for a Jew to associate with or to visit anyone of another nation . . ." (Acts 10:28). Whoa, Pete, maybe you should take some lessons in how to win friends and influence people! But we miss the point. Peter has let go of his previous understanding. He's there, fully present, ready to declare the whole counsel of God to these Gentiles – Romans who maliciously and militarily occupy his homeland. Pretty impressive. We're taught to think of Paul as the apostle to the Gentiles. Remember that before Paul was ministering to the household of Caesar from prison, the Galilean fisherman had already blazed that trail in Caesarea in a most surprising way.

I like to think of Peter in the Acts stories as a graduate student of spiritual formation. He's way past the introductory lessons. The terrain of rescripting expectations, letting go of previously cherished beliefs, is now familiar to him. He's an eager student making rapid progress. The vision on the Joppa rooftop might well have been a major obstacle for most of us. Peter understood the vision to mean letting go of some deeply cherished beliefs and practices – ideas that had rooted in his being through years of identity formation in his family and among his people. To deculturate is no easy challenge. Yet Peter is up to the task. He gets it quickly and moves immediately in obedience, fulfilling the great commission and establishing the new entity of the "Jew-plus-Gentile" body of Christ. We can learn a lot from Peter and we'll delve into that further below.

Ripple Effects

Picture a reverse time machine that would allow travel back in time surveying the history of the Jesus movement across various cultures, languages and places. As you wind back through time, the events would narrow as if swirling through a funnel. As you come into the book of Acts, Paul's apostolic team would figure large. Further still, we would see the scene in the home of Cornelius. It is a lightning strike to the heart of the Jewish identity of the church, splitting open the rock of Peter's confession as the river of God's grace spills over on people of every tribe and tongue. The ripple effects of this simple preaching trip, validated by the outpoured Spirit in the home of a Roman centurion, are still radiating around the world. Because Peter was prepared to move into uncharted territory, the world changed.

Paul was known as the apostle to the Gentiles; nevertheless, Paul did not arise out of a vacuum. Events had prepared the way for him. The early community of Jesus-followers awoke to the fact that the cross of Christ effected a cosmic redemption that demanded a gospel suited for all peoples and nations. The walls of cultural differentiation were broken down by the gospel. It was not an immediate awakening. Luke, the author of Acts, gives the sense that Peter's persuasiveness and pedigree as an early disciple plays the lead role in this gradual realization. Because it is so critical, there are three, perhaps four, tellings of the Cornelius story in the book of Acts. The first is the actual event (Acts 10), related in great detail by the author. Then there is Peter's relating the story to the church in Jerusalem (Acts 11). He had some obstacles to overcome as a faction of the church insisted on the necessity of circumcision and adherence to the Jewish traditions. It's revealing that they criticized Peter, not for preaching to the Gentiles, but for eating with them! The gospel revelation, at its core, is about acceptance, reconciliation, fellowship, adoption, becoming part of the family of God. Is it any wonder that the old practices of restrictive table fellowship would have to be laid aside as the gospel penetrated every ethnicity and culture of the world? That may explain why Peter was given a vision of unclean animals.

The third telling of the Cornelius event is in Acts 15 – the pivotal chapter of Acts. Paul and Barnabas have returned to Jerusalem to report all that God has accomplished among the Gentiles. The pillars of the church are all in attendance, reviewing and deliberating on what is transpiring in Roman cities and towns. What happened at Cornelius's home through Peter, the Rock, supplied the standard by which the elders of Jerusalem would reluctantly accede to God's sovereign work among the Gentiles. Peter's inference, "We believe that we will be saved through the grace of the Lord Jesus, just as they will" (Acts 15:11), is unequivocal. He upholds the beauty and freedom of the gospel as well as the fact that all stand as equals at the foot of the cross. The fourth telling of the event is by James as he brings the council to its conclusion. The decision is made. The die is cast. So we owe our faith, in large measure, to Peter. His radical following of Jesus into unknown territory opened the way for you and me to come under the protective covering of Jesus's atoning death and resurrection. He really did hold the keys. Thank you, Peter, the Rock!

Exiting the Stage of the Biblical Story

It is puzzling that Peter, after the Jerusalem Council, virtually disappears from the pages of Scripture. Paul's apostolic travels become the focus of the Acts narrative – his letters to various churches of Asia Minor and Europe figure large in our understanding of the gospel. Peter, much later in life, authors two letters which we will consider in epilogue 2. Nevertheless, he virtually disappears from consideration in the biblical story. Even when Paul visits Jerusalem (Acts 21), James is mentioned but Peter is not. Why? Was he still there?

We are not entirely at a loss as we try to fill in the blanks of Peter's more mature years. We have bits and pieces of church history as well as the arc of

Peter's spiritual development that allow us to surmise how he ended his years on earth.

Tradition holds that Peter died as a martyr outside Rome. That's a long way from Jerusalem and a very different ethnic and cultural context. If that tradition can be trusted, it begs us to consider what factors might have led Peter to such a distant location to end his days. Our minds do not resist the idea of Paul's travels culminating in Rome. His erudition and linguistic skill allow us to envision him moving freely among the Roman provinces. We know that story and anticipate that he went further still, to Spain. But for Peter, the Aramaic-speaking fisherman from Galilee, moving his livelihood to Rome, the urbane and sophisticated capital of the empire, stretches the boundaries of plausibility.

What's the story? Could it have happened? And how? We don't know, but indulge me as I attempt to paint the picture.

Michael Card suggests that Peter "disappears into a sea of these so-called unclean."[1] Before his arrival in Rome, the tradition suggests he moved first to Antioch, then possibly to Corinth and finally to Rome. His death by crucifixion took place outside Rome, in roughly the same timeframe as Paul's martyrdom. Fathers of the church, including Eusebius, Irenaeus and Tertullian, left us this record.[2] We know of Peter's first visit to Antioch from Paul's writings. We'll look at it in the next chapter as the final station of his spiritual formation. So the tradition of the church fits what we know from Scripture in terms of Peter's whereabouts, though admittedly, for critical historians, it is the subject of much debate.

What concerns us most is how it fits with the arc of Peter's journey of spiritual formation. He must have had a good gig in Jerusalem. Thousands of Jews had believed (Acts 21:20). The horrific destruction of Jerusalem in AD 70 was still years in the future. Peter might well have set himself up in the holy city as the Christ-appointed keeper of the keys – the bishop-apostle. Apparently, he did not.

With his rooftop vision and the Cornelius event echoing in his mind, Peter set out. He left Jerusalem. He had already begun to travel and preach in the Acts narrative. We find him in Joppa and Lydda with an unexpected excursion which opened his eyes to what he should have seen, but could not see, before. Once he saw it, there was no un-seeing it. Peter didn't have to be nudged again.

---

1. Card, *Fragile Stone*, 175.
2. Helyer, *Life and Witness of Peter*, 276.

His journey led him through multiple cities of the Roman world, serving his scattered Jewish compatriots. He also became a shepherd to many Gentiles who were cascading into Christ just as he observed in Cornelius and his household.

You may recall that Paul spent fifteen days with Peter in Jerusalem (Gal 1:18–20). The word Paul chose to describe his visit (1:18) indicates it wasn't a social call. Paul went intentionally to "get to know" Peter. Doubtless, Peter's firsthand experience of following Jesus provided much-needed background for Paul's understanding of the gospel, honed by his three-year sojourn in the wilderness of Arabia (1:17). We wonder if Paul's clear call to the Gentiles intrigued Peter, perhaps stimulating his thinking in a similar direction. If he was slower than Paul in embracing the imperative of taking the gospel to all nations, he was no less committed to it after he grasped it. He launched out in that direction, never looking back.

Peter likely recalled the basin and towel that his Master used to such great effect. He saw himself, not as a sedentary keeper of the keys, but as a shepherd, sent to seek and care for the lost sheep of his master. He recalled, I suppose, Jesus's delight in a conversation with an immoral Samaritan woman, his marvel at the faith of a Roman soldier, and his satisfaction that a renegade Jew-turned-tax-collector (Zacchaeus) came home. Peter knew that the Good Shepherd leaves the ninety-nine and goes in search of the lost one. In light of what transpired with Cornelius, Peter needed no further directive concerning where to go searching for lost sheep. He was moved by a deep desire to bring the "other sheep" to Jesus – the ones from outside the Jewish fold (John 10:16).

Peter's Reorientation and Ours

Let us attempt to move from Peter's world to ours, to appropriate his reorientation to our lives. It's no easy task. We are different from Peter as individuals, and his context is far removed from ours. Nevertheless, as Peter's story is Spirit-inspired Scripture, let us dive in.

We should ban the thought from our minds that Peter, because of his restoration by Jesus (John 21) or the amazing results of his preaching at Pentecost, reached a point where he was no longer challenged, no longer grew. For those of us who are "professional" believers, the trap is exceedingly subtle. As we teach and lead others, we unconsciously move ourselves into the category of "maturity." That's a trap if we understand maturity as a stoppage or even a slowing down of change. Maturity should mean we quickly realize our need of change and respond to the promptings of the Spirit willingly and freely.

A prominent Christian publication recently featured a friend of mine, describing his fruitful ministry. I admit a tinge of envy. Ouch! It struck the chord of my own hope for fruitfulness and, what is more difficult to admit, a desire for notoriety. The emotional reaction alerted me to a sinful reflex on the one hand, but perhaps also a calling that lay dormant, now being stirred again. I'm still working out that latter part. But the point is, I'm not overly shocked by my own egotistic inclinations. I have had them a long time and maturity allows me to recognize them. Maturity also points me in a possible direction of growth. I am eager to move in that direction, testing it in my conversations with my spouse and other friends. If, however, I suppress or deny the trace of envy, then the opportunity for growth will disappear. Peter learned to recognize when his inclinations were out of step with the Spirit of Jesus and he eagerly moved to learn the new lesson, despite the difficulty.

Emotions are key in identifying opportunities for growth. Disappointment, anger, bitterness, envy, passion, longing, hope . . . all are human responses that act as a spiritual meter. Rather than suppress them or deny their power, try bringing them to the surface in your conversations with spiritual friends. Describe the situation and your emotional response as clearly as you can. It helps to journal it. Then ask the Lord and your friends what he could be saying.

Emotions are key in identifying opportunities for growth. Disappointment, anger, bitterness, envy, passion, longing, hope . . . all are human responses that act as a spiritual meter.

Second, we can almost trace a line along Peter's journey so as to anticipate this lesson. Though it surprised him, it didn't surprise us at all. We knew Peter had nationalistic expectations of the Messiah. We knew his vision of Jesus's kingdom had to be vastly expanded from the shrunken vision he had absorbed from his religious and social network. The Cornelius event was the final brush stroke of the master artist, painting the landscape of a new understanding of the kingdom. God did not begrudgingly permit the Gentiles to occupy the margins of the church. They were fully and honorably included as sons and daughters. No hierarchy. In fact, God chose and blessed Israel *for the purpose* of blessing the nations (Gen 12:3). So naturally, they were given the Spirit, "just as we were."

Peter's spiritual transformation was rooted in his context. It drew from his upbringing, his culture and his education, often challenging it or reshaping it. If we have ears to hear, Peter will serve us masterfully, reorienting and broadening our vision beyond the bounds of our culture and background. Peter thought he had it right in his Jewish upbringing. Like him, we are taught to hold our lines and positions, fearing the slippery slope that threatens our way of life. Peter had to drop his ethnocentrism. He had to lay aside Jewish nationalism. In Acts 10, he is moving beautifully in that direction.

What about us? Are our positions prohibiting our embrace of people that God may be calling to himself? God is not changing us merely so that we'll be better people. Being formed in the Jesus way is about fulfilling our personal and collective mission. He's changing us into the image of Jesus who sought and saved the lost. To be specific, has my position on some heated social issues blunted my willingness to move in obedience to love the mentally ill, the person of fluid gender identity, the Muslim, the Jew, the Hindu, the Sikh, the immigrant, the conservative, the liberal, the wealthy, the poor, the white woman, the black man? Being formed in the way of Jesus will always push us to conformity with the purpose of the Father-Son-Spirit God, extending his embrace of love in our world.

Internalizing Spiritual Reflexes Modeled by Peter

In response to this chapter, take a few moments to journal about the kind of people you struggle with – the ones you avoid when you see them on the street, the ones your find difficult to listen to. We all have them. Look at Peter's embrace of Cornelius – a Roman officer of a military occupation – and ask if you need to adapt. Make it specific. Peter invited them to be his guests. Then he got up and went with them and entered a Gentile home. All of it was unthinkable to a pious Jew! So how can I follow Peter's lead? Again, sharing this in your small community of spiritual friends will reinforce the lesson. It also invites them to give input or reflect on their own journey.

One last application: Peter must have left Jerusalem, traveling on to Antioch, Corinth and Rome. His letter was to the scattered believers of Asia Minor, both Jews and Gentiles. I admit that we can't be certain of this, but it appears that Peter moved out of a well-established ministry where he was "top of the heap" and accepted to serve among the Gentiles and scattered Jewish communities of Asia Minor and Europe. If this is an accurate reading of Peter's life, the man refused to be satisfied with what he had achieved. Like Paul, he pushed out into new frontiers. He left the place of comfort and embraced challenge and newness.

I confess, travel has been a big part of my history. I've lived nearly thirty years in foreign cultures. So I'm intrigued by this aspect of Peter's life. However, my most difficult move was not to a foreign culture, but back to my home culture. That move pulled out many of my security props. For our purposes, the focus is not geography per se. Changing places almost always extracts us from our comfort zone, which gets us closer to the heart of the matter. So ask yourself these questions:

- Where is my comfort zone? What do I do regularly that makes me feel value and worth?
- Is it time to hand that off?
- Given Peter's example, what is my next frontier? A change in location? A shift in my social engagements? A personal risk as I move out of my comfort zone?
- Is laying aside my security the next step in my spiritual journey?
- Am I willing to lower my status?

Again, journaling your response accompanied by conversation with spiritual friends can help clarify the way forward.

In the next chapter, we get another window into Peter's ongoing growth as a mature disciple. You might be surprised at how costly his commitment to growth continues to be.

12

The Confrontation

A Disciple's Humility

"Yes," said the fox. "I'll explain. To me, you are just a little boy like any other, like a hundred thousand other little boys. I have no need of you and you have no need of me. To you I am a fox like any other, like a hundred thousand other foxes. But if you tame me, you and I, we will have created a relationship, and so we will need one another. You will be unique in the world for me . . . If you were to tame me, my whole life would be so much more fun. I would come to know the sound of your footstep, and it would be different from all the others. At the sound of any other footstep I would be down in my hole in the earth as quick as you like. But your footstep would be like music to my ears, and I would come running up out of my hole, quick as you like."

Antoine de Saint-Exupéry, *The Little Prince*

Galatians 2:11–14

But when Cephas [Peter] came to Antioch, I opposed him to his face, because he stood condemned. For before certain men came from James, he was eating with the Gentiles; but when they came he drew back and separated himself, fearing the circumcision party. And the rest of the Jews acted hypocritically along with him, so that even Barnabas was led astray by their hypocrisy. But when I saw that their conduct was not in step with the truth of the gospel, I said to Cephas before them all, "If you, though a Jew, live like a Gentile and not like a Jew, how can you force the Gentiles to live like Jews?"

2 Peter 3:14–18

Therefore, beloved, since you are waiting for these, be diligent to be found by him without spot or blemish, and at peace. And count the patience of our Lord as salvation, just as our beloved brother Paul also wrote to you according to the wisdom given him, as he does in all his letters when he speaks in them of these matters. There are some things in them that are hard to understand, which the ignorant and unstable twist to their own destruction, as they do the other Scriptures. You therefore, beloved, knowing this beforehand, take care that you are not carried away with the error of lawless people and lose your own stability. But grow in the grace and knowledge of our Lord and Savior Jesus Christ. To him be the glory both now and to the day of eternity. Amen.

[IN ANTIOCH]

Being here is a breath of fresh air . . . people are engaged, seeking Jesus without all the synagogue stuff! No one is looking over their shoulder and God's love comes through loud and clear. They've started calling themselves "little Christs." Ha! I'm loving it. Barnabas and Paul and the others are doing an amazing job!

Watching non-Jews get the gospel helps me see how it can change the whole world. It makes sense that Jesus told us to go and disciple all nations.

Uh-oh. Oh man, what are they doing here? Rabbi Harun and some of his people. So I'm not the only one to visit the Gentile church.

What'll they say? Man! Seeing those guys puts me right back in the middle of all that. I feel it in my gut.

They're checking this place out . . . and here I am, enjoying the table fellowship. Guess I'm between a rock and a hard place.

[SPEAKING TO HIS FRIENDS AT THE TABLE]

"Excuse me for a minute, will ya? Some friends from down south just came in. I wanna go over and say hi."

[MAKING HIS WAY TO HIS JERUSALEM FRIENDS]

I see their eyes scanning . . . heads nodding . . . wrinkled foreheads . . . whispers.

I know exactly what they're thinking. I've heard it all before.

If I play my cards right, maybe I can persuade them . . . I speak their language. But if they see me taking the other side, against them, it's all over. Yeah. They know I'm one of their own . . . I don't wanna lose that tactical advantage. The rabbi could make a lot of trouble back in Jerusalem. It'll take a little time, but I'll work with him.

After all we've been through in Jerusalem, I can't risk alienating my leaders. I'll pull back a bit . . . mentor my Jerusalem people to avoid them making a big scene. The last thing I want to do is lose Rabbi Harun. Besides, Antioch is in good hands.

[LATER]

Paul sent word that he wants to talk to me. Wonder what that's about??

Centering Our Tribe

St. Exupery's delightful account of *The Little Prince* features a fox (a typical enemy) imploring the young prince to see him differently, to "tame him." It would require the young prince to discover a new vision of his antagonist – to think, act and feel differently towards him. He would move from being an enemy to a friend, from a threat to a companion. The fox issues a challenge, inviting the prince to tame him, radically changing their relationship from avoidance and exclusion to mutual enjoyment.

We tend to evaluate events and people through the lens of the way we were raised. We are socialized during our formative years, developing our views of what is right and wrong, what is wise and foolish, what is worthwhile and wasteful. Those views are woven into our surroundings, our people, our tribe. Many collectivist cultures know the concept of "tribes" well. Western Europeans and Americans are generally die-hard individualists, but we also belong to tribes, meaning we identify as part of a social group. We rarely question that group's values because they conform to our own. Those outside our tribe represent a threat, making it difficult, if not impossible, to step outside our tribe and see others empathetically. To do so, we must first see ourselves as others see us. The different perspective is shocking. I'll share a couple of examples and then tie this back to Peter.

I was a young cross-cultural minister and I had heroes. They were the older generation who labored decades in the resistant areas of Muslim North Africa. A recent breakthrough had seen the establishment of a thriving church in Algeria. I recall gathering with the older, more experienced members of our mission to listen to their stories of years of patient sowing and how now, at long last, prayers were being answered. There was a harvest. My respect for my senior colleagues deepened and I felt affirmed that I was on the right path, that patient labor and prayer would eventually produce a harvest. It never occurred to me to question whether these heroes of mine were the change-agents that brought about this breakthrough.

Years later, I had the opportunity to hear the story of the "breakthrough" that established a thriving church in Algeria. This time, the story was recounted by one of the Algerian pastors. I listened intently, expecting to hear the names of my missionary heroes whom I believed to have been "key players" in the birth of the Algerian church. To my surprise, the speaker related the history of his church with no reference to foreign cross-cultural ministers. After his talk, I approached him and asked about some of these individuals. He was aware of one or two of them, but unaware of others. He expressed gratitude for their service, but it was apparent that he did not view them as "key players." They were peripheral to the history of the church as he saw it.

The realization hit me hard. Again, these were my vocational role-models, the people whose path I followed. I aspired to be like them. Suddenly I realized that they were little more than a footnote to the history of the Algerian church. Of course, they never claimed to be "key players" – it was an assumption on my part. No doubt, had they been there listening to the Algerian pastor, they would have rejoiced at every aspect of his account. Nevertheless, the point for me was how easily I moved them into the focus of consideration. They were my tribe. I made them central and marginalized others, without even realizing I was doing so. In reality, my tribe was peripheral. I'm not saying God didn't use these heroes of mine. He certainly did. However, the central role I attributed to them was inaccurate. More importantly, it was unfair to the Algerian Christians. I had to listen empathetically to those outside my tribe to get that.

A second and more recent example arises from the turbulent days of demonstrations around the death of George Floyd, a Black man, at the hands of police (Summer 2020). A group of Christian ministers held a panel discussion on race relations. I was eager to attend, hoping for an even-handed treatment of the topic that was so prevalent in the news media. The White facilitator spoke first, sharing his hopes for this panel discussion. He introduced the participants including both Black and White Christian leaders. Then he proceeded to ask the White pastors what they anticipated from this forum. We all listened for the first twenty minutes of the hour-long discussion while the White pastors shared their hopes for race relations in the American church.

Frankly, I found that bizarre. I hope you see the irony. It was Black people who were being killed unjustly. A tsunami of demonstrations had swept across the country claiming that Black lives did not hold the same value as White lives in a predominantly White society. If we truly desired to understand the experience of Blacks in America, wouldn't we listen to our African American pastors first?! I was also baffled that none of the White pastors deferred to their African American colleagues. They all felt it was legitimate for them to speak first on the topic of race relations in the church.

I'm not suggesting that being White should exclude a Christian leader from discussions of race relations. All have a place at the table. However, in that critical moment in our nation, those Christian leaders had an opportunity to center the Black experience by listening empathetically and learning experientially. They missed a chance to give preference to the other. Prioritizing the White pastors confirmed Black suspicion that their plight is not heard, nor is their oppression felt in the White church. It was a revealing moment, demonstrating that the American church has a long road ahead in pursuit of repairing race relations.

But what does this have to do with Peter?

What's Up with Peter?

Jesus has been progressively deconstructing Peter's core beliefs and assumptions. Peter often held these unconsciously. He was socialized in this way, discipled by his Jewish society. One of the themes of Peter's spiritual formation is ethnocentrism. Peter is reflexively loyal to his own tribe; he centers his own people in his understanding of Jesus's kingdom. Jesus began to challenge Peter's beliefs years earlier as he interacted with Samaritans and Roman soldiers. The experience in Cornelius's home dealt a deathblow to Peter's centering of the Jewish people in his vision of Jesus's kingdom. Nevertheless, in Antioch, Peter is forced to confront, yet again, the remnants of his tendency to center his own people and the implications for his call as an apostle of Jesus. The confrontation in Antioch may well represent the nail in the coffin of Peter's ethnocentricity. His master's class in "deculturation" continues.

I suspect Peter's retreat from table fellowship with the Gentiles was not premeditated. He didn't plan to withdraw from breaking bread with them. He was taken unawares. Jewish people of influence showed up from Jerusalem. Peter had to negotiate in his own mind what steps he should take in response. He wanted, I suppose, to preserve the peace in the Jerusalem church. Doing so required upholding the Jewish traditions and Mosaic dietary laws. Peter pulled back to keep the peace. He must have felt that he had more to gain in holding to his position of influence with the Jerusalem Jews than he did by an unguarded participation in Gentile fellowship. He assumed, probably unconsciously, that his Jewish tribe was the centerpiece of God's purposes. His Jewish belonging caused him to look through Jewish lenses. He still could not completely lay them aside. He needed some help from a bold brother. Enter Paul.

But before we talk about Paul, you may be asking if this event should really be considered a station in Peter's spiritual formation. You may be tempted to tune out of this conversation. Wasn't this an adjustment? Did what transpired in Antioch really shape Peter into the image of Christ? Wasn't it more like a policy shift than a heart transformation? Is this really the stuff of spiritual formation?

I'm glad you asked.

In this book, we've made the case that Jesus forms us spiritually. We respond to his action, but it *is* his action. Like Eustace, we have to lie down on our backs, desperate for Aslan to strip off the dragon skin. Our spiritual formation is not so much about doing things – disciplines, studies, sermons, mission trips, lectures, etc. – nor is it about producing or acquiring. It is about being stripped, laying aside, leaving behind the old – our old vision, our former understanding. It is more about losing than gaining. Of course, we do gain, but we lose first and then receive.

Our spiritual formation is not so much about doing things –
disciplines, studies, sermons, mission trips, lectures, etc. – nor
is it about producing or acquiring. It is about being stripped,
laying aside, leaving behind the old – our old vision, our
former understanding. It is more about losing than gaining.

Peter's journey reveals just how deeply we hold to our old way of life. He's a mature apostle, fruitful in ministry, discipled by Jesus himself. Yet he needs the help of another brother to see himself for who he really is. His core beliefs still cling to him. His assumptions are the colored lenses through which he sees the world. They influence his actions. Jesus is determined that Peter will release those beliefs and embrace the new reality of his kingdom. He never stops working in Peter, and he will continually work in us as well if we are alert to his movement, aware of his ways.

Paul Is No Pushover!

To get a sense of the crucial nature of this confrontation between Paul and Peter, it's important to consider Paul's accusations, which are plain in the text of Galatians 2. Remember, this is Peter, the keeper of the keys, the leader of the apostles of Christ. The fact that Paul could say these things about one so highly esteemed tells us a lot about how Jesus views leadership and how we, if we are leaders, must view ourselves. I find it amazing that this confrontation between the two key leaders of the early church is preserved for us in Scripture.

Here are Paul's accusations:

Peter stood condemned (Gal 2:11). This is the man that Jesus had reinstated, instructing him to care for his sheep. He played the lead role at Pentecost and in the Jerusalem church. Yet, for Paul, it was clear. Peter's stance was condemnable. He was clearly in the wrong. There's a crack in the rock!

He feared the circumcision party (Gal 2:12). I can't imagine a more damaging and disqualifying accusation for an apostle of Jesus than the "fear of man." Peter had shown himself to be incredibly bold, facing down the temple elite, confronting them with the fact that they crucified the Messiah. Yet, in this instance, Paul, not one to mince his words, states that Peter is acting out of fear.

He influenced other leaders, leading them astray (Gal 2:13). This one must have been the kicker for Paul because Barnabas had been his mentor, the "son of encouragement," who brought Paul to Antioch to launch his public ministry. Now even Barnabas is being led astray because of Peter's lack of principle!

He was out of step with the gospel (Gal 2:14). Can you imagine? The keeper of the keys of the kingdom is out of line? His actions do not correspond to the truth of the gospel that Jesus gave his life to secure. This is weighty. We can almost feel the timbers that hold the structure of the early church together creaking and groaning under the weight of this confrontation. Will the gospel be lost? Will the church survive?

Paul "said to Cephas before them all" (Gal 2:14). Paul was "type A." He wasn't one to keep things quiet. My preference would have been a backroom conversation. Had I been in Paul's place, I would have offered Peter a chance to explain himself privately, deferring to his pedigree as an early apostle. Not Paul! He smells blood in the water and he's in attack mode. Peter's actions compromise the gospel in a public action with public consequences so he goes for a public rebuke. Paul pulls no punches.

Paul doesn't tell us how Peter responded. I would love to know and I'll tell you what I think below; but first, consider the weightiness of these accusations. Peter is being publicly shamed. I confess that when I read this account, I don't like it. My identification with Peter makes me want to say, "Come on Paul. You've been hard-headed yourself a few times. Take a more humble approach and let's try to resolve this thing amicably. Show some respect to Jesus's man."

One would expect the early church to split over this confrontation. Antioch would become the Pauline denomination and Jerusalem would be the Petrine denomination. Public and shameful confrontations throughout history, not unlike this one, have been resolved by denominations taking the names of their founders who were considered heretics by their accusers. Paul's accusations are no less weighty than those. The fact that we do not have a church of the Paulites and one of the Peterites tells us something about Peter's response. Surely if Peter had bristled and rejected Paul's accusation, Paul would have told us about that in recounting the story. The fact that he does not suggests that Peter accepts the rebuke. He allows himself to be corrected, publicly. Stunning!

What Do You Have to Say for Yourself, Peter?

In fact, we don't have to read between the lines of history. Peter voices his opinion on Paul. Near the end of his life, he writes a couple of letters to the "churches in exile" in Asia Minor. As he closes his final letter, the aged Peter, soon to die as a martyr, mentions Paul in passing.

This letter from Peter (2 Peter) is written to correct some things in the churches. Specifically, they have misunderstood the return of Christ. Paul was the one who said that Christ would return like a thief in the night (1 Thess 5:2), so this could be an opportunity for Peter to set the record straight. He could easily have said to the churches:

> You are aware that Paul and I have had conflict in the past on other matters. Back then, Paul insisted on freedom from the law. Now he is causing confusion regarding the Lord's return. To get the correct understanding, you churches will need to get your authoritative teaching from us – the true apostles, the original ones. Paul's teaching is convoluted and unhelpful. Allow me to give the proper understanding.

Peter could have taken advantage of the situation to incriminate Paul. I'm a little embarrassed to admit that this comes to my mind. Perhaps it reveals more about my reaction to conflict than it does Peter's. Nevertheless, I think you can imagine this kind of response from an offended church leader. In fact, you might have seen it. It serves to highlight the contrast of Peter's response.

Peter affirms Paul's teaching at the end of chapter 3, making explicit that Paul is not one of the false teachers that Peter has been writing against. He voices his agreement with Paul that the Lord's slowness to return should be understood as his patience, bringing salvation to more people. He embraces Paul as a "beloved brother." No bitterness or revenge here. He shows deference to Paul as one whom God has given wisdom. He grants that some of the things Paul writes are difficult to understand; however, rather than censure Paul, he recognizes that unstable people twist what Paul says, distorting it. It is they who will be judged. Last of all, Peter says these unstable people do this with the "other Scriptures." Implicitly, Peter is recognizing that all Paul's letters are Scripture and therefore his teaching is to be held in honor (3:16). We could not ask for a higher endorsement of Paul from Peter. There is no hint of anger or malice in Peter's words, only respect and brotherhood. How refreshing!

This must tell us something about how Peter received the rebuke back in Antioch. We can only surmise that he received it graciously. The keeper of the keys was called on the carpet in Antioch. He must have humbly confessed his error and asked for forgiveness. He acted in humility, ensuring the unity of the church across the many cultures, ethnicities and languages of the Mediterranean world. Why would an apostle do anything less? This apostle, now well-formed in the way of Jesus, was adequately prepared to accept correction. He had learned to be suspicious of his own deeply embedded beliefs and assumptions. It is a tremendous testimony to his spiritual formation. We are blessed to know you, Peter. Thank-you for such an honorable ministry!

The keeper of the keys was called on the carpet in Antioch. He must have humbly confessed his error and asked for forgiveness. He acted in humility, ensuring the unity of the church across the many cultures, ethnicities and languages of the Mediterranean world. Why would an apostle do anything less?

Why Is This Lesson Crucial?

We may wonder why this lesson is featured as the final station of Peter's spiritual formation. Is "ethnocentrism" Peter's besetting sin, or at least his primary character defect that must be eliminated? It doesn't seem like such a big deal, plus it may be hard for many of us to relate to. Let's try to put it in perspective.

Christians have come to understand the God of the Scriptures as one God in a triunity – a community of self-giving love and reciprocity. God didn't *become* a triunity so that he could save us (sometimes called the "economic Trinity"), it's *how he is in reality* (the "ontological Trinity") from eternity past. Christians came to understand that God existed for all eternity as a community of love, relating to and preferring the other. The first time humans got an inkling of this was when God created the universe. He placed humanity in an ideal setting for growth intellectually, relationally, aesthetically. His creation of humanity and the cosmos is best understood as an overflow of God's self-giving love, lavished primarily on human beings who were created in his image. When humankind chose to flee from the self-giving love of God, God did not give up the pursuit. He clothed Adam and Eve, covering the shame of their rebellion and promising that their enemy would be defeated – the crushing of the head of the serpent.

The unfolding biblical story reveals God's continual pursuit of a relationship with human beings. Though God is separate and unapproachable, he still shows up all through the story of the Bible, talking with the patriarchs and revealing himself continually to the prophets in both word and vision. This can only be explained by a God whose very nature is love. His deepest and most profound essence is self-giving love to others. It reached a climax when Jesus was born into this world as a human being – another overflow of the Trinitarian love community. He didn't insist on a throne and a fleet of servants. On the contrary, God went to the utter limit of love, identifying with the worst evil human alienation could conjure up. The gospel teaches that Jesus did that to restore humanity's relationship with God and to redeem creation. It's a stupendous claim. No wonder so many find it hard to believe!

What is God's intention for us as human beings? We can answer that in the little phrase from Genesis, "in the image of God." God wants his human beings to enter into the self-giving love relationship that he shares. His relational love was extended to human beings – creatures very different from himself, limited and fallen. For God, that is the good life, the beautiful life, the abundant life. So he doesn't rest until human beings are drawn back into that circle of relational love that both receives the eternal love of God and also extends it to other human beings.

His relational love was extended to human beings – creatures very different from himself, limited and fallen. For God, that is the good life, the beautiful life, the abundant life. So he doesn't rest until human beings are drawn back into that circle of relational love that both receives the eternal love of God and also extends it to other human beings.

If you need to read those last three paragraphs again, please do. They are critical to the message of this book. They also help us understand why Jesus dealt with Peter the way he did. He was constantly confronting Peter with himself, his core beliefs and assumptions, challenging those and inviting Peter to a new and different vision. Peter had to get rid of his old way of seeing the world because it was an obstacle to the free flow of God's love through him. Peter had to stop centering his own people, his own culture, his own traditions. Why? It was essential that the love of God flow through him as Jesus's apostle to people of all backgrounds, cultures, beliefs and ethnicities. It flows from God's identity, from who he is. If we are to be made in the image of the Father-Son-Spirit God, we will go through a similar process, decentering some of our cherished assumptions that impede the flow of God's love through us to others who are different.

Peter's Story, My Story

In my life, God has used my vocation of cross-cultural ministry to do some deep work in me as he did in Peter. As I read Peter's story, I recognize more fully what God's Spirit was doing, and is still doing, in my life. I realize that you may not be involved in cross-cultural ministry; still, bear with me. I think it will help you see how this might apply in your life as well. We'll discuss that further as we end the chapter.

As a young man, I was just getting into the Arabic language. I was an eager student then and even now, I still love languages. I had learned the word for "cross" because I was also eager to share the truth of Jesus with my friends. My mention of the word prompted a friend to share his utter disgust for "cross people" or "cross-ites." Even as a new Arabic student, I knew he was using a derivative of the word "cross" and I could tell he was using it negatively. I discovered he was using an Arabic word for Crusaders. I was only vaguely aware of the Crusades as a Roman Catholic attempt to retake the holy land from Muslim invaders. The Europeans emblazoned the cross on their shields and banners so they came to be known in Arabic as "the Cross-ites." I had no sense that the Crusades involved me in any way. In fact, I was shocked that the issue was still very much alive in his mind and that he viewed any attempt from "Christian Europe" (including the US) to change his culture and people as an extension of the Crusades. I realized my friend saw me through the lens of the Crusades. It took some time, but I came to realize that the association wasn't as far off base as I originally thought. I was motivated by a zeal similar to the Crusaders, although I didn't carry a sword. I tended to look at Christian influence territorially. Along with my Christian friends, I prayed and longed for the displacement of the dominant religious system with the one I represented. In order to share God's love in Christ with my Muslim friends, I needed to do some internal work. I needed to face how my own background had shaped me. That shadow-self would have to be laid aside, but it would not happen overnight! My understanding of God's purposes is still "under construction."

There are many other instances of God confronting me with the need to lay aside the "dragon skin" of my background and upbringing.

- Wealth is an issue: Because I have resources, I also have a degree of power that my friends of the other culture felt instinctively. They know I have leverage, influence, etc., that they will likely never enjoy. Believe me, that has been a wake-up call for a guy who views himself as strictly "middle class."

- Education: I enjoy a good education to a post-graduate level. Few of them can achieve that level of learning.
- Travel and mobility: I carry a recognized passport and am funded through a Western organization. That means I can easily move between countries and continents. They cannot.
- Outlook and ambition: I approach life with an optimism my friends in other cultures do not naturally share. Though I would like to think that optimism is due to my faith in God and my natural disposition, I now know that's not true. It grows out of my privilege as the son of an advanced nation which dominates the world economically and militarily, a land whose motto is "dream big." Don't get me wrong. My upbringing has also been a huge blessing, but I have to come to terms with the fact that it's a result of privilege, not a result of personal effort or moral superiority. My upbringing sets the trajectory for my expectations from life. I can "dream big" whereas others I am in touch with have to accept their lot in life.

The cultures I serve in act as a kind of spiritual mirror that enable me to see myself more clearly. There are other mirrors in my life. My marriage relationship continues to be a huge one. I can't imagine a more effective spiritual pruning than marriage, provided one pays attention to what God teaches through that relationship. I am blessed that my wife Stephanie wants to help me pursue transformation. As a result, she speaks up. She feels freer as we have gotten older, but she has always been able to tell it like it is, and I'm forever grateful. Of course, she is on her own journey of transformation, so that has helped me to receive from her. I have never felt she was seeking her own advantage against me. She tells me the truth and I know that I must deal with it.

Having kids is another mirror. I was slow to learn that I had to give my kids permission to tell me what they really thought. I wish I had done it earlier. They have to be secure, unafraid of speaking their mind, without fear of scolding or shame. That willingness to listen, to step outside ourselves and look back at ourselves through the eyes of another, is key to spiritual growth. Peter was willing to look at himself through the eyes of Paul and the Gentile believers there at Antioch. He must have realized Paul was telling him the truth. He had "ears to hear."

Peter's Humility and Ours

Now the challenging part: How do we carry this lesson from Peter into our own lives?

Peter unconsciously centered his own people, his own tribe. If our reading of this story is correct, the Spirit of Jesus wanted to rid him of that tendency, or at least to make him painfully aware of it so as to resist it in the future. To get a sense of this, make a list of the ways you identify socially. These include affiliations, loyalties, etc. Here's my sample list to help you get started. I am:

- Male, late 50's, heterosexual, married long-term, parent, grandparent
- American (from the south, originally), Caucasian (White)
- Middle income (though I realize I am in the top 5% globally)
- Well-educated (graduate degrees)
- Christian, evangelical
- Conservative fiscally
- Residency: mid-sized town, suburbia, home-owner
- English-speaker, well-read, high literacy

I should also list my political leanings, but I prefer to keep that to myself (smile). Anyway, you get the sense that I am asking you to profile yourself socially. When you've done that as thoroughly as you can, ask yourself the following questions:

- What percentage of my friends and family (the people I most often interact with) align with those characteristics?
- When is the last time I interacted intentionally with someone who shares less than 40 percent of them?
- How do I respond (emotionally, intellectually and physically) when someone who shares very few of those characteristics enters my sphere?

To illustrate, think of me, in the presence of a Mexican immigrant laborer, a "Black Lives Matter" activist or an Asian transgender person. How do I size them up? Do I posture myself to build a relationship or do I protect myself? Do I seek the security of my tribe – those who are more like me – or do I associate easily and freely with this person? Am I willing to "center" that person as an act of love, or do I resort to centering my tribe, assessing them by my tribal standards?

To be clear, I'm not asking you to transform yourself into this person's image. That would be inauthentic. We can't change our own skin. However, following Christ should equip us emotionally and mentally to move into that person's sphere with love and a reception of hospitality. Does our body language convey judgment and aloofness? Do we, like Peter, fear being seen by those of our own tribe as we relate to this outsider?

You may have never thought of challenging yourself to move beyond your social comfort zone as an act of spiritual formation. Surprise! This little experiment may prove challenging, but try it, and not just as a mental exercise. Do it in the real world. Listen to the Spirit. See what you learn about yourself and about the other person you're relating to. If you're struggling to see the point, remember that Jesus delighted to enter into relationship with the outsiders of his day – the Samaritans (read John 4 if you need a reminder). Also, remember that Peter took Paul's rebuke without a hint of bitterness or revenge. Let's join him in seeking to be a vessel of self-giving love to a needy world.

13

The Legacy

A Disciple's Courage to Change

The Leaning Oak

This year could be the last for the old leaning oak.
Somewhere in her past, lightning struck, leaving scar.
A branch fell out a few years back
When dad was here.

But she fought on and there she stands, still holding her ground,
Stooped over now, letting go of green and life,
Scouting out the ground below, where we know
She will fall.

"She'll come down some day," Dad would say,
"But not on the house, so let 'er fall
Where she may." That's what Dad would say.
And we still wait.

As is the way of oaks, she's left her mark. Her seedlings stand
Scattered round the woods of our land
In the shade where she stoops stand two or three
Every bit as tall as me.

And when she's gone, they'll carry on, all the better
Cause in her shade they were planted and stood
For a while before she stooped,
Before her planting was no more.

You, little Oak, who knows her time is near, do you fear?
And when the day arrives and her once-mighty timbers plow
The very ground around you where she has fallen
What then?

Little Oak, enjoy the shade of her branches just one more year
And when she falls, and you bend – yes – bend you will,
But you won't break, for she gave you her life
On the crest of that hill.

Contemplating Legacy

Legacy: The Merriam-Webster dictionary defines it as "something transmitted or received from an ancestor or from the past." "I have no silver and gold," said Peter, so we're searching for Peter's spiritual legacy – how his character was formed in relationship with Jesus and if he passed that on to the Jesus community, the early church, our spiritual ancestors. To use biological imagery, Jesus passed along his spiritual DNA to Peter who, along with the apostles and early followers, passed it on to us. Peter's legacy lives in the global church of Jesus Christ.

Peter left us his inheritance with little fanfare – no marketing scheme, no bling. For many, Paul is a more enticing candidate for the keeper of the keys. Admittedly, Paul's legacy is more accessible through his writings and the recorded history of his travel. But Jesus picked Peter, so it is worth our while to dig out his legacy, remembering, "if you seek it like silver and search for it as for hidden treasures, then you will understand the fear of the LORD and find the knowledge of God" (Prov 2:4–5).

Before delving into Peter's legacy, I want to share a personal note. I wrote the poem that opens this chapter in honor of my dad's legacy. Not unlike Peter, he was from a small place, respected in his community but having nothing of wealth or status to commend him. No bling. Yet, for his children and grandchildren, he towered over our lives. Like the small oaks around that leaning and wounded tree, we live because of him. His working man's wisdom and simple grace live on through his progeny, making the world a better place. Legacy is like that. It works silently, but so effectively. As we stand in that legacy, it roots us deeply in authentic life; not image but the real deal.

As this book draws to a close, I'm suggesting that Peter's spiritual formation in relationship with Jesus works like that. His example roots us in authentic life. Let's take a fresh look at the spiritual legacy of the "rock" on whom Jesus said he would build the church.

Peter's Voice

I begin contemplating Peter's legacy through my dad because dad was a man of very few words. Somehow, his silence made his presence weightier. Think of Peter that way. All we have from his pen are two brief letters written to churches whose light was eventually extinguished. A casual observer might be forgiven for thinking Peter's legacy failed to live up to its promise. He didn't leave much.

A research project once required me to spend long hours in libraries looking at medieval manuscripts. I quickly learned that I could not take for granted that a particular document was written by the person it claimed as author. I needed to be a little skeptical, searching for internal proofs that the author was indeed the person I was studying. I found myself looking for turns of phrase and common themes across the manuscripts. Gradually as I immersed myself in their writings, I became more confident that I was hearing their voice. I got to know them through their writing and was then able to discern what they said . . . and sometimes what had been added by an editor.

Once we learn to discern Peter's voice in the Gospels, we may realize that he was a lot more influential in their writing than we previously understood. It starts with the Gospel of Mark.

Peter and the Gospels

The early centuries of the church were characterized by persecutions. It was a fledgling church under constant pressure. Its history was passed on through the stories and memories of its leaders. Constantine's Edict of Milan (AD 313) changed all that as the church of Christ became a legal religion in the Roman Empire. Under this new situation, Christians began to collect the stories and traditions which had been passed on orally. Gradually, orally transmitted stories were recorded in writing by the church fathers.

One of those fathers, Eusebius, was the bishop of Caesarea, a coastal town of Israel between Tel Aviv and Haifa. He lived from AD 260 to 340 and collected many of the anecdotes passed down by the early leaders of the church. He learned the story of Peter from another bishop – Papias (from Hierapolis in Turkey). Born around AD 60, Papias heard the story from someone he referred to as "the elder." This may have been John the Apostle, the disciple whom Jesus loved. What did Eusebius write?

> Mark was the interpreter of Peter and wrote accurately but not in order whatever he remembered about the things which were said or done by the Lord. He [Mark] neither heard the Lord nor followed him, but later, as I said, [he relied upon] Peter who adapted his teachings to the needs [of his hearers] without setting forth an orderly account of the Lord's sayings. Therefore Mark did not err in writing various things as he remembered them, for he made it his first priority not to omit or falsify anything which he heard.[1]

---

1. Brooks, *Mark*, 18; citing ca. AD 325 Eusebius, *Church History* 3.39.15.

If we can trust Eusebius (and Papias and John), then Peter is the source of the Gospel of Mark. Have you considered that when you listen to Mark's gospel, you are hearing the voice of Peter? Peter is the source.[2] Mark accompanied Peter as is witnessed by Peter's passing on greetings from Mark, referred to as his son in 1 Peter 5:13.[3] Mark's gift was to capture Peter's anecdotal preaching about Jesus. Mark's gospel reveals the intense emotional reaction of the disciples as they observe Jesus's words and actions (see Mark 4:40–41; 10:32; 16:8). This would likely not be the case if the source of the gospel was Mark himself since he was not a close follower of Jesus.

Peter's Transparency in Mark's Gospel

Mark, more than the other Gospels, reveals Peter as a faltering disciple. Peter's name is mentioned twenty-three times in the Gospel. Often Jesus directly challenges some aspect of Peter's understanding and vision. We've seen those instances in previous chapters but recalling them here emphasizes the point that Peter took pains to transparently pass on his legacy.

- Mark's version of the walking on the water does not include Peter (Mark 6:45–51)[4]
- Peter's rebuke of Jesus after he predicts his suffering and death (Mark 8:33)
- Peter's awkward suggestion of building a tent for Jesus, Moses and Elijah on the Mount of Transfiguration (Mark 9:5–13)
- Peter's falling asleep with James and John in the Garden of Gethsemane. Only Mark records that when the disciples awoke, they didn't know what to say (Mark 14:40)

---

2. For the academic argument for Mark serving as Peter's secretary, see Gene Green, *Vox Petri* (Cascade, 2020) loc. 454–657 (ch. 1). Other voices of the church fathers add their testimony: Irenaeus (Bishop of Lyons ca AD 130–202) adds that Mark wrote the record of Peter's preaching in Rome after Peter's death; Clement of Alexandria (c. AD 200) adds that the people of Rome who heard Peter preach pressed Mark to do this. Stott, *Story of the New Testament*, 17.

3. Mark is John Mark. His mother, Mary, was likely the owner of a large house in Jerusalem that became the gathering place of the disciples (Acts 12:12). He was Barnabas's cousin (Col 4:10) and accompanied Paul and Barnabas on their first ministry journey (Acts 13:5). Mark returned home (Acts 13:13) and experienced Paul's disapproval (15:38), while Barnabas took Mark on subsequent ministry journeys (15:37–39). Paul later requested him as a useful companion in ministry (2 Tim 4:11). Tradition holds that he became the Bishop of Alexandria and the founder of the Coptic Church of Egypt.

4. My friend, Jon Woodroof, pointed this out to me. Though Mark's silence on this point could have other motivations, it may lie in Peter's desire not to portray himself above his companions.

- Peter's denial with cursing (Mark 14:71)[5]

It's worth contemplating this as we consider Peter's legacy. If Mark is preserving Peter's "Jesus stories," it becomes clear that Peter is eager to put himself in his proper place. We simply do not find him insisting on his role as the keeper of the keys or his title of "the Rock." Rather, Peter is keen to put his failures on display with no need to touch up the impression he would make. He invites public scrutiny of himself, as he centers Jesus as the focal point of his gospel. There is a refreshing honesty and humility in Peter's simple recounting of Jesus's great acts. Apparently, he had moved beyond shame to claim his legacy as a person in process. Rather than insist on title or rank, Peter invites us to join him in a journey of following.

Metanoia – A Renewed Mind

This attitude is captured in a word – a key word in the Gospel of Mark. It is translated to English as "repent." It is the first message presented in the Gospel and the theme of Jesus's ministry (Mark 1:15) as well as John the Baptist's (1:4). It was the word the disciples preached as he sent them out (6:12). Perhaps that word has a moralizing connotation for you – a righteous insistence that you should be better and act differently. The Greek word, however, offers a broader concept. It is *metanoia* – a compound word from two Greek words *meta* meaning "beyond," and *nous* meaning "the mind," referring to one's thought life. In essence, following Christ requires a new way of perceiving, of thinking. Inevitably, a transformed mind results in new behaviors, but it is important not to get the cart before the horse. Peter, through his journey of spiritual formation with Jesus, moves into a new dimension of thinking relative to himself, Jesus and his society. He is the exemplar of a renewed mind (repentance). He has done the hard work of replacing his own expectations with the realities of Christ's kingdom. His actions follow naturally.

It's fair to say that the Gospel of Mark is the gospel according to Peter as recorded by Mark. That's a significant piece of Peter's legacy, but Mark is the shortest gospel, right? So again, a casual observer might dismiss its importance in favor of the longer versions. But, not so fast. The first three gospels (Matthew, Mark and Luke) are called the "Synoptic Gospels." The title means they see things from the same optic. They are organized in a similar fashion and relate

---

5. Stott, *Story of the New Testament*, 19. Stott also suggests: "Perhaps the friendship between Peter and Mark was cemented by their shared experience of failure and restoration. Quite possibly the Gospel itself was born out of this shared experience." John Stott, 16.

similar content. As scholars have compared the three gospels, most conclude that the Gospel of Mark was a primary source of both Matthew and Luke. Matthew and Luke provide lengthier accounts and additional material, but they are still based on Peter's telling of the Jesus stories. So Mark's notes from Peter become the primary source of the first three Gospels. That's quite important in assessing Peter's legacy.

Wouldn't you agree that Peter's legacy is growing?

The Peter-Paul Relationship

Before considering Peter's letters, probing his interaction with Paul will also reveal echoes of his spiritual legacy.

Paul sometimes overshadows Peter when we consider those early days of the church. He is a rare combination of gifts and abilities, a "type A" personality, an ascetic, a scholar, a pioneer. Inspired by unspeakable visions of Christ, Paul becomes the impassioned Pharisee convert, taking the gospel to the far reaches of the Roman world, becoming "all things to all people." No doubt, Paul is a hero of the faith. Nevertheless, consider that, by Paul's own account, he opened himself to a mutual accountability to the early apostles of Jesus, chief of whom was Peter.

Paul provides a revealing defense of his apostleship in his letter to the Galatians. False teachers were ravaging the early church, forcing him to defend his apostolic credentials. In his self-defense, he appeals to two visits to Jerusalem. The first visit took place after Paul's stunning conversion and sojourn in the Arabian desert. It's true that he does not immediately consult other leaders; his apostleship was received directly from Christ. Yet, after three years, he goes to Jerusalem specifically to visit Cephas. Paul uses the Aramaic name for Peter meaning "Rock" – the same name Jesus gave him in their native language. He spent fifteen days with Peter (Gal 1:18). He specifically says he saw no other apostle except James the brother of Jesus.

Think about that a moment. This visionary, pioneering apostle felt it important to go spend an extended time with Peter. He shared that with the Galatians, some of whom were dubious about his apostleship. What did Peter and Paul discuss? Was there a mutual give and take? Did Paul share his visions with Peter? Did Peter share what happened on the Mount of Transfiguration? What other memories did Peter share from his personal experience of following Jesus in Judea and Galilee for three years? The questions are tantalizing. At minimum, the two had enough time to become personally acquainted and bond as brothers in service of the one gospel of Christ. As Paul himself expresses it, he went to Jerusalem to "get to know" Peter (Gal 1:18). Our English translations render the verb "visit," but that does not capture the full sense. Paul went to interview Peter, to gather information. Paul was filling in the gaps of his understanding of Jesus. But beyond that, he went to nurture a partnership in the gospel with Peter.

In this self-defense to the Galatians, Paul mentions a second visit to Jerusalem, fourteen years later (Gal 2:1–10). Paul made this visit in response to a vision. He went "to make sure I was not running or had not run in vain." He sets before them his gospel. There must have been some resistance from the Jewish Christians of Jerusalem because Paul mentions that he "did not yield in submission for even a moment." The result of this apostolic consultation is that James and Cephas and John, pillars of the Jerusalem church, gave Paul and Barnabas the right hand of fellowship (Gal 2:9). Notice that Paul again refers to Peter by the title given him by Jesus. Together, these apostles declare they are partners in ministry.

Interestingly, Paul compares himself to Peter noting that as Peter was entrusted with the gospel for the Jews, Paul had also been entrusted with the gospel for the Gentiles. The three pillars of the Jerusalem church agreed that Paul and Barnabas should fulfill their ministry among the Gentiles while they continued their labor among the Jews. James was put to death in Jerusalem, but unfolding events for Peter and John demonstrate that they both actively ministered to churches consisting of Jews and Gentiles. These were the churches of Asia Minor who were the recipients of Peter's letters and John's Apocalypse (the book of Revelation). So, the two early apostles, by the end of their lives, ventured well beyond the confines of Judaism. We do them a disservice if we keep them in the box of Jewish ministry only. As we've suggested earlier, perhaps Paul's influence nudged the apostles in that direction.

We are suggesting that though Paul was a pioneer, he opened himself up to relationship with the apostles, especially with Peter. There was a mutual give and take between the two leaders and we assume that the two men influenced one another. As we've seen, Peter apparently received Paul's rebuke in Antioch and later revealed great respect for Paul, his ministry and his writings (2 Pet 3:15–16). Furthermore, the apostolic bond did not end simply because we have no record of them seeing one another after the book of Acts. There were other links. For instance, Peter's scribe who wrote or perhaps carried his letters was Silvanus (1 Pet 5:12). Most think that Silvanus is Silas, the same Silas who was an early traveling companion of Paul (Acts 15:22, 40). If Silas is writing down or carrying Peter's messages, this may indicate some overlap between Paul's traveling team and Peter's associates. We've already mentioned Mark who apparently worked alongside both Peter and Paul at different times. Finally, if we accept the early traditions of the church, Paul and Peter may have spent their last days together before martyrdom near Rome in AD 65–67.

As we consider the legacy of Peter, we should avoid seeing Paul as preeminent in the leadership of the early Christian community. Paul is certainly prominent, but his apostolic credentials owe, in part, to his relationship with "the Rock." Peter's voice did not go silent as the gospel began to spread through the Mediterranean basin among Jewish and Gentile communities. On the contrary, Peter's voice continued to influence and provide leadership for those communities as did Paul's.

Peter's Letters

It would require a full commentary to adequately assess Peter's spiritual legacy through his letters. Epilogue 2 of this book highlights some aspects. At this point, I will simply underscore Peter's expectation that the gospel will effect a deep transformation in the community of Jesus followers.

The apostle has now lived a long life. His journey has led through significant turns, deconstructing his expectations, and rebuilding them on the sure foundation of Christ. Surveying his own life, he turns to the community of Jesus-followers, those whom Jesus commissioned him to care for and shepherd. Is it any surprise then, that his final exhortation to the disciples is that they love one another earnestly from a pure heart (1 Pet 1:22–23)? Is this not the same exhortation that Jesus left his disciples (John 13:34)? Peter's life was now on display in the early community of Christ-followers as one who had purified his soul by obedience to Christ (1 Pet 1:22). That means, as we have seen, that his defects had to be preserved in the stories the believers told and the Gospels that were to be written. Yes, that was his story. Now he casts a glance over his shoulder, calling his brothers and sisters to follow the same path. The final result of obedience to the truth, is not sinlessness, but a purity of soul that allows the transformed Jesus-follower to love the other.

Peter realizes that his journey with Jesus was not a mechanical unfolding of events. The presence and power of God was at work through his relationship with the Lord. "His divine power has granted to us all things that pertain to life and godliness *through the knowledge of him* who called us to his own glory and excellence" (2 Pet 1:3 emphasis added). This divine power withholds nothing from the believer, permitting them to become "partakers of the divine nature" (1:4). The immensity of that claim has captured the minds of Jesus-followers in East and West. How can our finite spirits partake in the infinity of God, the Creator and source of our being? Peter confines himself to an economy of words to express the magnificent hope of the believer.

Nevertheless, Peter has shown us enough. He had become a friend of Jesus with all that implied of self-awareness and *metanoia* (transformation of thought). His life pointed the way to a sharing in the life of his friend and Lord. Peter shows us that if he can do it, we can too. We need not hang back in fear and trepidation. Surely Peter was in no better place than we when he started his journey. Like him, we are invited into the divine life, invited to become the friends of our Lord, even the sons and daughters of God. Peter is not compelled to explain it to us in systematic language. It is, after all, a relationship. From the first call – "follow me and I will make you a fisher of people" – to the point of return from alienation – "feed my lambs" – to the provocative – "rise, kill and eat" – Peter has demonstrated a slow but steady willingness to be transformed. He has moved into a sharing in the life of God (the Father-Son-Spirit God) through a tenacious following of Jesus.

Peter says to us, in the most reassuring language of all, that of real-life experience, that we can follow, that we can enter into the divine love.

As I read Peter's letters, I cannot lightly pass over an exhortation in 1 Peter 5. It forms a direct line to Peter's final commission from Jesus on that familiar shore of the Sea of Galilee in the early morning hour. The older shepherd turns to those under his care and says,

> Shepherd the flock of God that is among you, exercising oversight, not under compulsion, but willingly, as God would have you; not for shameful gain, but eagerly; not domineering over those in your charge, but being examples to the flock. And when the chief Shepherd appears . . . Clothe yourselves, all of you, with humility toward one another, for "God opposes the proud but gives grace to the humble." (1 Pet 5:2–5)

It is fitting that Peter's legacy would conclude with this note – a plea to shepherds. I am convinced he is not talking to bishops, priests and prelates. He is talking to us, normal folks, who walk alongside God's people from many walks of life. He asks us to shepherd them with authenticity and humility, motivated by the soon return of our Chief Shepherd, who walks with us through all of life's ups and downs.

Peter's Legacy

Why is it important to recover Peter's spiritual legacy?

The Christian faith is a faith of relationship. It flows out of a relationship within God himself – the Father-Son-Spirit God – whose love overflowed to humanity through Jesus's becoming a human being. As a man, Jesus called Simon. He entered a life-giving relationship with him. Peter's journey with Jesus brought him face to face with himself and his unspoken beliefs and assumptions. Jesus's pursuit of Peter was tenacious, leaving no stone of Peter's former person – his shadow-self – unturned. His natural inclination to center himself as a leader had to be deconstructed. His deep affinity to his family and friends which served as a source of strength also became a searchlight, revealing Peter's deep flaws and misplaced loyalties. Peter's upbringing had rooted him in the scriptural and religious narrative of the Old Testament as understood by the religious establishment of his time and place. Jesus carefully, but thoroughly, uprooted that understanding, leaving the story intact, while placing himself at the center of the Old Testament promises and symbols.

Peter was no gilded saint. No halo graced his head. Putting Peter in our day, he was no eloquent churchman relying on his charisma and winsome words to impress and woo his constituency. He enjoyed no pedigree of education nor silver spoon of lineage. No, Peter's spiritual credentials are far more authentic. His real experience of following Christ speaks to us in our

---

Peter was no gilded saint. No halo graced his head. Putting Peter in our day, he was no eloquent churchman relying on his charisma and winsome words to impress and woo his constituency. He enjoyed no pedigree of education nor silver spoon of lineage. No, Peter's spiritual credentials are far more authentic.

---

humanity, our need, our poverty, our alienation. He gives us hope in the real world. The apostle, key-keeper, true to his Galilean fisherman nature, was prepared to do the hard work. He was willing to get knocked off his horse, more than once, and yet get back on and keep riding for, "to whom else could we go? You have the words of life."

Let's make this so simple that we can't forget it. Peter was willing to CHANGE.

Peter was willing to have his preconceived ideas stripped away for the sake of relationship with Jesus, for the honor of following. His friendship to Jesus became the axis of his life, naturally moving all other relationships to the periphery. All beliefs and priorities came under the scrutinizing searchlight of Jesus's lordship. All were re-situated around the axis of Jesus's person and his call to Peter, "follow me." In that overused word, Peter was transformed. He saw himself differently, because he learned to see Jesus as he was. He saw his people differently. He came to view servanthood and leadership through a new lens. His story, personally and collectively, was rewritten in light of following Jesus.

I'm getting older and I suppose it is normal in one's senior years to recall and review the early decades. I wonder how I, as one who saw myself so "right," could now so readily admit that I don't know. This sense that following Jesus implicates us in a total rewrite of life's expectations is destabilizing. I recall attempting to walk across a desert dune in Egypt. The sand kept shifting under my feet causing me to question if I was making any progress. Life feels like that sometimes.

Peter's life assures us that the shifting sand is OK. In fact, that is the way of following Jesus. Our presuppositions must be ripped out as our life script is rewritten.

Scholars of ancient literature know of the "palimpsest." In ancient times, parchment or papyrus was rare and difficult to obtain. To supply their need, scribes would scrape off parchments already filled with words to reuse them. The old passes away. The new comes. Modern techniques in paleography (the study of ancient writings) have managed to look behind the later script, uncovering the original writings of the palimpsest. Take it is a metaphor of our life story. Its lines have been erased and then overwritten with new ideas, new priorities. Like the palimpsest, it may be that what is being written the second time around, or third, is closer to capturing the truth of our lives.

For Peter, the old writing remained as a faded script. He could recall it. Sometimes the old stories still influenced him. Nevertheless, the new words, the words he received from Jesus, were the bedrock reality of his life. They were the source of his transformation. The old had to be overwritten by the new – his in-Christ destiny.

Peter's example is life-giving in that he urges us forward to find the in-Christ destiny of our lives, which is the only script that matters. He exhorts us not to settle for the old story with its false claims on our beliefs and practices. He shows us how important it is to find the courage to change. No change means we are not following. For Peter, following Jesus meant placing his life at the fulcrum of personal transformation.

Though it sometimes feels that the foundations are crumbling, a life centered on Jesus is the only secure foothold. Peter enables us to accept the challenge of a new identity – an "in Christ" personhood. He demonstrates that jargon is useless. Words, if unaccompanied by deep change, only serve to mask our idolatry. Following Jesus means letting go of the old and receiving the new. It is a transformative journey as Jesus puts his finger on aspects of our lives that await his transforming touch. The old assumptions, beliefs and practices lay faded under the new script issuing from Jesus's call on our lives. The old loses its power as we receive words of life from Jesus. Peter became a true human being. His authentic identity was uncovered as he tenaciously set his course for following Jesus, doing the hard work of laying aside the old, and receiving the new script of God's love in Christ.

Peter's Legacy and Ours

Stephen Covey is a famous leadership guru. One of his famed "seven habits of highly effective people" is to begin with the end in mind – to see the end from the beginning. The idea is to know where you are headed so that you are not deterred. In a dramatic illustration, he asks his readers to imagine themselves at their funeral. Gulp! The point is to imagine what you would want your family, friends and work associates to say about you at that moment. What lasting impression do you hope to leave in their memory? What will be your legacy?

This book has sought to reframe Peter's legacy as a spiritually formed disciple of Jesus. Now it is our turn to probe our legacy.

In response to this chapter, take a few moments to consider the spheres of relationship of your life – your acquaintances, associates, friends and family. Choose one key representative from each sphere and write out what you would want them to say about you at your life's end. Keep those statements at hand, perhaps referring to them in a journal from time to time. Those words from your loved ones are an expression of your hoped-for legacy. Keep pressing in to them, not allowing yourself to be turned aside by other urgent business. Keep pressing toward the end that you desire.

Epilogue 1

Going Deeper: Centering Christ in the Old Testament

He is the image of the invisible God, the firstborn
of all creation. . . . All things were created
through him and for him. And he is before all
things, and in him all things hold together.

Colossians 1:15–17

Introduction: Are We Taking This Too Far?

A critical aspect of Peter's spiritual formation was learning to center his understanding of the Old Testament story around Jesus. The Old Testament was the normative story of life for the Jewish people of that era. In order for Peter to see Jesus as the center and fulfillment of that story, he had to release his assumptions and prior enculturation around that story. It was a massive transfer of trust. Peter was able to make that transfer, as his Pentecost sermon reveals.

In our day, our challenge is different from Peter's but equally difficult. Our claim that Jesus is the center and fulfillment of the Old Testament story is a dangerous proposition. Trying to read the Old Testament with a Christ-centered focus can get us in trouble. First, the Old Testament is a Jewish book. It belonged to the Jews first. So how do we Christians get off saying that Jesus is the central point and theme of the Old Testament? Isn't that disrespectful to Jews? After all, aren't we just borrowing a Jewish book as background to the New Testament?

Second, Jesus's explicit teaching is contained in the New Testament. Should we not make that our starting point? At least saying the New Testament is Christ-centered has credibility, but claiming that the Old Testament is Christ-centered is, well, stretching it. Shouldn't we Christians stay in our lane?

Third, Christians disagree about the Old Testament. Through history, some Christians wanted to eliminate most of the Old Testament, and with good reason. Some of it makes us cringe – exile, sieges, murders, slavery, incest, polygamy, plagues, patriarchy, etc. There's a lot there that isn't pretty. Some claim that the Old Testament law should be applied today. Others say that Jesus did away with it or that the Holy Spirit's presence makes it superfluous. Some say that the promises to Old Testament Israel still apply to the ethnic Israelites, or even specifically to the state of Israel. Others say that they apply to an expanded Israel including all followers of Jesus – Jews and Gentiles. Let's face it, we disagree a lot about the Old Testament.

Fourth, if we surveyed the history of the church, some of its leaders have made outlandish claims of Christ in the Old Testament. In the hindsight of history, we can see that they were reading their own understanding into the Old Testament rather than understanding it on its own terms. Hasn't reading the Old Testament with Jesus Christ as its focal point been tried and found deficient? Why repeat the mistakes of history?

So how can we claim that the Old Testament should be Christ-centered or read in a way that anticipates and points to Jesus Christ? Isn't that a hard sell?

Jesus's View of the Old Testament

Admittedly, there are some challenges, but we start with a basic assumption – that Jesus is who he claims to be. With that assumption, his view of the Old Testament is of utmost importance. If he was, in fact, the one who inspired the Old Testament, we should attempt to see it as he did. In fact, that would be the only legitimate reading of the Old Testament. Truth is, he was clear-eyed in his view of the Old Testament and if we look at it as he did, our confusion may clear up considerably.

For instance, in his "Sermon on the Mount," Jesus says that not an iota or a dot will pass away from the law until all is accomplished (Matt 5:18). The reference is to the tiny markings in Hebrew writing, similar to a dot of an "i" or the cross of a "t." Jesus is making the point that none of the Old Testament Scriptures will fall by the way. They will all come to an ultimate fulfillment.

He faced down the Old Testament scholars of his day on more than one occasion. He had the audacity to say, "You search the Scriptures because you think that in them you have eternal life; and it is they that bear witness about me" (John 5:39). He accused them of not believing Moses. Remember these guys lived and breathed Moses, so to make that claim is crazy on the surface. So why did Jesus say that? He tells us. "If you believed Moses, you would believe me; for he wrote of me" (John 5:46). Moses authored the first five books of the Bible – the Pentateuch. "He wrote of me." Either Jesus is psychotic or he's speaking sober truth, correcting the Pharisees' understanding of the Old Testament. Which will it be?

On another occasion, he told more Jewish theologians and scholars that "your father Abraham rejoiced to see my day. He saw it and was glad" (John 8:56). I used to think that meant that Abraham looked ahead through time and, by faith, had a hazy premonition of Jesus coming to earth. In recent years I've changed that view . . . but I'm getting ahead of myself. Then Jesus said words that were absolute blasphemy for anyone other than the Son of God: "Before Abraham was, I am." As he identifies himself with Yahweh, the religious leaders pick up stones.

There were other instances as well, but none so explicit and revealing as Jesus's reunion with his disciples after his crucifixion and resurrection. It's all in Luke 24. First, the two disciples on the road to Emmaus got the best kind of heartburn! Their hearts were burning as Jesus opened the Scriptures of the *Old Testament* to them (Luke 24:32). They must have been seeing it with new eyes, hearing it with new ears. When Jesus left them, they made a beeline back to Jerusalem to share with the other disciples their passionate joy of discovering Jesus alive in person *and* in the Hebrew Scriptures.

But Jesus showed up there too! This time, he "opened their minds" to understand the Scriptures, showing them how everything written about him in the Law of Moses, the Psalms and the Prophets had to be fulfilled (Luke 24:44–45). In mentioning the three divisions of the Hebrew Scriptures, Jesus does not exclude any part of the Old Testament. What he shared with them became the refrain of the apostles' preaching and teaching, setting the church of Jesus Christ on a trajectory to spread to all nations of the earth. Peter was the vanguard of this renewed Old Testament understanding:

> God foretold by the mouth of all the prophets, that his Christ
> would suffer . . . Jesus, whom heaven must receive until the time
> for restoring all the things about which God spoke by the mouth
> of his holy prophets long ago. Moses said, "The Lord will raise
> up for you a prophet like me from your brothers. You shall listen
> to him in whatever he tells you . . ." And all the prophets who

have spoken, from Samuel and those who came after him, also proclaimed these days." (Acts 3:18, 21–22, 24)

Peter proclaimed before his fellow Jews and the Gentile God-fearers that "all the prophets bear witness that everyone who believes in him receives forgiveness of sins through his name" (Acts 10:43). Later, Paul defended himself against charges brought by his own people. He was saying "nothing but what the prophets and Moses said would come to pass: that the Christ must suffer and that, by being the first to rise from the dead, he would proclaim light both to our people and to the Gentiles" (Acts 26:22b–23).

Both Jesus and his disciples saw him as the main point of the Old Testament. So by making the claim that Jesus is central to the Old Testament, we're not advocating some wacky, marginal view. We are actually taking it from the source. We are rooting ourselves in an ancient way of reading the Old Testament that was taught by Jesus and practiced by his disciples. The fact that it is viewed as a strange way to read the Bible should alert us that something is wrong. We've allowed ourselves to be pressed into the mold of our society and the worldview of our culture. We've lost a distinctive element of our faith – something that is core. We need to get that back.

How Does the Old Testament Reveal Christ?

But there are dangers, right? If we see Christ in the Old Testament, doesn't that take away from the stories of the Old Testament themselves? If all we are looking for is Jesus Christ, then we miss much of the passion and drama of the stories. We might miss what God was doing in that time and place. We need to see the Old Testament on its own terms. Right? Let's think about it.

When we say Jesus is central to the Old Testament, we don't deny the value of those stories for discipleship, teaching and preaching. If anything, we recognize the true depth and value of the Old Testament narrative. The Spirit of Christ who inspired the writing of those stories wove them together masterfully so that we would meditate on them, finding Jesus in them and seeing their fulfillment in him. As Paul said in Galatians, the Old Testament law becomes a tutor that leads us to Christ. Borrowing Paul's image, the Old Testament's objective is Christ. Some refer to this as the "Christotelic" nature of the Old Testament. It comes from *telos* meaning "end goal."

Though the disciples needed help (as do we) to get their minds around Jesus as the center of the Old Testament, it was not an innovation. In fact, several New Testament believers indicate they are awaiting the one who would fulfill the Scriptures. Zechariah's prophecy (Luke 1:67–79), the blessing of Simeon (Luke 2:25–32), and Mary's song (Luke 1:46–55) reveal a longing for the fulfillment of the Old Testament prophecies and a recognition that they were fulfilled in Jesus. Philip says to Nathanael, "We have found him of whom Moses in the Law and also the prophets wrote" (John 1:45).

Charles Spurgeon used this analogy. An English village, at first glance, appears remote and unrelated to the capital, London. A small road passes through it, but that road leads to a larger town which connects to a highway which ultimately leads to London. The application is that from every passage of the Old Testament, there is a road which leads to Christ.[1] Spurgeon would agree that the Old Testament is "Christotelic"; however, we might borrow the analogy and push it further by saying that London is not "Christ" in the analogy. Christ is the road. He is present in the Old Testament, engaging with the prophets, revealing the Father, drawing the nations to himself. Christ is not merely the end goal of the Old Testament, but also the beginning. "In the beginning was the Word" (John 1:1). His presence is constant throughout the Old Testament.

Following are four avenues of discerning the Christ-centered Old Testament story. They are:

1. The visible and audible presence of Christ

2. The unfolding covenant that leads to Christ

3. Old Testament characters, events and institutions that foreshadow Christ

4. Prophets foretell aspects of Christ's person and work

The first of these avenues is the most surprising and a rich resource for spiritual formation. So I begin with it. The other three are more familiar to us, but also reveal important aspects of Jesus's identity and work. Each of them could easily take up a whole book, but let's try to get the gist of this way of reading the whole Bible as one united story with Jesus as its beginning and end goal.

1. The Visible and Audible Presence of Christ

I never thought much about those stories in the Old Testament where God speaks audibly or appears visibly until I lived among Muslims. Orthodox Islam

---

1. G. K. Beale, "Finding Christ in the Old Testament." JETS 63.1 (2020): 46–48.

teaches that God cannot be seen or heard because that depicts God with human traits (physicality, voice, etc.). Allah, in Islamic thought, must not be conceived of in human terms. In fact, he should not be conceived of at all except in what he has revealed as he is unknowable in his essence. In brief, he cannot be seen, heard or experienced by the physical senses. (Note: Not all Muslims adhere strictly to this understanding, but it is the standard of classic Islamic theology.)

I had some obstacles to discovering the presence of Christ in the Old Testament. I was an heir of the enlightenment, as were those who taught me not to read the New Testament back into the Old Testament. That was "eisegesis" – reading *into* the text rather than letting the text itself inform the reader. I was told the church fathers gradually understood Christ as fully God and fully man, finally formulating that doctrine into a creed in the fourth century AD. Seeing Christ in the Old Testament, therefore, was chronologically out of place. I should not commit the error of reading the Bible according to doctrines established much later in time.

It was a conundrum. If Jesus existed eternally, as the New Testament says, should we not see indicators of that before he was born in Bethlehem? But I didn't want to be rash in my exegesis of Scripture. How would I resolve it? An early clue came through an icon of an Eastern Orthodox church. It was Moses in front of the burning bush. Inside the bush, was the child Christ. Clearly, these Orthodox Christians thought Jesus was speaking to Moses from the burning bush.

It was the "angel of the LORD" that called to Moses from the bush (Exod 3:2). I envisioned angels as luminous beings with wings, but created beings, not divine. But this angel was different. He is identified as the LORD (Yahweh) himself and therefore, his word was God's word. The Hebrew word for angel is best translated "sent one." The Old Testament "angel of the LORD" is the "sent one" of Yahweh – the same descriptor Jesus used of himself, "sent by the Father," forty times in the Gospel of John alone. So that icon I saw in the Orthodox church identified the angel of the Lord as the "sent one of Yahweh." As you know, that sent one of Yahweh appears through much of the Old Testament.

As I looked into this further, I realized that this way of reading the Old Testament was commonplace in the Eastern church. It began to make sense to me because the Fathers of the church who determined Jesus was fully God and fully man were Eastern Fathers – Athanasius, Basil, Gregory of Nazianzus, etc. As I dipped into their writings, it was clear that Christ as the eternal Word of the Father was the main character of the Old Testament. They naturally read it that way. For them, the whole Bible was full of Jesus, who was the vehicle of God's revelation to humanity. As I looked into it further, I realized that some from my own evangelical tradition also read the Bible in this way. A great example is Jonathan Edwards, the eighteenth-century Congregationalist pastor and leader of the Great Awakening:

> Seeing that there is one of the persons of the Trinity united to the human nature, God chooses in all his transactions with mankind to transact by him. He did so of old, in his discoveries of himself to the patriarchs and in giving the law and in leading the children of Israel through the wilderness and in the manifestations he made of himself in the tabernacle and temple.[2]

The Scripture that encapsulates this thinking is John 1:18: "No one has seen God at any time. The only begotten God, in the bosom [or chest] of the Father, he has revealed [or explained] him."

That verse deserves a closer look. No one has ever seen God. As that phrase stands, it is perfectly consistent with the Islamic view of God. God cannot be perceived by human faculties. But there is a resolution, and it is not God sending down a book. It is God sending the Son – a person who fully reveals himself, but in human terms. The Fathers of the church followed this basic principle. The God of the Old Testament, who could not be seen or heard by human beings, was nevertheless seen and heard. How? It was by the medium of the eternal Son. He was always God's means of making himself known. It is a theological interpretation of the Old Testament, one that naturally commends itself based on the understanding of Jesus's divine nature. I was beginning to see this concept was not chronologically incorrect, nor was it reading the New Testament back into the Old. It is consistent with Jesus's teaching about himself and many church leaders through history have recognized it.

That realization helped me begin to read the Old Testament appearances of God as appearances of Christ – the second person of the Trinity. He was the one who revealed or explained God in terms we humans could understand. Of course, that revelation reached its pinnacle when he entered humanity as Immanuel – God with us – but it was anticipated through multiple appearances of the eternal Son of God in the Old Testament. Following are a few examples, taken only from Genesis. Each reveals a God who is present to us, interacting with us in ways our senses can understand. Note that when the word LORD appears in upper case letters, it is the name Yahweh in Hebrew. Recall that for the Jews, this name was God's self-revealed name – "I am who I am" (Exod 3:14). Many Jews felt this sacred name was too holy to pronounce. Yet, here

---

2. Edwards, *Works of Jonathan Edwards*, 518.

is Yahweh engaging in normal human activities such as walking, speaking and eating.

- Gen 1:26–27: Man is created, by the spoken word of God, in the image of God.
- Gen 2:7: God breathes into man's nostrils as he becomes a living being.
- Gen 3:8–10: The sound of the LORD God walking in the Garden, calling out "where are you?" Actually, Christ himself promises the "seed of the woman" will crush the serpent!
- Gen 6:5–8: The LORD sees the evil of man and is grieved.
- Gen 8:21–22: The LORD smells the aroma of Noah's sacrifice and promises not to destroy the earth.
- Gen 11:7: The LORD goes down to confuse the language of humanity at Babel.
- Gen 12:1–3: The LORD calls Abram and gives him promises.
- Gen 15:1, 4: The "word of the LORD" comes to Abram in a vision.
- Gen 16:7: The angel (or messenger) of the LORD pursues and finds Hagar who recognizes the messenger as Yahweh.
- Gen 17: The LORD appears to Abram, changing his name, promising a son through Sarah.
- Gen 18: The LORD appears to Abraham, receives his generous hospitality and discusses his plans for Sodom and Gomorrah. Might this be Abraham seeing the day of Jesus in joy? (John 8:56).
- Gen 22:15: The angel of the LORD calls to Abraham from heaven.
- Gen 26:2, 24: The LORD appears to Isaac (twice).
- Gen 28:13: The LORD appears to Jacob in the dream of a ladder to heaven.
- Gen 32:24–32: Jacob's night-time wrestling match: He sees God "face to face."
- Gen 35:9: The LORD appears to Jacob, renewing covenant promises.

You can imagine that as I read Genesis now, I'm very aware of and alive to the presence of the person of Christ seen and heard in these stories. Genesis becomes a gospel encounter as Christ is constantly reaching out to human beings in love, drawing them to himself, engaging in their conflicts and calling them to follow him in confusing circumstances. It becomes clear that the Old Testament believers believed in Christ, just as the New Testament believers. The journeys of Abraham and Isaac are not unlike that of Peter. Hagar was given hard commands to follow and yet she learned that God hears her, which must have given her courage to keep walking a hard road. We see Jacob's dark night of the soul as he clings to God for a blessing while wrestling in the dust, all the while, fearing for his very life.

Genesis is only the beginning. God's self-revelation continues through the Old Testament story. He reveals himself to Moses from the burning bush (Exod 3). He shares a covenant meal with seventy of Israel's leaders on top of Mount Sinai (Exod 24). He speaks with Moses face to face, as a friend to a friend (Exod 33:11). He goes before the children of Israel in a pillar of cloud and fire (Exod 13:21–22; Num 14:14). He reveals himself to the judges (Judg 6:12; 13:3), Samuel (1 Sam 3 and 16), David (1 Chr 21:16; 2 Chr 3:1) and the prophets.

The list of sources at the end of this chapter will give some more detailed resources on seeing the Old Testament story in this way. As we conclude, let's recall that Peter had to learn this skill. His "seeing Jesus in the Old Testament" featured large in the post-resurrection appearances of Jesus to his disciples. The early preaching of the apostles drew from these lessons, proclaiming "all the prophets testify to Christ." The story of the Bible is one unified story with Christ as its focal point and fulfillment. If we can begin to see that as our story, we will be helped immensely to walk the path of spiritual formation on which Jesus led Peter.

2. The Unfolding Covenant Leads to Christ

We don't use the word "covenant" very often in our normal interactions. We are somewhat familiar with it from attending weddings which are sometimes called a "covenant." We also hear the word in communion (mass or Eucharist) – Jesus's words at the final meal he shared with the disciples: "This cup is the new covenant in my blood" (1 Cor 11:25).

Covenant is an Old Testament word for relationship. It is a relationship based on God's promise which we trust he will fulfill. The covenants of the Bible are God's way of re-establishing relationship with us. They are an expression of his nature, his love. As we think of the Old Testament covenants in this way, it is important to remember that God always set the terms for how we are to be in relationship with him. It is a relationship, but not among equals. It is the creature in relationship with the Creator. The dynamics of this relationship are not casual or flippant as may be the case in human relationships. In fact, the Old Testament language for making a covenant is "cut the covenant." It referred to the act of cutting animals as a solemn testimony to the penalty of breaking the covenant. If one betrays the covenant, he or she declares, "may

I forfeit my life like this animal." For this reason, one scholar has defined the covenant as "a bond in blood, sovereignly administered."[3]

We can identify several covenants in the Old Testament: Adam and Eve,[4] Noah, Abraham, Moses, David and a promised new or "renewed" covenant (Isa 54:1–10; Jer 31:31–40; 33:14–26; Ezek 33:11–31; 37:26–28).

So there are six covenants? Well, no. Really, *there is only one covenant* that has several iterations or episodes. Each one relates how God brings humanity into relationship with himself and each one is mediated by Christ. The covenant frames the story as it moves towards fulfillment. God pursues relationship with humanity as his holy and eternal son becomes a man to die in our place, effecting a full reconciliation with him. Actually, we're still in the story as we await a consummation of that covenant, when Jesus returns and we return to our intended purpose as God's image bearers in the renewed creation.

I will include some resources below that give more detail on the covenant. Here, allow me to emphasize that in different ways, each covenant expresses God's grace – his undeserved love – to humanity. That may be different from what you have heard in the past. Others may speak of dispensations (innocence, government, law, etc.) or a covenant of works (Adam and Eve were required to perfectly obey God). These descriptors highlight aspects of the covenant, but they sometimes mask the simple truth that God's grace and love dominate each of the covenant episodes. When this is foremost in our thinking, we see God as unchanging and his interactions with us, his creatures, as consistent and reliable, always centered around Christ.

Here is a brief synopsis:

Adam and Eve: God's love is seen in that he created a world of beauty and diversity as a perfect home for Adam and Eve – a temple where they would flourish as his image-bearers. Every relational, aesthetic and intellectual need of humanity was fully provided for in God's creation. The breath of life, God's Spirit, was breathed into the man and the woman by God who was present in the garden – a pre-incarnate appearance of Christ. They shared the life of God in perfect intimacy with one another. They did nothing to earn this. However, the Tree of the Knowledge of Good and Evil gave Adam and Eve the opportunity to reject God's good gifts and betray their relationship to him. Disastrously, they chose to determine their own destiny by eating from that tree. Though it was a blatant rejection of God's love, still God comes walking

---

3. Robertson, *Christ of the Covenants*, 3.

4. Not all agree that Adam and Eve represent a covenant; however, the significant elements of a covenant are present and Hosea 6:7 refers to the "covenant" made with Adam.

in the garden, seeking humanity (Christ again). He decrees that the man and woman will not be allied with the serpent – their mortal enemy and the cause of their fall. His head will be crushed by the seed of the woman (Christ). God acts to cover Adam and Eve's shame of nakedness with the skin of an animal after their tragic breaking of the covenant. So even at this initial stage, shedding blood is necessary to resolve the dilemma of a broken covenant.

Noah: Noah found favor with God despite the very corrupt and evil society he lived in. The favor he found was not so much due to his own righteousness as to God's love. God had promised to save humankind through the seed of the woman. Now he determines to intervene so that humankind would not self-destruct through rampant evil. Noah trusts God, building the ark and preserving creation and humanity. The covenant with Noah reminds us that humanity's alienation from God has devastating effects and that God's judgment on evil preserves his creation and us.

Abraham: God (Yahweh) promises that Abraham will become a great nation, will have a great name, and will be a great blessing (to all the nations). The LORD (Yahweh) appears to Abraham multiple times. Abraham trusts Yahweh and the Lord counts that to him as righteousness (Gen 15:6). Abraham is justified by faith in Christ. He begins his journey through the ancient world as a pilgrim by faith in God. God's covenant of love always evokes action in response to his promise. God delights to fulfill his promises against all odds. Abraham and Sarah conceive in their old age and Isaac becomes the son through whom the promise will unfold. In an unexpected turn of events, Abraham is commanded by God to sacrifice his own son, Isaac. The Angel of the LORD intervenes at the last minute, providing a substitute for Abraham's only son on Mt. Moriah – the place where Jesus was crucified. The anticipation of God's offering his only Son could not be more evident.

Moses: The covenant with Moses is often described as a covenant of law, since the law was a big part of what God gave through Moses. However, bear in mind that, *before* the law, the Exodus from Egypt was God's *salvation* of the Old Testament people. The blood of a Passover lamb secured their deliverance. He did not give them a law and *then* save them because they obeyed. He saved them, delivered them from oppression, established them as his people – his kingdom of priests – and *then* gave them the Torah, a teaching to live by. Similar to the other covenants, the people of Israel were given God's love and favor without condition. They then had a choice – to live in the light of God's teaching or to reject it. It is also critical to note that God himself came to dwell among them (see: Exod 13:21; 14:19, 24; 40:34; Num 10:34; 14:14). What distinguished them from the other peoples was that God was in their midst.

This is the person of Christ dwelling among his covenant people. Their history, as we know, is mixed with moments of great faithfulness and many failures.

David: After a long line of judges, the Lord chooses a young man from Jesse's family. He literally takes him from behind the sheep and sets him on the throne of Israel (2 Sam 7:8). As a "man after God's own heart," David trusts God to keep his promises. He was flawed as were all the other covenantal leaders; nevertheless, God promises him that his throne will endure forever, vanquishing all enemies, and that David's son will build the dwelling of God among his people – the temple.

The New Covenant: When Jesus shares his final words with his disciples before he is crucified, he does it over a meal. Most of the Old Testament covenants had a sacrifice and a meal as a seal of the covenant – a reminder that now they were in a committed relationship to God. Jesus says, "this cup that is poured out for you is the *new* covenant in my blood" (Luke 22:20, emphasis added). Isaiah anticipates the death of the "suffering servant" as a "covenant" (Isa 42:6; 49:8). His death saves us, but he also invites us into relationship. We are given a new way of life – the Torah of Jesus. We are also given the Holy Spirit to empower and deepen that life of Jesus in us. Jesus takes the covenant to the next level as the presence of God is no longer in a building but in the living stones (people) of his church. He graciously brings us in as his brothers and sisters. We eat at the Father's table and follow our "older brother" through this life until the covenant will someday be consummated, completed, as we see him face to face and are made like him.

Though the covenant of Jesus is freely given, it is also a solemn covenantal relationship. Jesus's blood testifies to the serious nature of our covenant relationship with him. The same warnings that applied to the Old Testament people of God still apply to us as new covenant people. The writer of Hebrews warns, "How much worse punishment, do you think, will be deserved by the one who has trampled underfoot the Son of God, and has profaned the blood of the covenant by which he was sanctified, and has outraged the Spirit of grace?" (Heb 10:29)

In Peter's spiritual formation, we saw repeatedly that his story was the Old Testament story. His people were the Old Testament people. Like us, Peter needed to understand Jesus as the focal point and fulfillment of the Hebrew Scriptures. That is our challenge as well. The story of the covenant is our story – the story of God pursuing a renewed relationship with humanity. We live in the last episode of that covenant relationship walking in the light of Jesus's truth, awaiting a final consummation.

3. Old Testament Persons, Events and Institutions Foreshadow Christ

This way of seeing Christ in the Old Testament, through foreshadowing, is familiar to us. It is most famously portrayed by the book of Hebrews which is a long litany of Old Testament images which Christ fulfills. For instance, Christ is a true representative of humanity – fully human (Heb 2:14), better than Moses (Heb 3:1–6), better than the Old Testament priests (Heb 5:6–11; 7:1–10:22), better than the Old Testament sacrifices (Heb 10:1–22), and he brings about a covenant better than the old covenant (Heb 8:6–13). What Jesus does is eternal, not temporary. It will never pass away as the Old Testament "shadows" did.

Biblical scholars speak of this foreshadowing of Jesus as "types," from the Greek word *tupos* which indicates a "pattern." The study of these types is called "typology." One of those scholars helpfully defined typology:

> Typology is the study of analogical correspondences between persons, events, institutions, and other things within the historical framework of God's special revelation, which, from a retrospective view, are of a prophetic nature.[5]

While these persons, events and institutions – types – play an important role in the Old Testament story, they also anticipate a fuller meaning seen in the unfolding history of redemption. They point forward to something that comes later in the story of the Bible, which is called the "antitype." The antitype fulfills the type or, saying it another way, the New Testament reality in Christ fulfills the Old Testament image. Thinking of the type as a "pattern" brings to mind an article of clothing. A tailor cuts the cloth from a pattern. The point is not the pattern, but the fulfillment of it in the clothing. So the patterns, or types, of the Old Testament point to the fulfillment in Jesus.

What contemporary theologians call "types" and "antitypes" are similar to what Paul and the author of Hebrews called "shadows" and "reality." As an object located between us and the sun produces a shadow, it signals that something real is there. The shadow is not the object, but it signals us to look for the object. The Old Testament shadows were never intended to be the whole story. Their purpose was to alert us to a reality so that we would not miss it! Both Paul and the author of the Hebrews said the substance or the "true form" is Jesus Christ (Col 2:17; Heb 8:5; 10:1).

It's important to remember that, in fulfilling the type, the antitype always raises the bar. Some of the Old Testament characters did despicable things. So as they point forward to Jesus, they also reveal a desperate need for a real savior,

---

5. Beale, "Finding Christ in the Old Testament," 29.

a just king, a faithful prophet, a merciful priest. These Old Testament characters include Adam, Noah, Melchizedek, Abraham, Isaac, Jacob, Joseph, Moses, Aaron (and the priests) Joshua, the judges, Samuel, David and the prophets.

In fact, the nation of Israel itself is a type of Christ. As Israel was to be a light to the world and a source of blessing to the nations, so Jesus comes to bring the peace and reconciliation of God to humanity. Israel accomplished her purpose imperfectly, through many failures and shortcomings. Jesus, on the other hand, achieved it fully. The New Testament overflows with this idea of Jesus fulfilling the purpose and calling of Israel. Those "shadows" mentioned in Hebrews point to Jesus as a fulfilled Israel. Paul made it explicit by saying that Jesus was the seed of Abraham (Gal 3:16) and, as such, the covenant promises were made through him to his people.

Finally, when we speak of types and shadows, we should not infer that the real presence of Christ came only in the New Testament. The types and shadows were pictures and patterns pointing to Christ who was *present and active in the Old Testament* and became *incarnate in the New Testament.*

To own the Old Testament as our story, we must read it with Jesus lenses. It is a disastrous story in many ways, culminating in a brutal exile and a tentative return from exile. It is a story of prophetic warnings of impending judgment and promise of a return to God's favor. It is a story of corruption and injustice more than a story of justice and truth. The Old Testament ends in search of a conclusion. That conclusion that sums up the Old Testament and fulfills it is found in Jesus Christ and his gospel.

4. Prophets Foretell Aspects of Christ's Person and Work

There is no need to take up a lot of space here as this is the way we're most familiar with approaching Jesus in the Old Testament. Micah said that a Son of David would be born in Bethlehem (Matt 2:6, from Micah 5:2). Isaiah spoke of the suffering servant cited by Matthew (12:18–21). The Psalms are cited by Jesus showing that he recognized them as speaking of himself (e.g. "My God, my God, why have you forsaken me?" Ps 22:1). Matthew quoted abundantly from the Old Testament, applying it to Christ. For example, "Behold, the virgin shall conceive and bear a son, and they shall call his name Immanuel" (Matt 1:23, from Isa 7:14).

Rather than painstakingly go through these passages, let us recall that if the New Testament writers had not pointed out these things to us, we might also find these applications to Jesus strange and out of place. Because they have become familiar to us as we read the Bible, we no longer deem them strange.

Putting ourselves in the shoes of Peter and the apostles, who grew up in a synagogue setting, should help us see how mind-blowing it was for them to see these passages referring to Jesus with whom they lived and ate and traveled. It took time for it to come together for them, but when it did, they began to see Christ himself *and* anticipations of Christ in pictures and patterns all through the Old Testament.

As an example, think about Paul's claim that Christ was the rock from which the people of God drank in Exodus 17:6 (1 Cor 10:4). Matthew took a promise that was clearly applied to Israel as a nation and applied it to Jesus without hesitation: "Out of Egypt I called my Son" (Matt 2:15, from Hosea 11:1). The author of Hebrews noted Melchizedek was a priest without a genealogy related to Aaron. In fact, he preceded Aaron. Jesus, also from outside the tribe of Levi and Aaron, was a priest after the order of Melchizedek (Heb 5:6; Ps 110:4). Sometimes the New Testament writers surprise us by claiming that the Old Testament prophets saw Jesus. For instance, John says that Isaiah "saw the glory of Christ and spoke of him" (John 12:41), and Peter claims that David "foresaw and spoke about the resurrection of Christ" (Acts 2:31).

As we reflect on these and many other New Testament references to prophecies fulfilled in Jesus, we begin to get a sense of how Peter and the apostles viewed the Old Testament story. They saw it originating in Christ and fulfilled by him. We should allow the apostles, and Jesus himself, to be our tutors in understanding the Old Testament.

Resources
Christ in the Old Testament

Al-Massira. "Walk with the Prophets . . . and Meet the Messiah." https://almassira. org/. (Note: The documents that are provided to Al-Massira trainers are helpful in seeing Christ in the Old Testament.)

Beale, G. K. "Finding Christ in the Old Testament." *JETS* 63, no. 1 (2020): 25–50.

Blackham, Paul. *Frameworks: Volume 1 – Roots: 30 Days of Theology and Bible Study.* Independently published, 2019.

Christ The Truth. "Jesus Is the Word of God: Christ in OT." https://christthetruth. net/christ-in-ot/. (Note: Glen Scrivener presents Christ in the Old Testament as "pictured, prophesied and present." His blogs on this site provide more details on Christ in the Old Testament.)

Clowney, Edmund P. *Preaching Christ in All the Scripture.* Wheaton: Crossway, 2003.

———. *The Unfolding Mystery: Discovering Christ in the Old Testament.* Phillipsburg: P&R Publishing, 2013.

Greidanus, Sidney. *Preaching Christ from the Old Testament*. Grand Rapids: Eerdmans, 1999.

The Unified Story of Scripture

Bartholomew, Craig G., and Michael W. Goheen. *The Drama of Scripture: Finding Our Place in the Biblical Story*. Grand Rapids: Baker Academic, 2004.

Beale, G. K. *Handbook on the New Testament Use of the Old Testament*. Grand Rapids: Baker Academic, 2012.

Fuller, Daniel P. *The Unity of the Bible: Unfolding God's Plan for Humanity*. Grand Rapids: Zondervan, 1992.

Goldsworthy, Graeme. *Preaching the Whole Bible as Christian Scripture*. Grand Rapids: Eerdmans, 2000.

Robertson, O. Palmer. *The Christ of the Covenants*. Phillipsburg: P&R Publishing, 1980.

Williams, Michael D. *Far as the Curse Is Found: The Covenant Story of Redemption*. Phillipsburg: P&R Publishing, 2005.

Epilogue 2

Peter's Letters

As he who called you is holy, you also
be holy in all your conduct.

1 Peter 1:15

Introduction: Identity

Who is the follower of Jesus?

Though it is difficult to determine an overarching theme of Peter's letters, I suggest that it is the identity of Jesus's followers. Their sense of personhood has migrated to form around the person of Jesus. The Father has caused them "to be born again to a living hope through the resurrection of Jesus Christ from the dead" (1 Pet 1:3). They claim a new inheritance, "imperishable, undefiled and unfading" (1:4). Though rejected by the world they enter the community of love constituted by Jesus's disciples. Beyond this new birth to a living hope, they receive a pure spiritual milk, enabling a growth to maturity (2:2). It is in solidarity with brothers and sisters that they form a solid spiritual house, serving the world as a mediating priesthood. This community was called out of darkness to become a holy nation, a people of God's possession, proclaiming his excellencies in the beauty of an all-enveloping light (2:5, 9–10).

Peter moves into the multi-dimensional nature of human relationships, surrounding the believer from all sides to forge this new collective identity of the redeemed. They are a distinct people, a set-apart community. Yet their lives intersect with the web of normal human relationships – institutions, government, employers, families (2:13–3:7). Peter's concern is that this community's conduct reflects its identity as people redeemed by Jesus, brought into the fellowship of Father, Son and Spirit. Ultimately, they are to be a people of blessing, pursuing good in a world estranged from God.

It all fits. Peter's identity has passed through the refiner's fire, his assumptions rescripted, his core beliefs radically rewritten. He emerges from his journey of spiritual formation with a new identity, being progressively freed from the shackles of his past, he calls the community of Christ's followers to a more intentional following – a forging in the fires of transformation grounded in the truth of their redemption. Peter leads the church in the same journey he has undertaken. "Feed my sheep" was the last commission he received from Jesus. In his letters, we get a glimpse of how a shepherd, formed in the Jesus way, cares for the sheep.

Peter's Audience

To a casual reader of the Bible, the question of to whom Peter was writing might not be of great importance. The greater concern is application. What does his message say to us today? But understanding who is on the receiving end of his letters is a critical step to applying his words today.

He addresses his letter to "elect exiles of the dispersion in Pontus, Galatia, Cappadocia, Asia and Bithynia." These names are all located in what is today, Turkey. The area is often called Asia Minor. It is the Anatolian peninsula that separates the Mediterranean Sea from the Black Sea. This is noteworthy, given that Peter is often assumed to have focused his ministry on the Jews of Jerusalem. While Jews could well have been scattered in this area, they would not have been the majority population.

The use of "elect exiles" has also led some to assume that Peter is writing to Jews who had been scattered from Jerusalem. While those Jews are no doubt part of his audience, other factors indicate that he is not writing uniquely to Jews. There are repeated references to the pagan background of the recipients. For instance, in 1 Peter 1:14, Peter speaks of the "passions of your former ignorance." He likewise speaks of the "futile ways inherited from your forefathers" (1:18). In 2:10, Peter reminds the readers that they were once "not a people, but now are the people of God." And in 4:3–4 Peter reminds his readers to abandon their former lifestyle, "living in sensuality, passions, drunkenness, orgies, drinking parties and lawless idolatry." These indicate that Peter is not writing solely to Jewish people, but to a group of mixed churches in Asia Minor made up of Jews and Gentiles who now form the new people of God – followers of Jesus.

Why is this important? Because we have argued that much of Peter's spiritual formation was a rescripting of his ethnocentrism . . . his presupposition that the Jews were the sole focus of God's work in the world. Jesus did not allow that to remain in Peter, and in his mature years of apostleship, Peter's vision of the new people of God was generous and inclusive. Those of Gentile background and those of Jewish background were held together in his apostolic embrace. Our preoccupied attention span might skip right over that fact. Apply it. Whom do I center, assuming them to be God's focus? Might Peter's example move me beyond my small worldview to see Jesus's grace overflowing its bounds to people I might not have previously considered?

Whom do I center, assuming them to be God's focus? Might Peter's example move me beyond my small worldview to see Jesus's grace overflowing its bounds to people I might not have previously considered?

Prominent Themes in Peter's Letters

While the two letters that bear his name are not the sole representative of Peter's legacy, they represent his most mature and direct instruction. As a seasoned apostle and well-formed disciple, Peter leaves us a treasure trove of the Christ-follower's identity. In what follows, we briefly review a few of the outstanding themes of Peter's letters.

1. Salvation and Transformation

Peter's understanding of salvation and ongoing growth in conformity to Christ comes through clearly in his letters. God saves without conditions, motivating the disciple to a zealous pursuit of holiness. It is a quandary that many believers have faced: If God saves apart from my effort, why should I continue to strive for holiness? Peter's perspective arises from a long discipleship in close company with Jesus. *Because* God has pursued and saved, granting all that is needed for a life of faith and conformity to Christ, the disciple therefore seeks God in whole-hearted devotion. It is the unconditional nature of God's love that assures the believer that his salvation will not fail. Peter's introduction in 1 Peter 1:1–2 invokes the Father, Son and Spirit, all of whom are integrally involved in the full obtaining of salvation: "To those who are elect . . . according to the foreknowledge of God the Father, in the sanctification of the Spirit, for obedience to Jesus Christ and for sprinkling with his blood: May grace and peace be multiplied to you."

Peter blesses God the Father of our Lord Jesus Christ because he has "caused us to be born again to a living hope through the resurrection of Jesus Christ" (1 Pet 1:3). How then are we to respond to this new birth?

> Preparing your minds for action, and being sober-minded, set your hope fully on the grace that will be brought to you at the revelation of Jesus Christ. As obedient children, do not be conformed to the passions of your former ignorance, but as he who called you is holy, you also be holy in all your conduct. (1 Pet 1:13–15)

Peter's second letter opens in much the same fashion: "His divine power has granted to us all things that pertain to life and godliness, through the knowledge of him who called us to his own glory and excellence" (2 Pet 1:3). This all-encompassing gift allows believers to become "partakers of the divine nature" (1:4). This was a primary passage, leading Eastern churches to understand God's purpose for the believer as *theosis*. Though the word is translated "divinization," it should not be understood as "becoming god," but as receiving the divine Spirit and thereby entering into the fellowship of the Trinity.[1] It is the end goal (*telos*) of the believer's transformation. Peter portrays our salvation as a relational belonging. While Paul often used forensic or legal language (i.e. "justification"), Peter highlighted the complementary truth that Jesus's death was vicarious or substitutionary – he died in the place of sinners: "For Christ also suffered once for sins, the righteous for the unrighteous, that he might bring us to God . . ." (1 Pet 3:18a).

That full inclusion in the divine love allows the believer to escape the corruption that is in the world through lust.

> For this very reason, make every effort to supplement your faith with virtue, and virtue with knowledge, and knowledge with self-control, and self-control with steadfastness, and steadfastness with godliness, and godliness with brotherly affection, and brotherly affection with love. (2 Pet 1:5–7)

These qualities were to ensure the believers' fruitfulness in the knowledge of Jesus Christ (1:8). To fail to pursue those qualities is unthinkable, tantamount to forgetting one's purification from sin.

Peter's teaching, similar to Paul's, does not allow us to disassociate salvation and sanctification (lifestyle conformity to Christ). The latter flows from the former. Being in Christ means we live the life of Jesus, not perfectly, but with

---

1. See Fairbairn, *Life in the Trinity*.

an active pursuit of transformation. We may be grateful that Peter was not a schooled Pharisee as was his colleague Paul. It is amazing how much truth Peter manages to pack into a few words as seen in 1 Peter 2:24:

> He himself bore our sins in his body on the tree [the vicarious atonement],
> that we might die to sin and live to righteousness [total life transformation].
> By his wounds you have been healed [Jesus fulfilled Old Testament sacrifices].

Paul's scholarly mind unpacked these truths (and others) over several chapters of his letter to the Romans. Peter's orientation is more concrete. He avoids the complicating objections that Paul takes on. His formulations are succinct and memorable, providing handles for the believer who is to orient his or her life around God's love manifested in Christ.

If we are to apply Peter's teaching today, we quickly see that the only life of a Jesus-follower is a life of ongoing formation – of soul-purification for an obedience to the truth (1 Pet 1:22). The reader comes away with the impression that Peter would not be impressed by a testimony that basks in an experience of salvation fifteen years ago. He would want to know how a Jesus-follower is being changed today.

2. Christ Fulfills the Prophets of the Old Testament

Peter's citation of Isaiah above, "by his wounds you have been healed," indicates his understanding of the Old Testament as the story *fulfilled by Jesus Christ* (see epilogue 1). This key theme surfaces early in Peter's letters. The prophets of the Old Testament searched and inquired carefully concerning what the *Spirit of Christ* in them was revealing (1 Pet 1:10–12). These prophets spoke of the suffering of Jesus and his subsequent glory. Peter reflexively views the Spirit who inspired the Old Testament prophecies as the Spirit of Jesus himself. That same Spirit now inspires the preaching of the gospel which the Old Testament saints understood themselves to be serving. Thus, the gospel and the Old Testament prophecies are integral, intimately related, not disparate. They are inspired by one Spirit – the Spirit of Jesus Christ – who revealed mysteries so sublime that angels long to look into them (1 Pet 1:12).

In his second letter, Peter recalls Jesus on the Mount of Transfiguration (1:16), then replicates what Jesus had taught the disciples after his resurrection, declaring that this is "the prophetic word more fully confirmed" (1:19). He goes on to give an apostolic synopsis of biblical interpretation: "No prophecy of Scripture comes from someone's own interpretation . . . but men spoke from God as they were carried along by the Holy Spirit" (1:20–21). Having been so impressed by Jesus's post-resurrection teaching that he himself was the big idea of the Hebrew Scriptures, Peter leaves that understanding to the early disciples both in his early preaching and in the written letters.

Peter likens followers of Jesus to the exiles of the Old Testament (1 Pet 1:17). Their means of salvation are not perishable things like silver and gold, but the blood of Christ, like a lamb without blemish (1:18–19). Jesus's sacrifice on the cross fulfilled what the Exodus and the Passover lamb anticipated – a deliverance from slavery. The believer's freedom, however, does not lead to a promised land, but to a sincere love of the family of God from a pure heart (1:22). Isaiah's word of the Lord that remains forever is the preached word of the gospel (1:24–25).

This theme of Jesus's fulfillment of the Old Testament story and symbols reverberates through Peter's words in the book of Acts. It is a key element of his spiritual formation and one he bequeaths to the early church. Conflicting trends in biblical exegesis have muddied the waters of Peter's crystal-clear understanding. The contemporary church must embrace this element as a sure foothold in our pursuit of spiritual formation in the Jesus way.

A contemporary author underscores the importance of a single normative story through which we understand our lives and the world.

> The whole point of a basic story or grand narrative is to make sense of life as a whole, and such grand narratives cannot easily be mixed up with each other. Basic stories are in principle *normative* – they define starting points, ways of seeing what is true – and they are comprehensive since they give an account of the whole.[2]

As I've mentioned in previous chapters, the story of Scripture gets crowded out of our media-soaked minds. We are left as helpless prey of competing cultural narratives. Peter reminds us that it is critical to keep our mooring in the story of Scripture.

3. The Identity of the People of God/Israel

Peter deals with complex and thorny theological issues that are hotly debated to this day, all with a refreshing economy of words. One of those is the identity

---

2. Bartholomew and Goheen, *Drama of Scripture*, 20.

of the multi-cultural, multi-ethnic people of God in a post-Pentecost world. For Peter, there can be no doubt that the full inclusion of the Gentiles ends the ethnic distinction of Jew and Gentile which had so marked the Old Testament order. Writing to a joint Jew-Gentile audience, Peter draws on Moses's classic statement of the identity of the children of Israel found in Exodus 19:6 (and other passages) after God had saved Israel from the hand of Pharaoh and was constituting them as his own people:

> But you are a chosen race, a royal priesthood, a holy nation, a people for his own possession, that you may proclaim the excellencies of him who called you out of darkness and into his marvelous light. Once you were not a people, but now you are God's people; once you had not received mercy, but now you have received mercy. (1 Pet 2:9–10)

The people of Christ preserve the identity of God's Old Testament people, Israel; however, it is an expanded and inclusive people, now incorporating multitudes from other ethnic backgrounds.

The church of Christ will forever be a multi-cultural family. This does not do away with the Jewish people nor does it replace them with the church. It expands the identity boundaries of God's Old Testament people. The Jews become the elder brothers and sisters who welcome newly adopted non-Jews into the family.

The church of Christ will forever be a multi-cultural family. This does not do away with the Jewish people nor does it replace them with the church. It expands the identity boundaries of God's Old Testament people. The Jews become the elder brothers and sisters who welcome newly adopted non-Jews into the family.

In the introduction to his second letter, Peter addresses his words "to those who have obtained a faith of equal standing with ours . . ." (1:1). The apostle makes it clear that there is no hierarchy of belonging to Christ. Peter's faith, like that of Paul and the other New Testament writers, broke down the walls of separation. Not only are Gentile believers equal with their Jewish brothers and sisters, but the entire religious pecking order is destroyed. Peter does not see his apostleship as a superior status, a higher rank in faith, but as a function of faith. Each has received a gift and must "use it to serve one another, as good stewards of God's varied grace" (1 Pet 4:10).

Given that nothing was more sacred to Jewish religious and ethnic identity than the temple, Peter's embrace of an expanded temple concept is a stunning application of his new concept of God's people: "You yourselves like living stones are being built up as a spiritual house, to be a holy priesthood, to offer spiritual sacrifices acceptable to God through Jesus Christ" (1 Pet 2:5). The former function of the temple as a dwelling of God and a place of mediation through sacrifice is now fulfilled in the people of Christ, the community of the church. Much as Jesus used images to challenge the mindset of his disciples, Peter also draws on the image of the temple to instill the identity of the Jesus community among the early disciples.

Through following Jesus, Peter imbibed the lesson well: There is no distinction between Jews and Gentiles. The liberating truth, flowing from that lesson is that there is no hierarchy of spiritual value. It is the "divine power" of Christ that has granted us all that we need to become "partakers of the divine nature" (2 Pet 1:3–4).

Peter would likely be shocked to see that our contemporary churches revolve around a priest or pastor who functions as a sole leader of the community. He would call us all, as living stones of a new temple and co-equal members of Christ's body, to exercise our gifts in a unity of diversity. He would probably challenge the spectator sport that worship and general church life has become. He would call us back to the life of the body – a life of mutual care and shared ministry. Furthermore, he would expect the contemporary church to be integrated racially and culturally. It is a challenging path for us to follow and yet it was the path of the early church – multiple ethnicities worshipping together in the one body of Christ.

4. Suffering and Persecution

Both letters take on the thorny issue of persecution. As I have mentioned in past chapters, persecution is praised most by those who have little experience of it. For a church body to be exposed to the threat of torture, imprisonment, loss of employment, etc., is hugely destabilizing. In such situations, believers quickly learn how vulnerable our faith is and how dependent we are on brothers and sisters to sustain and support us. Peter, an apostle who walked that road, offers seasoned wisdom:

- Do not fear your persecutors. Respond to them with gentleness and respect. Be prepared to defend your hope. Keep a clear conscience and be prepared to suffer for doing good. 1 Peter 3:13–17
- "Since Jesus went through everything you're going through and more, learn to think like him. Think of your sufferings as a weaning from that old sinful habit of always expecting to get your own way. Then you'll be able to live out your days free to pursue what God wants instead of being tyrannized by what you want." 1 Peter 4:1–2 (from *The Message*)
- Don't be taken by surprise. Don't think that God is not paying attention. Count yourself privileged that you share in Christ's suffering. When his Spirit is on you, you will be insulted as he was. Suffering for the name "Christian" is no shame. So glorify God that you bear that name. 1 Peter 4:12–19

Peter's sober assessment of suffering helps persecuted communities walk that delicate balance, avoiding triumphalism but also affirming that Christ has ensured victory to his oppressed followers. In essence, we suffer for our faith because Christ did. As we follow him, persecution arises. We get through persecution as we follow him through it to the other side.

Perhaps Peter's call to endure persecution should warn us against seeing our faith as a vehicle to effect political change. Admittedly, there is a balance that is difficult to strike between seeing Jesus followers as salt and light, influencing and enlightening society on the one hand, and called to endure persecution on the other. Nevertheless, the remains of Christendom (inherited from Constantine and the Christian empires of Europe) govern our expectations for the role of Christians in the Western world. We subtly expect the state to cater to our Christian faith. It is a rude awakening for many to discover that is no longer the case. Peter's exhortations remind us that things are getting back to normal, or perhaps we allowed our flirtation with Christendom to deter us from the true nature of following Christ. The world's values and assumptions put our Lord on the cross. We should expect resistance as we follow Jesus in today's world. Peter's understanding of persecution remains a standard for many Christ-followers in the non-Western world where other worldviews produce a more strident resistance to the gospel.

5. Awaiting Jesus's Delayed Return

Peter also offers perspective as we await Christ's return. He perceives that false teaching will proliferate as Jesus's second coming draws near. Much of his second letter is given to warning the believers against false teachers who are declaring that the coming judgment is a false alarm. Isn't everything going along as usual, since the creation? (2 Pet 3:4) Peter takes a clear stand that a day of judgment is coming. Like the flood overtook the people of Noah's day, so a purification of fire will overtake unbelievers in the final judgment. Believers in Peter's day were puzzled over the delay in Christ's coming. Why so long?! Peter's explanation is that God's timing is not like ours. A thousand years is as a day (2 Pet 3:8). The Lord is not slow to fulfill his promises. Rather, he is patient towards us, unwilling that any should perish. But judgment will come swiftly, purging creation through fire, after which there will be a renewed heaven and earth – a home of righteousness (2 Pet 3). This cataclysmic end of history is not the end of creation. Peter awaits a new heaven and a new earth – a renewed home for God's people (2 Pet 3:13). Peter's exhortations to a set-apart life in the world and its systems suggests that our presence here and now in our society prepares the world for a future after Christ's return. We are to adopt attitudes and develop skills that will preserve the world until Christ has judged, refined and renewed creation. John's apocalypse informs us that the heavenly Jerusalem will descend from heaven to earth. It seems we will still inhabit this planet – a renewed planet, but the same dirt. At that time, the seed we have sown here and now will be reaped in eternal life in Christ's presence.

If the believers of Peter's day were struggling with the delay of Jesus's return – the *parousia* – how much more today, some 2,000 years later?! In affirming Paul's teaching and writing, Peter adopts Paul's attitude that the delay of Jesus's return allows God's mercy to spread bringing salvation to more and more people (2 Pet 3:15). I wonder how Peter might react knowing that the gospel he was entrusted with has been embraced by more than 2 billion people around the globe from thousands of tribes and nations. I think he would be pleased that the door he opened to the Gentiles has provided such an impetus to the spread of Christ's love to the nations.

6. Exhortations to Love, Humility and Unity

Peter's call to shepherd the people of God comes through clearly in exhortations to love, humility and unity. His repeated refrain is that the people of God should "have unity of mind, sympathy, brotherly love, a tender heart and a humble mind" (1 Pet 3:8). As a married apostle, Peter advises husbands and wives that a wife's adornment should be focused on internal character qualities. The imperishable beauty of a gentle and quiet spirit is precious to God (1 Pet 3:1–3). Husbands are to live with their wives in an understanding way, showing them deference and honor, remembering that they are also heirs of God's grace (1 Pet 3:7).

As believers await Christ's return, they are to continue to love one another fervently as love covers a multitude of sins. In practical terms, this implies hospitality (*philoxenia*), literally "loving the other," by receiving them into relationship (1 Pet 4:8–9). As Jesus commanded the disciples in the upper room to love one another, so Peter, the undershepherd, exhorts the believers of Asia Minor in a similar vein.

Peter's final exhortation in his first letter is directed to the shepherds of God's flock, which is fitting! Jesus's final exhortation to Peter was to shepherd his lambs. Now Peter similarly exhorts the caretakers of Christ's people. They are to shepherd willingly, not under compulsion, not domineering, but by being examples to their flocks (1 Pet 5:1–5).

A Final Appeal

Peter's letters make a case for a life of set-apart holiness in the world as a pilgrim, one who is passing through. While Peter makes it clear that our ultimate belonging is not to this world and its passing pleasures, he also urges us to remain in the world, engaged in it as sojourners. Peter mediates between two tendencies. The first is to overly personalize faith. This is prominent in a Western worldview that emphasizes privacy and personal liberty. Western beliefs are not open to scrutiny by the public because they are seen as a private matter. At most, we acknowledge them in the company of others who have made similar life commitments – our small group or pastoral leaders. Anything beyond that is deemed improper, overstepping the bounds of decorum. This personal faith makes few claims, if any, on our public life. To suggest it as a guide for others would be ill-advised. In this isolated individualistic faith, our primary concern is personal preservation.

A different perspective sees the world in terms of us-them. The world around us is dangerous in its allurement. To protect ourselves we readily discern the enemy in fields of education, media, politics, etc. We build high walls and engage the culture from behind them, often aiming our arrows of critique at the fortress that the enemy has built within our culture. In this "world against the church" paradigm, our concern is boundaries and keeping the church pure.

Peter offers a clear distinction to both perspectives. His is a personal and collective holiness of engagement in the world, neither a passive and personal preservation nor a "church against the world" paradigm to avoid sinful contamination.

This commitment to a collective life (a church) of set apart holiness as an act of engaging the world inevitably results in rejection by the world. "Be watchful. Your adversary the devil prowls around like a roaring lion, seeking someone to devour. Resist him, firm in your faith, knowing that the same kinds of suffering are being experienced by your brotherhood throughout the world" (1 Pet 5:8–9).

Peter's vision of holiness as engagement in the world creates a new collective identity for the community of Jesus followers. It warns against the fallacy that Rome (or whatever political power dominates our world) can be befriended for the sake of Jesus's kingdom. Peter writes from Rome, referring to it as "Babylon" (1 Pet 5:13). Babylon had carried the ancient children of Israel into exile. Using the label "Babylon" warns the early Christians not to grow comfortable in the empire. Though living under Roman dominance, those who follow Jesus are also in exile, living under the rule of Christ even while Rome holds temporal sovereignty.

Through his letters, Peter pleads that the new community of Christ followers embrace their identity as aliens and sojourners who engage the world as they follow Christ. It is a set apart community, but not an isolated one. It is a kingdom of priests, mediating the presence of God through the body of Christ to an estranged world.

Bibliography

Bartholomew, Craig G., and Michael W. Goheen. *The Drama of Scripture: Finding Our Place in the Biblical Story*. Grand Rapids: Baker Academic, 2004.

Blomberg, Craig. *Matthew*. The New American Commentary 22. Nashville: B&H, 1992.

Brooks, James A. *Mark*. The New American Commentary 23. Nashville: B&H, 1991.

Card, Michael. *A Fragile Stone: The Emotional Life of Simon Peter*. Downers Grove: InterVarsity Press, 2006.

Carson, D. A. *The Gospel according to John*. The Pillar New Testament Commentary. Grand Rapids: Eerdmans, 1990.

Edwards, James R. *The Gospel according to Mark*. The Pillar New Testament Commentary. Leicester: Apollos, 2002.

Edwards, Jonathan. *The Works of Jonathan Edwards: Sermons and Discourses, 1723–1729*, edited by Kenneth P. Minkema. London: Yale University Press, 1997.

Fairbairn, Donald. *Life in the Trinity: An Introduction to Theology with the Help of the Church Fathers*. Downers Grove: IVP Academic, 2009.

Green, Tim. "Conversion in the Light of Identity Theories." In *Longing for Community: Church, Ummah, or Somewhere in Between?*, edited by David Greenlee. Pasadena: William Carey Library, 2013.

Grudem, Wayne. *Systematic Theology: An Introduction to Biblical Doctrine*. Leicester: Inter-Varsity Press, 1994.

Helyer, Larry R. *The Life and Witness of Peter*. Downers Grove: IVP Academic, 2012.

Hendriksen, William. *The Gospel of Matthew*. Grand Rapids: Baker, 1973.

Irenaeus of Lyons. *Against Heresies*. N.p.: Createspace Independent Pub, 2012.

Keating, Thomas. *The Human Condition: Contemplation and Transformation*. New York: Paulist Press, 1999.

Lewis, C. S. "Surprised by Joy." In *The Inspirational Writings of C. S. Lewis*. New York: Inspirational Press, 1986.

Little, Don. *Effective Discipling in Muslim Communities*. Downers Grove: InterVarsity Press, 2015.

Lovelace, Richard F. *Dynamics of Spiritual Life: An Evangelical Theology of Renewal*. Downers Grove: InterVarsity Press, 1979.

Manning, Brennan. *Abba's Child: The Cry of the Heart for Intimate Belonging*. Colorado Springs, Colorado: NavPress, 2002.

Merton, Thomas. *Thomas Merton, Spiritual Master: The Essential Writings*. New York: Paulist Press, 1992.

Morris, Leon. *The Gospel according to Matthew*. The Pillar New Testament Commentary. Grand Rapids: Eerdmans, 1992.

Nouwen, Henri. *Life of the Beloved: Spiritual Living in a Secular World*. New York: Crossroad, 2002.

———. *The Way of the Heart*. United States: Ballantine Books, 2003.

Root, Andrew. *The Relational Pastor: Sharing in Christ by Sharing Ourselves*. Downers Grove: InterVarsity Press, 2013.

St Irenaeus. *Adversus Haereses (Against Heresies)*.

Stott, John. *The Story of the New Testament*. Oxford: Candle Books, 1994.

Taylor, Barbara Brown. Smashing Idols Through Pain (Video). See: https://www.huffpost.com/entry/barbara-brown-taylor-smash-idols-through-pain_b_2043989.

Torrance, Thomas F. *Space, Time and Incarnation*. London: T&T Clark, 2005.

Wright, N. T. "How Can the Bible Be Authoritative?" *Vox Evangelica* 21 (1991): 7–32. https://biblicalstudies.org.uk/pdf/vox/vol21/bible_wright.pdf.

———. *The New Testament and the People of God*. Christian Origins and the Question of God, Vol. 1. Minneapolis: Fortress Press, 1992.

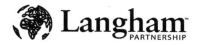

Langham Literature and its imprints are a ministry of Langham Partnership.

Langham Partnership is a global fellowship working in pursuit of the vision God entrusted to its founder John Stott –

> *to facilitate the growth of the church in maturity and Christ-likeness through raising the standards of biblical preaching and teaching.*

Our vision is to see churches in the Majority World equipped for mission and growing to maturity in Christ through the ministry of pastors and leaders who believe, teach and live by the word of God.

Our mission is to strengthen the ministry of the word of God through:
- nurturing national movements for biblical preaching
- fostering the creation and distribution of evangelical literature
- enhancing evangelical theological education

especially in countries where churches are under-resourced.

Our ministry

Langham Preaching partners with national leaders to nurture indigenous biblical preaching movements for pastors and lay preachers all around the world. With the support of a team of trainers from many countries, a multi-level programme of seminars provides practical training, and is followed by a programme for training local facilitators. Local preachers' groups and national and regional networks ensure continuity and ongoing development, seeking to build vigorous movements committed to Bible exposition.

Langham Literature provides Majority World preachers, scholars and seminary libraries with evangelical books and electronic resources through publishing and distribution, grants and discounts. The programme also fosters the creation of indigenous evangelical books in many languages, through writer's grants, strengthening local evangelical publishing houses, and investment in major regional literature projects, such as one volume Bible commentaries like *The Africa Bible Commentary* and *The South Asia Bible Commentary*.

Langham Scholars provides financial support for evangelical doctoral students from the Majority World so that, when they return home, they may train pastors and other Christian leaders with sound, biblical and theological teaching. This programme equips those who equip others. Langham Scholars also works in partnership with Majority World seminaries in strengthening evangelical theological education. A growing number of Langham Scholars study in high quality doctoral programmes in the Majority World itself. As well as teaching the next generation of pastors, graduated Langham Scholars exercise significant influence through their writing and leadership.

To learn more about Langham Partnership and the work we do visit **langham.org**

9 781839 736049